W9-BHK-720

SERIOUS FACE

BY JON MOOALLEM

Serious Face

This Is Chance!

Wild Ones

SERIOUS FACE

| ESSAYS |

Jon Mooallem

RANDOM HOUSE

NEW YORK

Published in the United States by Random House, an imprint and division of Penguin Random House LLC, New York.

RANDOM HOUSE and the HOUSE colophon are registered trademarks of Penguin Random House LLC.

All of the essays in this work have been previously published, some in different form:

"A House at the End of the World" as "One Man's Quest to Change the Way We Die," *The New York Times Magazine,* January 3, 2017; "Why These Instead of Others" as "The Senseless Logic of the Wild," *The New York Times Magazine,* March 20, 2019; "Can You Even Believe This Is Happening? (A Monk Seal Murder Mystery)" as "Who Would Kill a Monk Seal?," *The New York Times Magazine,* May 8, 2013; "The Outsiders" as "You Just Got Out of Prison. Now What?," *The New York Times Magazine,* July 16, 2015; "At the Precise Center of a Dream" as "A Journey to the Center of the World," *The New York Times Magazine,* February 19, 2014; "We Have Fire Everywhere," *The New York Times Magazine,* July 31, 2019; "This Story About Charlie Kaufman Has Changed" as "This Profile About Charlie Kaufman Has Changed," *The New York Times Magazine,* July 2, 2020; "Swing State" as "What's a Monkey to Do in Tampa?," *The New York Times Magazine,* August 22, 2012; "Birdman," *The New York Times Magazine,* March 6, 2015; "A Cloud Society" as "The Amateur Cloud Society That (Sort Of) Rattled the Scientific Community," *The New York Times Magazine,* May 4, 2016; "Neanderthals Were People, Too," *The New York Times Magazine,* January 11, 2017; and "Take Me Out" as "I Had a Chance to Travel Anywhere. Why Did I Pick Spokane?," *The New York Times Magazine,* September 21, 2021.

Hardback ISBN 978-0-525-50994-3
Ebook ISBN 978-0-525-50996-7

Printed in Canada on acid-free paper

randomhousebooks.com

9 8 7 6 5 4 3 2 1

First Edition

Book design by Caroline Cunningham

Contents

Introduction

Twenty years years ago, I was working at a small literary magazine in New York City, screening the bulging slush pile of poetry submissions for anything that the editors might be interested in publishing. Please know that passing judgment on all these people's poems made me queasy. I was twenty-two years old, not especially well-read, and my only previous full-time employment had been as a kosher butcher. I could only like what I liked.

Also, I was extraordinarily sad. My father had died a year earlier, and the grief and bewilderment I'd kept tamped down were beginning to burble upward. I felt alone. I felt lost. And I was fixated on figuring out why everything was so hard, what I was doing wrong. Some evenings, I'd walk the fifty-eight blocks home from the office, excessively serious-faced, wrenching my mind around like a Rubik's Cube, struggling to make it show a brighter color. My point here is, I'm sure this made me less patient and open-minded than I ought to have been whenever I opened another envelope from the slush pile and found someone else's delicate clump of pentameter about pear blossoms or regret.

In fact, of the thousands of poems I must have read at that job, there's apparently only one that I allowed to leave an indelible impression—and not even the whole poem, just one line. The poem is called "Frost on the Fields." I know because I just went Googling for it, and found it reprinted in an obituary for the poet, Eric Trethewey, who died in 2014. It's twenty-three lines long and describes a typical November day, somewhere cold and rural: "An oak leaf still stemmed to a branch tugs away" and so on. There's a pond. A hillside. A turkey buzzard on a wooden post. But then, out of nowhere, there's a question: "Why are we not better than we are?"

I've been thinking hard about any common themes running through the pieces in this book, or whether there's some secret theory that explains why I've spent almost my entire adult life so far obsessing over the process of reporting and writing them. In other words: *Why these?* Also: *Why me?*

I'm tempted to say that it's all utterly random. But this morning, I suddenly remembered that line, *Why are we not better than we are?*, and felt the clarifying, boneheaded profundity of it all over again. I'm not sure—sincerely, I'm not—but if there's a question that all these stories have at their heart, and that a reader might keep wrestling with once they're done reading them, it could be that one. And just phrasing the question that way—*Why are we not better than we are?*—somehow conveys that it can't possibly be answered. It's just too damn big, like the sky.

But that's only the half of it. I also remembered the particular moment in my life when I encountered that poem, a moment when I was trying to write poetry myself, but also accepting how unnatural the medium felt to me, and wondering how long I could keep pretending. Meanwhile, I was reading magazine journalism for the first time and starting to wonder what *that* kind of writing was all about.

It wasn't lost on me that everything about "Frost on the Fields," beyond that quick, explosive question, felt lonely and cocooned. The entire poem—and I don't mean this as a knock against it as literature—is simply a guy noticing stuff on a walk, in a landscape where hardly anything is moving, where no else is around. Magazine writers, meanwhile, seemed to be circling around the same kinds of question, but only in the background while they whipped through our colossal, mystifying, stupidly beautiful world in rental cars and airplanes—the same world that I was feeling intimidated to fully enter.

I knew I'd spend my life asking questions like *Why are we not better than we are?* Like it or not, and often I didn't, this was evidently just the way I was wired. But here was a way to channel that impulse that felt more doable to me, and more fun. Instead of thumping my head against the biggest questions of my own life, I could go ask other people specific questions about their lives, then work hard to transmit whatever feelings I'd felt when I was with them and whatever insights I'd stitched together or absorbed.

I'd been puzzling over myself, torturously trying to unlock the truth of who I was. The truth is, I am the puzzling.

SERIOUS FACE

A House at the End of the World

| 2017 |

First, the backstory, because, B. J. Miller has found, the backstory is unavoidable when you are missing three limbs.

Miller was a sophomore at Princeton when, one Monday night in November 1990, he and two friends went out for drinks and, at around 4:00 a.m., found themselves ambling toward a convenience store for sandwiches. They decided to climb a commuter train parked at the adjacent rail station, for fun. Miller scaled it first. When he got to the top, electrical current arced out of a piece of equipment into the watch on his wrist. Eleven thousand volts shot through his left arm and down his legs. When his friends reached him on the roof of the train, smoke was rising from his feet.

Miller remembers none of this. His memories don't kick in until several days later, when he woke up in the burn unit of St. Barnabas Medical Center, in Livingston, New Jersey. Thinking he'd resurfaced from a terrible dream, he tried to shamble across his hospital room on the charred crusts of his legs until he used up the slack of his catheter tube and the device tore out of his body. Then all the pain hit him at once.

Doctors took each leg just below the knee, one at a time. Then they turned to his arm, which triggered in Miller a deeper grief. ("Hands do stuff," he explains. "Your foot is just a stinky, clunky little platform.") For weeks, the hospital staff considered him close to death. But Miller, in a devastated haze, didn't know that. He only worried about who he would be when he survived.

No visitors were allowed in his hospital room; the burn unit was a sterile environment. But on the morning Miller's arm was going to be amputated, just below the elbow, a dozen friends and family members packed into a ten-foot-long corridor between the burn unit and the elevator, just to catch a glimpse of him as he was rolled to surgery. "They all dared to show up," Miller remembers thinking. "They all dared to look at me. They were proving that I was lovable even when I couldn't see it." This reassured Miller, as did the example of his mother, Susan, a polio survivor who has used a wheelchair since Miller was a child: *She* had never seemed diminished. After the operation, when Miller was rolled through the hallway again, he opened his eyes as he passed her and said: "Mom, Mom. Now you and me have more in common."

It wasn't that Miller was suddenly enlightened; internally, he was in turmoil. But in retrospect, he credits himself with doing one thing right: He saw a good way to look at his situation and committed to faking that perspective, hoping that his genuine self might eventually catch up. Miller refused, for example, to let himself believe that his life was extra difficult now, only *uniquely* difficult, as all lives are. He resolved to think of his suffering as simply a "variation on a theme we all deal with: to be human is really hard," he says. His life had never felt easy, even as a privileged, able-bodied suburban boy with two adoring parents, but he never felt entitled to any angst. He saw unhappiness as an illegitimate intrusion into the carefree reality he was supposed to inhabit. And don't we all do that, he realized. Don't we all treat suffering as a disruption to existence, instead of an inevitable part of it? He wondered what would happen if you could "reincorporate your version of reality, of normalcy, to accommodate suffering." As a person with a disability, he was getting all kinds of signals that he was different and separated from everyone else. But he worked hard to see himself as merely sitting somewhere on a continuum between the man on his deathbed and the woman who misplaced her car keys, to let his accident heighten his connectedness to others, instead of isolating him. This was the only way, he thought, to keep from hating his injuries and, by extension, himself.

Miller returned to Princeton the following year. He had three prosthetics and rode around campus in a golf cart with a rambunctious service dog named Vermont who, in truth, was too much of a misfit to perform any concrete service. Miller had wanted to work in foreign relations, in China; now he started studying art history. He found it to be a good lens through which to keep making sense of his injuries.

First, there was the discipline's implicit conviction that every work is shaped by the viewer's perspective. He remembers looking at slides of ancient sculptures in a dark lecture hall, all of them missing arms or noses or ears, and suddenly recognizing them for what they were: fellow amputees. "We were, as a class, all calling these works monumental, beautiful, and important, but we'd never seen them whole," he says. Time's effect on these marble bodies—their suffering, really—was understood as part of the art. Medicine didn't think about bodies this way, Miller realized. Embedded in words like "disability" and "rehabilitation" was a less generous view: "There was an aberrant moment in your life and, with some help, you could get back to what you were, or approximate it." So, instead of regarding his injuries as something to get over, Miller tried to get *into* them, to see his new life as its own novel challenge, like traveling through a country whose language he didn't speak.

This positivity was still mostly aspirational. Miller spent years repulsed by the "chopped meat" where his arm ended and crushed with shame when he noticed people wince or look away. But he slowly became more confident and playful. He replaced the sock-like covering many amputees wear over their arm stumps with an actual sock: first a plain sock, then stripes and argyles. Then one day he forgot to put on any sock and—just like that—"I was done with it. I was no longer ashamed of my arm." He became fascinated by architects who stripped the veneer off their buildings and let the strength of their construction shine through. And suddenly, the standard-issue foam covers he'd been wearing over his prosthetics seemed like a clunky charade— Potemkin legs. The exquisitely engineered artificial limbs they hid were actually pretty interesting, even sexy, made of the same carbon fiber used as a finish on expensive sports cars. *Why not tear that stuff off and delight in what actually is?* Miller recalled thinking. So he did.

For years Miller collected small, half-formed insights like these. Then he entered medical school and discovered palliative care, an approach to medicine rooted in similar ideas. He now talks about his recovery as a creative act, "a transformation," and argues that all suffering offers the same opportunity, even at the end of life, which gradually became his professional focus. "Parts of me died early on," he said recently. "And that's something, one way or another, we can all say. I got to redesign my life around this fact, and I tell you it has been a liberation to realize you can always find a shock of beauty or meaning in what life you have left."

One morning in July 2015, Miller took his seat at a regular meeting of palliative-care doctors at the University of California San Francisco's cancer center. The head of the team, Dr. Michael Rabow, started with a poem. It was a tradition, he later told me, meant to remind everyone that this was a different sort of hour in their schedule, and that, as palliative-care physicians, they were seeking different varieties of outcomes for their patients: things like comfort, beauty, and meaning. The poem was called "Sinkhole," and it seemed to offer some sneaky, syntactically muddled wisdom about letting go. When it was over, there was a beat of silence. (It was sort of a confusing poem.) Then Rabow encouraged everyone to talk about any patients who had died since their last meeting. Miller was the first to speak up.

Miller, now forty-five years old, with deep brown eyes and a scruffy, silver-threaded beard, saw patients one day a week at the hospital. He was also entering his fifth year as executive director of a small, pioneering hospice called the Zen Hospice Project, which originated as a kind of compassionate improvisation at the height of the AIDS crisis, when members of the San Francisco Zen Center began taking in sick, often stigmatized young men and doing what they could to help them die comfortably. The hospice is now an independent nonprofit group that trains volunteers for San Francisco's Laguna Honda public hospital as well as for its own revered, small-scale residential operation. (Two of the facility's six beds are reserved for UCSF, which sends patients there; the rest are funded through sliding-scale fees and private donations.) Once an outlier, Zen Hospice had come to embody a growing nationwide effort to reclaim the end of life as a human experience instead of primarily a medical one. The goal, as Miller likes to put it, is to "de-pathologize death."

Around the table at UCSF, Miller stood out. The other doctors wore dress pants and pressed button-downs—physician-casual—while he wore a sky blue corduroy shirt with a tear in the sleeve and a pair of rumpled khakis; he could have come straight from camping or Bonnaroo. Even just sitting there, he transmitted a strange charisma—a magnetism that people kept telling me was hard to explain but also *necessary* to explain, since the rapport that Miller seems to instantly establish with everyone is a part of his gift as a clinician.

"It's reasonable to say that it's impossible to describe what it feels like to be with him," Rabow told me. "People feel accepted. I think they feel loved." It's in the way Miller swaddles you in his attention, the way his goofiness punctures any pretensions. (Miller, who has an unrepentant knucklehead side, habitually addresses other men as "Brother man" or "Mon" and insisted to me many times that he hasn't finished a book in twenty years.) For people who know him, his magic has almost become an exasperating joke. When I spoke to Miller's childhood friend Justin Burke, he told me a story about Miller running around on a beach with his dog in San Francisco years ago. Another man came hobbling over and explained to Miller that he was about to have his own leg amputated and that just watching Miller run around like this, on two prosthetics, had instantaneously reassured him that he was going to be OK. I told Burke, Wait a second: Someone at Zen Hospice had already told me this story, except that in her version, Miller was running on a trail in Texas. "Ask him how many times it's happened," Burke deadpanned.

Now Miller seemed to be on the cusp of modest celebrity. He'd started speaking about death and dying at medical schools and conferences around the country and would soon surface in Oprah's living room, chatting about palliative care on her *Super Soul Sunday* TV show. Several of Miller's colleagues described him to me as exactly the kind of public ambassador their field needed. "What B.J. accomplishes is to talk about death without making it sound scary and horrible," explained Rita Charon, a professor of medicine at Columbia University College of Physicians and Surgeons. "We know from seeing him standing in front of us that he has suffered. We know that he has been at the brink of the abyss that he's talking about. That gives him an authority that others may not have." Vicki Jackson, the chief of palliative care at Massachusetts General Hospital, agreed: Nobody welcomes conversations about dying, not even about making the experience less miserable. "But people will listen to B.J.," she said. "They want to."

Jackson pointed to the talk Miller gave to close the TED conference in 2015. Miller described languishing in a windowless, antiseptic burn unit after his amputations. He heard there was a blizzard outside but couldn't see it himself. Then a nurse smuggled him a snowball and allowed him to hold it. This was against hospital regulations, and that was Miller's point: There are parts of ourselves that the conventional health care system isn't equipped to heal or nourish, and this adds to our suffering. He described holding that snowball as "a stolen moment," and said, "I cannot tell you the rapture I felt holding that in my hand, and the coldness dripping onto my burning skin, the miracle of it all, the fascination as I watched it melt and turn into water. In that moment, just being any part of this planet, in this universe, mattered more to me than whether I lived or died." Miller's talk has been watched more than five million times. And yet, Jackson told me: "If I said all that—'Oh, I could feel the coldness of the snowball . . . '—you'd be like: 'Shut. Up. Shut up!' But no one is going to question B.J."

Now, after the poem at the morning meeting, Miller began describing the case of a young man named Randy Sloan, a patient at UCSF who died of an aggressive cancer a few weeks earlier after a brief stay at Zen Hospice. In a way, Sloan's case was typical. It passed through all the same medical decision points and existential themes the doctors knew from working with their own terminal patients. But here, the timeline was so compressed that those themes felt distilled and heightened.

And then there was the bracing idiosyncrasy of everything Miller's staff had been able to do for Sloan at Zen Hospice. Rabow told me that all palliative-care departments and home-hospice agencies believe patients' wishes should be honored, but Zen Hospice's small size allows it to live up to these ideals more fully. When Miller relayed one detail about Sloan's stay at the hospice—it was either the part about the sailing trip or the wedding—one doctor across the conference table expelled what seemed to be an involuntary, admiring "What?"

Everything Miller was saying had a way of sharpening an essential set of questions: What is a good death? How do you judge? In the end, what matters? You got the sense that looking closely at Sloan's case might even get you close to some answers or, at least, less hopelessly far away.

This is the story he told.

It started with an email late one night, in April 2015. "I'm the mother of Randy Sloan," a woman named Melany Baldwin wrote to Miller. She reminded Miller that he'd met her son the previous year. And then: "Anyway, last week my dear son was diagnosed with mesothelioma," a rare, terminal cancer. "We are devastated. He is only 27 years old."

Miller got emails, texts, and calls like this almost daily from friends, friends of friends, or total strangers. And he put pressure on himself to help as much as he could. But it was also exhausting, and he put equal and opposing pressure on himself to live his own life fully—a by-product of his extreme intimacy with mortality. "The lessons I get from my patients and their families, and from this work," Miller said, "is to enjoy this big, huge, mystical, crazy, beautiful, wacky world. And I'm too often not doing that. That can feel distressing to me." A few months earlier, Miller had another brush with death—a pancreatic-cancer scare that turned out to be nothing—and he told me that "it was interesting to watch myself play with that thought. Where my mind went was: 'Cool. Now I get to quit all this work.'" Maybe he would just disappear, get weird, grow weed.

And so, as it happens, Miller didn't get Baldwin's email for several days, because he'd decided to experiment with going off the grid. He went on a weeklong, aimless road trip around the West with his mutt, Maysie, riding shotgun, and he rode his treasured motorcycle—a sleek, black, heavily customized Aprilia— up to Sonoma for a weekend with old friends. He was pulled over for speeding on the bike twice. The first cop approached a little freaked out; unable to compute a one-limbed man riding a motorcycle, he mistook Miller's prosthetic arm for a weapon.

"I love bikes," Miller told me. "I love gyroscopic, two-wheel action!" Mountain biking had become his way of releasing pressure in the turbulent decade after his accident. (Miller sued Princeton and New Jersey Transit, which operated the train, charging that they failed to make safety upgrades after similar accidents in the past. He won settlements totaling nearly $6 million, but was blindsided when some in the press excoriated him as a symbol of America's binge-drinking youth and their lack of personal responsibility.) He had returned to cycling quickly, tooling around trails with a specialized arm clipped to the handlebar and two prosthetics pedaling. It allowed him to be alone without being lonely, to remind himself that his life still allowed for adventure and risk. Soon, he was wandering into motorcycle dealerships, explaining how badly he wanted to get back on a motorcycle, too, asking if anyone could build him one. But for years, none of the mechanics Miller approached would touch the idea: Engineering a machine for a triple-amputee seemed nearly impossible, the potential liability too great.

Then, in late 2013, Miller checked out Scuderia West, a boutique motorcycle shop not far from Zen Hospice, in the Mission District. Scuderia was staffed by a crew of young, wisecracking gear-heads, who, after finishing their shifts, stayed late drinking beer and rehabilitating decrepit old bikes for fun. Right away, Miller noticed a different vibe. These people were excited by the challenge of retrofitting a bike for him. This was especially true of the young tech who ultimately volunteered to take on the project: Melany Baldwin's son, Randy Sloan.

Sloan grew up in Texas. He was bald, with a bushy, reddish beard and a disarming, contented smile. His social life in San Francisco revolved around Scuderia, and he was the baby of the group: not just younger, but more sensitive and trusting. "He was way too nice to work here," his friend and co-worker Katie Putman told me. Sloan's closest relationship may have been with his dog, a husky named Desmo, whom he rescued from a disreputable breeder. The dog was weird-looking: It had one blue eye and one eye that was half-brown and half-blue. "He would always select the misfit," Baldwin said.

Sloan threw himself into overhauling a bike for Miller. For six months, he confronted a cascade of problems—like how to run all the controls to a single handlebar so Miller could accelerate and brake with one hand—while Miller made excuses to frequently check in on his progress and hang out. "It was just an immediate man crush," Miller told me. "The guy was helping me build this dream."

Sloan was feeling it, too. Everyone at Scuderia was. They stalked Miller online, learning about his career at Zen Hospice. His work with the dying impressed them as fearless, just as his conviction to ride a motorcycle again did. Sloan never carried on about people or even talked that much, but he frequently referred to Miller as "a legend," and those close to him knew what that meant. "There were not many 'legends' in Randy's eyes," Putman said.

Sloan finished Miller's motorcycle in April 2014. A crowd gathered at Scuderia to watch Miller take possession. Sloan had him climb on, then clambered around and under the bike, making final adjustments. Then he stepped back and started, quietly, to cry.

Miller was tearing up under his helmet, too. But he didn't drag things out. He started the engine, said thank you, then streaked down the alleyway at the back of the shop. Everyone hollered and applauded as they watched him disappear down Valencia Street—very fast, but with a pronounced, unsettling wobble.

Miller had been lying. He'd never ridden a motorcycle before.

A year later, Miller got Melany Baldwin's email. Once he was back from his road trip, he contacted Sloan's doctors at UCSF to learn more about his case.

Sloan had been walking Desmo up a hill a few weeks earlier, in April, and found he couldn't catch his breath. He was rushed into surgery, to fix an apparent collapsed lung. But the surgeon discovered a raft of tumors spread across his lung, diaphragm, and heart: mesothelioma. The diagnosis alone was improbable. Mesothelioma is typically seen in older people, after long-term asbestos or radiation exposure. And the way the cancer was moving through Sloan's body was shocking. A subsequent PET scan revealed it had already spread to his pancreas and brain.

His doctors at UCSF believed the tumor on his brainstem would paralyze him within weeks. And so, Sloan underwent whole-brain radiation to shrink it before attacking everything else. He didn't want to be cut off from his body—he wanted to be as much like his old self as possible. "I'm sick of being sick, and I'm sick of talking about being sick," he kept telling his mother. He insisted that she go back home to Illinois while he returned to the small apartment he shared with two roommates, waiting to start chemo.

The next two weeks were grim. Tumors crusted over Sloan's heart, hindering it from pumping blood through his body. His capillaries began seeping water into his tissues. Soon, his feet were literally leaking, and the retained water cracked his skin from the shins down, mashing him with pain. Sloan's ankles grew as wide as logs. He started walking with a cane. And because the pain in his torso kept him from lying down or even sitting comfortably, one night he fell asleep standing up and cut his head open when he collapsed.

Putman, Sloan's friend from Scuderia, had swept in to take care of Desmo, the husky. Now she transitioned into Sloan's de facto nurse. But Sloan was a bad patient. He played down his condition and seemed to resent Putman's help, out of shame or guilt. Several times, Putman told me, she had to race to his apartment and take him to the emergency room: "I started calling it our date night." Finally, she asked Sloan if she should just sleep over. Sloan accepted her offer this way: "I think Desmo would like that."

Early in June, Sloan was readmitted to UCSF, and Baldwin, his mother, returned to San Francisco to be with him. Miller saw both of them for an appointment that morning, and when he walked in, it hit him how quickly Sloan's body was failing: In roughly six weeks, Sloan had gone from a functioning, happy twenty-seven-year-old, walking his dog up a hill, to very clearly dying. His decline was relentless, by any standard. At no point had any doctor been able to give him a single bit of good news. Even now, Sloan's oncologist was reporting that after the first dose of chemotherapy, his heart was likely too frail to take more.

Still, Sloan talked to Miller about "doing battle" with the cancer and "winning this thing"; about getting back to work at Scuderia and flying to Illinois, where his mother would be getting married later that summer. He also wanted to go to Tokyo Disneyland, he said. Miller looked at Sloan, then looked at Baldwin, trying to intuit who knew what and who might have been pretending not to know and how best to gently reconcile everyone's hopes with the merciless reality.

Good palliative-care doctors recognize there's an art to navigating clinical interactions like this, and Miller seems particularly sensitive to its subtleties. In this case, Miller realized, his job was to "disillusion" Sloan without devastating him. Hope is a tricky thing, Miller told me. Some terminal patients keep chasing hope through round after round of chemo. But it's amazing how easily others "re-proportion," or recalibrate, their expectations: how the hope of making it to a grandchild's birthday or finishing *Game of Thrones* becomes sufficiently meaningful. "The question becomes," Miller says, "how do you incorporate those hard facts into your moment-by-moment life instead of trying to run away from them?"

At an initial appointment with Sloan, two weeks earlier, Miller made the calculation not to steer Sloan toward any crushing realizations. He worried that if he pushed too hard, Sloan might feel alienated and shut down. ("I needed his allegiance," Miller later explained; it was more important, in the long term, that

Sloan see him as an advocate.) At the second meeting, Miller remembered, "I felt the need to be more brutal." And, he imagined, by now Sloan would have started to suspect that the story he'd been telling himself didn't fit the reality. "I just said, 'Randy, this is not going like any of us want for you,'" and Miller began, calmly, to level with him.

Miller explained that traveling was out of the question; best guess, Sloan had a few months to live. "You could just watch his world collapse," Miller recalled. "With each sentence, you're taking another possibility away." Sloan started crying. And yet, Baldwin also knew that her son had been waiting for his doctors to say this out loud. Sloan couldn't understand why, if he had Stage 4 of an incurable cancer, he was still taking seventy pills every day, with the doses laid out in a dizzying flowchart. And as Miller went on, he was stunned by how well Sloan seemed to be absorbing this new information, without buckling under its weight. "He was actually kind of keeping up with his grief, reconciling the facts of his life," he says. "It was a moving target, and he kept hitting it." Baldwin told me: "Randy was a simple guy. He would say to me, 'Mom, all I want is one ordinary day.'" He was sick of being sick—just like he'd been saying. He wanted to go back to living, as best he could.

Quickly the conversation turned to what was next. A standard question in palliative care is "What's important to you now?" But Sloan didn't muster much of a response, so Miller retooled the question. He told Sloan that nothing about his life was going the way he expected, and his body was only going to keep breaking down. "So, what's your favorite part of yourself? What character trait do we want to make sure to protect as everything else falls apart?" Sloan had an immediate answer for this one. "I love everybody I've ever met," he said.

Baldwin had heard her son say this before, with total earnestness. And he said it with such conviction now that Miller immediately believed it, too. Besides, Miller had already *felt* it to be true, a year earlier, when he drove the motorcycle Sloan had built for him away from Scuderia. "He was an amazing person that way," Miller told me.

Sloan got apprehensive when Miller started telling him about Zen Hospice's residential facility, known as the Guest House; it sounded as if it was for old people. But Miller explained that it was probably the best chance he had for living the last act of his life the way he wanted. His other options were to tough it out at home with two weekly visits from a home hospice nurse or go to a nursing home. At Zen Hospice, Sloan's friends would always be welcome, and Sloan could come and go as he pleased as long as someone went with him. He could eat what he wanted. He could step out for a cigarette. He could even walk up the street and smoke on his own stoop—the Guest House was just two blocks from Sloan's apartment. Besides, Miller told him: "It's where I work. I'll be there."

Sloan agreed but didn't seem entirely comfortable with the idea of a hospice. He told one of his friends from Scuderia: "I'm moving in with B.J."

Sloan arrived at the Guest House with his mother five days later, on the morning of June 9. He insisted on walking there, trundling the two blocks from his apartment with his cane.

The Guest House is a calm, unpretentious space: a large Victorian home with six beds in five bedrooms, vaulted ceilings, slightly shabby furniture, and warm, vintage rugs. There is a large wooden Buddha in the dining room. The kitchen is light-filled and bursting with flowers. There's always a pot of tea and often freshly baked cookies. And while Zen Hospice has a rotating, twenty-four-hour nursing staff, the tiny nursing station is literally tucked into a kind of cabinet in the hall upstairs. The house, in other words, feels very much like a house, not a hospital.

You don't have to spend much time there to realize that the most crucial, and distinctive, piece of the operation is its staff of volunteers. Freed of most medical duties by the nursing staff, the volunteers act almost as existential nurses. They sit with residents and chat, offering their full attention, unencumbered by the turmoil a family member might feel. The volunteers are ordinary people: retired Macy's executives, social workers, bakers, underemployed millennials, or kibitzing empty-nesters. Many are practicing Buddhists. Many are not. (Miller isn't.) But Buddhism informs their training. There's an emphasis on accepting suffering, on not getting tripped up by one's own discomfort around it. "You train people not to run away from hard things, not to run away from the suffering of others," Miller explained. This liberates residents to feel whatever they're going to feel in their final days, even to fall apart.

At first, many volunteers experience a confused apprehension. They arrive expecting nonstop, penetrating metaphysical conversations with wise elderly people and instead just wind up plying them for family recipes or knitting advice or watching *Wheel of Fortune* with them or restocking latex gloves for the Guest House nurses. But one especially well-liked volunteer, Josh Kornbluth, told me that, after a year working at the Guest House, he understood that the value of Zen Hospice is actually "in the quotidian—the holding of someone's hand, bringing them food that's been beautifully arranged on the plate, all the small ways of showing respect to that person as a living person and not as 'predeceased.' Those are actually deep things. And I say that as the least Zen person!" In fact, Kornbluth was raised by Jewish Communists in New York City, and once, after a woman died at the Guest House and no more-senior volunteer was on hand to take charge, I watched him—adrenalized, uneasy, perspiring—fumble around on his iPhone for something to say over the body before they wheeled it away, then mangle the pronunciation of "Thich Nhat Hanh."

Sloan didn't appreciate any of this at first; the Guest House creeped him out. Shortly after he arrived, a nurse showed him to one of the smaller rooms at the top of the stairs: "Bed 5," it was called. It had a twin bed, an ornate wooden chest, and a large framed photo of a Tibetan boy in a red robe. The rest of the rooms were occupied by old women: one who spoke no English and kept her television tuned to blaring Russian talk shows; a retired teacher in the final throes of cervical cancer; an unflappable, perpetually crocheting ninety-nine-year-old who had recently gained back some weight and taken to playing piano and who, everyone suspected, wasn't actually dying anymore. Sloan worried that he had exiled himself to a nursing home, and nothing he was seeing now reassured him. He told his mother he needed to "take a day off." Then he went downstairs and walked back to his apartment. The staff of Zen Hospice, considering it part of their job to accept his trepidation, let him go.

He returned the next morning. He was ready to move in now, he said, and came trailed by a squad of friends who'd tossed his possessions into boxes and were now hauling them up the Guest House stairs. They started hammering things into walls, mounting Sloan's flat-screen television, wiring his stereo and gaming console, claiming unused furniture from elsewhere in the Guest House. Soon the room was filled with Sloan's motorcycle-racing posters and helmets and a small garden gnome lying in a provocative position. Erin Singer, the house's kitchen manager, loved watching it happen. "All of a sudden, it was a late-twenties-dude's room," she said.

Once Sloan was settled, the feeling was one of profound relief. His little collective had been caring for him as best they could. But now he had chefs eager to cook for him and nurses and volunteers to ensure that he was comfortable. His mother and his friends didn't have to nag him about taking his pain medication anymore or try, ineptly, to clean and dress the wounds on his feet that caused him such shame. Baldwin told me, "At Zen, they talk about being unburdened and unburdening." And that's what happened: They could just be Sloan's mother and friends again, and Sloan no longer had to be their patient, either.

From then on, throngs of Scuderia co-workers and other friends passed through the Guest House. Desmo, the dog, hung out, too. "His entourage was either one-deep or ten-deep," Jolene Scarella, then the director of nursing, told me. They sat around playing video games and drinking Bud Light, just like they always did, or they swept Sloan around the city for dinner at his favorite restaurants. The Guest House isn't a somber place, but still, the volunteers weren't accustomed to this level of freewheeling autonomy or raucousness or youth. "They brought so much joy to the house," Singer said. And yet, some volunteers also had a hard time shaking the acute tragedy of Sloan's case. All that Buddhist, contemplative nonattachment was easier to buy into with the elderly; with Sloan, it was hard to feel as if you were helping someone transition through a cosmic crescendo at the end of a life well lived. Some of the staff, like Singer, were only slightly older than Sloan. Others had children his age. It felt cruel.

Sloan's body, meanwhile, continued to fail faster than anyone had anticipated. Within days, breathing became more onerous and the weeping ulcerations on his feet became rawer; there was blood draining from his right foot now, and a terrible odor. On Thursday, just three days after Sloan arrived, he needed to transition from OxyContin to methadone.

The next day, he went wedding-dress shopping. Baldwin and her fiancé had scrapped their wedding plans in Illinois. But a chaplain at UCSF volunteered to perform the ceremony at the tiny park next to the Guest House instead, and Singer offered to throw together a little reception inside. For Sloan, the best man, planning the wedding with his mother became a fun distraction. He was too swollen to wear a suit, but found a purple-and-gold velour tracksuit he liked online—the tuxedo of sweat suits, called a "Sweatsedo." Baldwin ordered one with RANDY embroidered on the breast.

The wedding was scheduled for the following Thursday. The Friday before, Sloan's fourth day at the Guest House, Baldwin drove him to a David's Bridal and helped him arrange himself on a chair. He seemed much foggier all of a sudden. As she came out of the dressing room, modeling each gown, Sloan mostly managed a thumbs-up or thumbs-down.

That night, Baldwin called Sloan's sisters in Texas and his father in Tennessee and said that it didn't seem as if Randy had months anymore, or even weeks. She told them to come right away.

Miller hardly saw Sloan at the Guest House. As Zen Hospice's executive director, he was consumed by fundraising and strategic planning or throttled by administrative work. The week Sloan arrived, Miller was courting producers from *60 Minutes,* hoping they would do a segment on the Guest House, and meeting with the Silicon Valley design firm IDEO, which he had retained to help put Zen Hospice forward as a national model for end-of-life care. IDEO, meanwhile, was calling Miller to consult on its own projects—helping entrepreneurs disrupt what some had taken to calling the "death space."

And yet, Miller's rising prominence made him uneasy. "If I want to keep doing this work, I have to be seeing patients," he told me. "It's really easy to get unhelpfully abstract." He was spending too much time in the wrong death space.

Still, it wasn't that Miller was too busy to visit with Sloan. He stopped by his room a couple of times, early on, but eventually made a therapeutic decision to keep his distance. It was obvious to Miller that his presence in the room upset the fragile sense of normalcy that Sloan and his friends were managing to create. As soon as Miller poked his head in, someone from Scuderia would start retelling the motorcycle story, saying how much Sloan loved building that bike for him, how he was "a legend." "No one knew what to say," Miller remembered. "Their suffering was palpable, and some of their suffering was these spastic efforts to put a smiley face on things."

It was also easy to wonder how much of Sloan's own composure was projected for their benefit. A friend from the shop, Steve Magri, told me that even when Sloan was healthy, "he would never let you feel uncomfortable around him." Moreover, the whole-brain radiation had clearly changed Sloan, sent him deeper within himself. The pain medication had, too. He occasionally said things that even he seemed surprised by or that seemed ludicrously out of character. He had always been a vulnerable, childlike man, but there were moments, in his last days, when his mother couldn't tell whether he'd achieved some higher state of openheartedness or was just disoriented. At one point, Sloan asked her to drive him to Scuderia so he could tell his boss that he was sorry, but he probably wouldn't be coming back to work after all. "I hate to let you guys down," Sloan said tenderly, as if he were breaking this news for the first time.

I never met Randy Sloan. But as I heard these stories in the months after his death, it became impossible for me not to fixate on the unfathomability of his interior life, or anyone's interior life, at the end—to wonder how well Sloan had come to terms with what was happening to him, how much agony he might have felt. Erin Singer, the kitchen manager, told me that Sloan seemed intent on keeping his distance from the Guest House— his physical distance. Usually, she said, he sat under a tree in the park next door, silently smoking a cigarette. And it struck Singer as significant that Sloan "didn't sit looking at the street or the garden. He always sat looking at the house," as if he was wrestling with what it would mean to go back inside.

The question that was unsettling me was about regret: How sure was everyone that Sloan didn't have desires he would have liked to express or anguish he would have liked to work through—and should someone have helped him express and work through them, instead of just letting him play video games and fart around with his friends? My real question, I guess, was: Is this all there is?

Later, when I admitted this to Miller, he told me he understood this kind of anxiety well, but was able, with practice, to resist it. "Learning to love not knowing," he said. "That's a key part of this story. Obviously, I don't know the depths of Randy's soul, either. Was Randy enlightened or did he just not have the right vocabulary for this, if any of us do? We'll never know. And maybe the difference between those things is unimportant. I think of it as: Randy got to play himself out."

This is a favorite phrase of Miller's. It means that Randy's ability to be Randy was never unnecessarily constrained. What Sloan chose to do with that freedom at the Guest House was up to him. Miller was suggesting that I'd misunderstood the mission of Zen Hospice. Yes, it's about wresting death from the one-size-fits-all approach of hospitals, but it's also about puncturing a competing impulse, the one I was scuffling with now: our need for death to be a hyper-transcendent experience. "Most people aren't having these transformative deathbed moments," Miller said. "And if you hold that out as a goal, they're just going to feel like they're failing." The truth was, Zen Hospice had done something almost miraculous: It had allowed Sloan and those who loved him to live a succession of relatively ordinary, relatively satisfying present moments together, until Sloan's share of present moments ran out.

By Sloan's sixth day at Zen Hospice, he'd become unsteady on his feet and was falling asleep in the middle of sentences. But when a nurse went to check on him at the start of her shift that morning, he smirked mischievously and told her, "I have cancer, so my mom wants me to go sailing."

In truth, the trip was Sloan's idea. The Scuderia gang had a tradition of Sunday trips to Angel Island, a forested state park in the middle of San Francisco Bay. And so, that morning, they met on a dock in Sausalito, motored over, dropped anchor, and started barbecuing and drinking Coronas—a low-key "simulated rager," as one friend put it. Sloan barely spoke. He smiled occasionally. He pounded his pain medication. He returned to the Guest House that evening, sunburned and dehydrated and three hours later than he'd promised. (The nurses were upset, concerned mainly that Sloan could have been in pain all day.)

Then he went out to dinner. After days of driving, Sloan's father, Randy Senior—Big Randy, everyone called him—had reached San Francisco from Tennessee, and Sloan was adamant that the two of them get some food. They ate huge plates of eggs and hash browns at a nearby diner. Big Randy noticed that Sloan was struggling to grip his fork and that he'd ordered a beer but didn't touch it. Big Randy was recovering from foot surgery—he was hobbled himself. So when they were finished, he found he had to prop Sloan against a tree outside while he staggered to the curb to hail a cab. "Like Laurel and Hardy," Big Randy said. Sloan, slumped against the tree trunk, lit a cigarette and couldn't stop laughing.

He died thirty-six hours later, early on Tuesday morning, his eighth day at the Guest House. Baldwin hadn't yet arrived for the day and Big Randy, who spent the night with his son, had just left to take a shower. Two nurses were changing Sloan's clothes when it happened, and one of them, Derrick Guerra, who'd grown particularly close to Sloan, told me that, until the last instant, he could feel the young man's hand gripping his arm. The strength still left in his body was unreal, Guerra said.

Sloan's family arrived. Scuderia people arrived. As Sloan's body was wheeled through the Guest House garden toward the back gate, they all placed flower petals around his head and over his chest—a ritual at Zen Hospice known as the Flower Petal Ceremony. Desmo, the husky, leapt up and licked his face.

"It was amazing," Miller now said, telling the doctors around the table at UCSF, summing up Sloan's story. And there was a postscript, too. Two days after Sloan died, Baldwin and her fiancé woke up and decided to go ahead with the wedding they'd planned, in the park next to the Guest House. Afterward, the hospice staff invited everyone in for what can only be described as a joint wedding-reception-funeral.

One staff member later told me that the Guest House felt a little like a house on Thanksgiving that day—full and bustling, in a comforting way. Upstairs in the bedrooms, the same women were still moving through the ends of their lives, each in her own way. But downstairs, there were tubs of beer and cheese plates and a handle of Jameson and someone playing guitar. Miller, who made a point of riding his motorcycle to work, invited Big Randy outside to see it. There were toasts to the happy couple. There were toasts to the dead young man. And there was his grieving mother, in a new off-white gown.

The scene was all mixed-up, upside-down, and unexpectedly joyful, Miller told the doctors: If you'd walked in off the street, it would have been impossible to explain. "It makes you happy for a place like the Guest House where such things can happen," he said, "a roof where these things can coexist."

"Have you had many weddings?" one of the other doctors asked.

"Not a ton," Miller joked. "We haven't put it in the brochure yet."

It was a Wednesday, the day Miller had his cancer clinic at the hospital, and he excused himself from the meeting to dash to another floor. His first patient, heavily medicated but still tearing up from pain in his spine and legs, fumbled through his symptoms and worries, still wondering how this had happened to him. Miller mostly listened and said things like: "There's nothing you could have done to cause this, pal. That's important for you to know." A lot of his patients were like this, he later told me. He couldn't do much for them, medically. "But I'm letting them know I see their suffering," he said. "That message helps somehow, some way, a little."

It did help, all morning. It was an astonishing thing to witness. Over the previous weeks, I noticed Miller struggling with his administrative role at Zen Hospice, looking depleted after a long lunch with a donor or while being talked at about options for optimizing the Guest House's automated phone directory. Now, he seemed in his element: The bedside was his natural habitat. When his next patient, a hunched older woman, arrived, Miller started by asking her not just about her pain, sleep, and meds but also about how she was doing since her dog died. "It's a big hole to fill in the heart," Miller told her. She whimpered, "The space is just so big." She seemed relieved just to admit that.

Not long after that, Miller decided to step down as Zen Hospice's executive director. He spent months trying to create the right part-time role for himself—something less administrative and managerial that would get him back at people's bedsides again—but finally resigned. He continued to see patients at UCSF, began co-writing a kind of field guide to dying, and started raising seed money for a dream of his, something he's calling the Center for Dying and Living: a combination "skunk works and design lab," as he puts it, to dig into more imaginative possibilities for palliative care. He also ramped up his public speaking, and as he traveled around the world, he usually did so wearing Randy Sloan's favorite beat-up belt, a gift from Sloan's mother. Only Miller, with his deep appreciation of one, maybe trite-sounding truth—that the dying are still very much alive, and we all are dying—could have thought about Sloan's life, even the last phase of it, and decided, without hesitation, to wear that belt "for good luck."

He was still hopelessly busy, still chastened by the volume of good work he saw in front of him but couldn't do. But it felt right. Miller hadn't unburdened himself, exactly, but rearranged and rebalanced the weight. He was committing to the parts of himself that felt most meaningful and trying to shake free of all the other, unhelpful expectations. "It's the same thing I would counsel a patient," Miller told me. It's what he had counseled Randy Sloan.

Why These Instead of Others?

The whale sighting happened right away, minutes into Day One. Jon, Dave, and I had just been dropped off on a remote Alaskan shoreline, an hour and a half by boat from the closest speck of a town. Jon was working as a sea-kayaking guide that summer in Glacier Bay National Park, and he had invited us up for a seven-day excursion during his week off. As the boat that delivered us vanished, the drone of its engine dampening into a murmur and then finally trailing off, it became unthinkably quiet on the beach, and the largeness and strangeness of our surroundings were suddenly apparent. It was a familiar phenomenon for Jon from the start of all his trips: a moment that people instinctually paused to soak in. To me, it felt like those scenes of astronauts who, having finally rattled free of the earth's atmosphere, slip into the stillness of space. Except we weren't in space. We were on earth—finally, really on earth.

We were only starting to move around again, packing our gear into the kayaks, when we heard the first huff of a blowhole, not far offshore.

Jon was ecstatic. It seemed to him as if the animal were putting on a show, swimming playfully in the kelp, diving, resurfacing, then plowing its open mouth across the surface to feed. He took it as a good omen. Though I had no idea at the time, he was anxious that Dave and I might feel intimidated about making the trip; such a big payoff, so quickly, would get us excited and defuse any apprehensions.

For Dave, the whale sighting had exactly the opposite effect. Once, when he was a kid, his dad took him scuba diving with dolphins. They were friendly, awe-inspiring creatures, purportedly, but they terrified Dave. He could still conjure the feeling of hanging defenselessly in that water while the animals deftly swirled around him, less like solid objects than flashes of reflected light, while he could move only in comparative slow motion. Ever since, he had harbored a fear of large sea creatures—a niche phobia, particularly for a young man who lived in the Bronx, but a genuine one still. And so, even as Dave understood that a chance to see whales up close like this was a major draw of a kayaking trip in Alaska, and though he feigned being thrilled, some second thoughts were kicking in: We were *going* out there, he realized.

The whale left me exhilarated and gleeful, like Jon; but deeper down, I also remember feeling shaken, like Dave. Nothing about the animal registered to me as playful or welcoming. It just appeared in the distance, then transited quickly past us, from left to right. My uneasiness had something to do with the whale's great size and indifference—its obliviousness—as it passed. Watching it made me feel profoundly out of place and register how large that wilderness was, relative to me.

At the time, I was working at a literary magazine in New York City called *The Hudson Review*, mailing poetry submissions to an outside panel of editorial advisers. I was trying hard in my letters to impress one of them: Hayden Carruth, a gruff and irreverent eighty-one-year-old poet who lived far upstate. I loved Carruth's work but was more enamored with his persona: his yeoman life in the woods, his intolerance for phoniness, and, most of all, the precision with which he articulated common suffering, including one strain of his own suffering that I related to, particularly in those years, but wouldn't have had the courage, or clarity, to examine.

"I had always been aware," Carruth once wrote of his youth, "that the Universe is sad; everything in it, animate or inanimate, the wild creatures, the stones, the stars, was enveloped in the great sadness, pervaded by it. . . . Never then or now have I been able to look at a cloudless sky at night and see beauty there. A kind of grandeur, yes—but not beauty. The profusion and variety of celestial lights have always frightened me. Why are they there? Why these instead of others? Why these instead of nothing?"

That was how I felt, watching the whale from the beach: afraid that everything was accidents. Then again, maybe it's just hard to picture the start of the trip in retrospect without amplifying some feeling of foreboding. Something else Carruth wrote that has always stuck with me: "The wilderness begins at the edge of my body, at the edge of my consciousness, and extends to the edge of the universe, and it is filled with menace."

It was mid-August 2002, and we were twenty-three, twenty-four, and twenty-five. We had graduated from college together two years earlier. Dave, whom I also grew up with, shot out of undergrad knowing he wanted to be a doctor and had just finished his first year of medical school. Any similar momentum I had after graduation was instantly sapped. Three nights after I returned to my parents' house from school, I found myself driving my father to the emergency room. Three weeks after that, he died. My grief was disorienting and total; at a moment in life when everything is supposed to feel possible, making any single decision became impossible. I gave in to that sadness for the better part of a year, resettling at home in New Jersey with my widowed mother and sliding back to the summer job I worked during school, glumly breaking down beef at a butcher shop two towns over.

I coped with my fatherlessness and confusion in ways I'm not proud of and still don't understand. I read a lot of books about Ronald Reagan, for example, even the collection of his love letters to Nancy. I also lashed out at Dave, who was living at home that summer, too, studying for the MCAT. He withdrew awkwardly after the funeral, and I suppose I was happy to hold that against him. It triggered some long-standing jealousy. A part of me always resented how he seemed unfairly exempt from the self-doubt and heaviness that I was prone to.

Jon, meanwhile, was teaching at a rustic little boarding school in Switzerland, where his mother was from. The summer after graduation, before starting the job, he set out for Alaska with a friend, sleeping in the bed of their old pickup. In the minuscule town of Gustavus, the gateway to Glacier Bay, he picked up seasonal work in the warehouse of a kayak-tour company. Jon had little actual experience of sea kayaking but had always felt drawn to the ocean in the abstract. In college, he and another friend plotted out a paddling expedition near Glacier Bay, across the border in Canada, and applied for a grant from our school to fund it. The grant was set up in memory of an alumnus who died in an avalanche while mountaineering. It was meant to encour-

age the "responsible and conscientious pursuit of wilderness expeditions." Safety was key. But the committee rejected Jon and
his partner's application. They seemed insufficiently prepared.

That wasn't surprising. Jon grew up doing a lot of backcountry
camping and was a competent outdoorsman, but putting together a grant application required a kind of administrative
fastidiousness he didn't always possess. He was bright but
scatterbrained, forever picking up things and putting them
down, both figuratively (music projects, conversations) but also
literally. I can still picture him hustling around the house we
shared in college, hunting for his keys or his soldering iron, having gotten in over his head rewiring some device. He was an
artist; one piece I remember consisted of a half-peeled banana,
implanted with circuitry and suspended in a jar of formalde-
hyde. Once, he grew grass in our upstairs bathroom—a living
bath mat, he said—until the turf became muddy and flooded the
downstairs.

This was Jon's third summer in Alaska, and he'd worked his
way up to leading expeditions, taking out vacationers for days at
a time. Our trip, however, would venture beyond the typical cir-
cuit, into a remote corner of the park that he'd never been to.
Jon had no serious concerns about our safety, but he felt he bore
responsibility for our emotional well-being. To enjoy ourselves,
we would need to feel comfortable, not just in the wilderness
but also with him as a leader.

He suspected we wouldn't trust him entirely. We didn't. We
knew him before he became a professional guide, and our perception of his expertise lagged behind the reality. "With Jon,"
Dave told me, "it was always unclear to what extent he'd thought
everything through." Dave remembered landing in Gustavus the
night before we got underway and casually asking Jon a lot of
questions: Where are we going, exactly? Do we have everything

we need? Jon seemed to have solid answers for all of them. As we headed back to his place for a good night's sleep, he told us to wait in the yard. He was living alone for the summer in a house that an acquaintance was building in the woods. The structure was framed-up but largely wall-less, and Jon, to be safe, needed to check that no moose had wandered inside.

After a spectacular first day of paddling, we came ashore on a rocky tidal flat about two miles from where we were dropped. Jon gave us his detailed tutorial about bear safety while we set up our campsite. He taught us, for example, to holler "Hey, bear!" if we heard any rustling but also preventively, ahead of us, when we walked through the woods. The last thing you wanted was to come across a brown bear unannounced.

"Hey, bear!" Jon kept hollering, by way of demonstration. He said it goofily, like a children's TV host greeting some down-on-his-luck ursine neighbor at the doorway to their clubhouse. This was intentional. Jon had noticed that the people on his trips often resisted bellowing "Hey, bear!" into the wilderness. It was essential for their safety, but it felt silly or vulnerable somehow, like singing in public. So he learned to turn it into a shtick, spinning it into a stream-of-consciousness narration: *Hey, bear, I'm coming into the trees now. Hope you're having a fantastic evening, Mr. Bear!* It loosened everyone up. They were performing for their friends now; the whole group was in on the joke.

I had never seen a wild bear, though I had backpacked in bear country a handful of times. I felt comfortable with the animals in the abstract. But here, the bears weren't abstract; they breached the material plane. There were bear trails everywhere, leading from the tree line to the water, and disquietingly close, I felt, to where we were pitching our tent. We found heaps of their scat.

We saw trees where the animals had slashed off the bark to eat the inner layer, tufts of fur from their paws still plastered in the sap.

I pretended I was having fun. But that evening I grew increasingly petrified, almost delirious. My eyes tightened, scanning for bears. The sound of the wind became bears, and so did the mossy sticks cracking under our feet. I gave myself a migraine, then phased in and out of sleep.

At sunrise, I woke feeling foolish. While Jon cooked pancakes, I reasoned with myself, privately, in a notebook I'd brought on the trip. I tried to conceive of the situation as a geometry problem. Yes, some number of bears roved this landscape, I wrote: relatively tiny, independent blips, going about their business randomly, just like us. In all that empty space and confusion, a lethal collision of their moving blips and our moving blips would be an improbable coincidence. I'd been distorting those odds, mistaking myself for "the absolute focus of all bears' attention," I wrote. It was embarrassing, really. "To be afraid of bears," I concluded, "is to be narcissistic."

I was reminding myself that freakishly horrible things are, by definition, unlikely to happen. Even now, my reasoning feels sound.

Day Two was a slog. We paddled through a spitting drizzle in an endless straight line, along the high granite walls of the coast. We talked less and less, just pushed through the emerald chop. Then eventually we gave up, hauling in our boats and making camp in a wide, crescent-shaped cove, short of the site that Jon originally picked out on his map.

We had entered Dundas Bay, a rarely visited pocket of the national park that, I've since learned, has a storied history as a hideout for solitary misanthropes. In the 1930s, one prospector built a cabin not far from our campsite and brandished a gun at the Alaska Natives who passed through.

We intuited that the scenery was beautiful, but we could see very little of it through the fog. Our guidebook explained that "the east side of the bay"—where we were—"can get extremely rough during foul weather, since large waves roll in . . . and batter this shoreline." That was happening now: The weather that plinked at us all afternoon was roiling into a storm. Soon, the big rain started. We rushed through dinner, then loafed in our tent until, eventually, the loafing turned to sleep.

A local newspaper would later describe the storm as "short but intense." In Gustavus, a creek swelled to about a foot higher than its previous record. Gale winds, with gusts up to fifty-nine miles per hour, turned back two cruise ships in Skagway, about eighty-five miles north. Around 2:00 a.m., we woke to discover the wind had shorn the rain fly off our tent. Jon's sleeping bag and mine were soaked, while Dave was snug and dry between us. We heard torrents of water lashing down and the waves crashing in the cove.

We got up three or four hours later. The rain and wind no longer felt ferocious but were still too gnarly to paddle through; there was no question, Jon said, that we were staying put. We cooked breakfast and took turns playing chess in the tent. By late morning, the storm seemed to have passed. We were antsy. We figured we would take a look around.

The terrain was crammed with thickets of alder and spruce, underlain by ferns and a furor of prickly things. Jon pointed out devil's club: three or four feet tall and leafy, armored up and down with spines. The plant pierced fleece and hurt like fire.

There were no trails. We'd been trudging for some time when we reached a fast-moving stream, maybe twenty feet wide. Jon was surprised; it wasn't on his map, most likely just a drainage bloated by the storm. We followed it downstream, looking for a way across, and eventually found it bridged by a hefty tree trunk. It seemed like an easy crossing. Jon stepped up and led the way, and Dave and I waited in a single-file line on the stream bank behind him. The creek was loud, like a factory with all its gears and rollers churning. Looking down, Jon realized there was more water than he'd thought.

That's when I heard the snap in the woods behind me. After all my paranoia, I instantly understood that the many bears I'd thought I heard before were absolutely not bears—were *nothing*—because this sound was so unmistakable and crisp, so explicitly something. I turned and hollered, "Hey, bear!" then waited a beat. Maybe I said "Hey, bear!" again; I'm not sure. But I must have scanned those trees long enough to feel satisfied and safe, because I know I was turning my head, to go back to my friends, when I saw the dark shape rushing forward in my peripheral vision.

What I heard must have been roots popping. If a tree is large enough, you can apparently hear them cracking underground like gunfire.

The thud was seismic. The trunk crashed down right next to me. Mapping out bits of evidence later, we concluded that the tree must have been about eighty feet tall and perhaps two feet in diameter. It was some kind of conifer—a spruce or cedar. I screamed, involuntarily, "Look out!" then watched Dave, a few steps directly in front of me, dive sideways and hit the ground. When I got to him, he was crouching, stunned but OK. He looked up and said, "Go get Jon."

It hadn't clicked back in for me yet: There were *three* of us.

The sight of Dave going down had canceled out everything else. I scrambled out over the creek, running across the tree that had just fallen, shouting Jon's name, then spotted him in the water, tangled in a snarl of cleaved-off branches near the bank behind me—a cage, which kept him from hurtling downstream.

He did not know he'd been hit by a falling tree. It had narrowly missed his head, struck his left shoulder, shearing it from his collarbone and breaking many of his ribs. Later, a doctor would explain that the downward force had been so powerful that it had probably squashed Jon's entire upper body, and all the organs inside, down toward his waist, momentarily compressing him like a bellows; for a split second, his shoulders headed in the direction of his belly button, before his torso sprang up again.

Jon had heard nothing, seen nothing. He was turning around to help Dave onto the log—again, feeling responsible for our safety—and the next thing he knew, he was in the water. He tried to reach out his left arm but could not make it move. He could not move his legs. He felt a bolt of pain down his spine.

Jon later described flashing through an idiosyncratic sequence of thoughts, all in a few milliseconds, as if watching a deck of cards fanning across a table. One was an image of himself in a wheelchair, sitting behind a mixing console in a fancy recording studio. *I guess I can become a recording engineer in a wheelchair,* he remembered thinking. He had never worked in a recording studio and, though he played music, he had no particular plans to. Still, this vision apparently felt like an acceptable future and freed him to resurface in the present. That was when he registered me, screaming his name.

Jon told himself he shouldn't move. He knew from his many wilderness first-responder trainings that moving a person with spinal injuries risks paralysis. Then again, he also knew that most of his body was submerged in cold water, and he recognized that he risked dying of hypothermia if he didn't move. "If I'm already paralyzed," he concluded, "I may as well move."

He somehow hoisted himself out of the stream before Dave or I got to him, using his right arm and his chin and biting into something loamy with his teeth, for additional leverage. He reassessed the situation: better. Also: worse. He now realized that we were at least a mile inland from our camp.

Suddenly, his body was walking; his legs just started working. Dave and I put him between us, supporting his frame. He was moving faster than we expected, but uncoordinatedly. Then he crumpled between us. We tried again; Jon was deadweight. Dave noticed that his breathing was shallow and his voice was low—signs, Dave knew from med school, of a collapsed lung. He began battering Jon with a pep talk, telling him, firmly, that he had to get up, that we had to get out of here. Jon didn't need that explained to him; he was cogent and still trying to plot our next steps in his mind. He looked down to see why this log he was resting on was so lumpy and realized that he was, in fact, sitting on his left arm. The arm was slack, obviously broken; his sleeve, impaled up and down with devil's club. Jon had zero feeling in it. He found it amusing, this sensation of complete estrangement from one of his limbs.

Jon had been stressing that it was important to stay together. But this was another theory of wilderness survival that appeared to be breaking down in practice. Someone would have to get on the radio back at our camp. By chance, while marooned in our tent during the rainstorm the night before, Jon showed us how to use the device, though he did it almost as a formality; the handheld VHF unit was merely a line-of-sight radio, he told us, meaning its range was small, its signal too weak to pass through most obstacles. You were unlikely to reach anyone you couldn't see, and we hadn't seen anyone since a faraway fishing boat, early on Day One.

There was a moment of discussion, or maybe just an exchange of looks between me and Dave. I told Dave he should go. I didn't trust myself to find my way back. I also knew that I lacked the courage to try; whether I was being sensible or cowardly, I still don't know. Besides, I took for granted that Dave would make it. He was more capable in my mind, less likely to cinch himself in indecisive knots.

Recently, though, Dave told me: "You probably had no idea how much in my own head I was. I know that you, growing up, definitely felt insecure about things, and I think you looked at me and thought, *Dave has everything figured out.* But I had so much anxiety." He brought up the tremor he used to have in his hands. I knew about it; in high school, we'd waited tables together, and I occasionally had to carry out Dave's soup orders, so he wouldn't spill. But I guess I thought of the tremor as strictly physiological. I couldn't see the vulnerability causing it.

Now, as Dave sprinted away from me and Jon, swatting devil's club from his path with the rubberized sleeve of his rain jacket, his nerves rose up and rattled him. He worried he wouldn't be able to find the radio once he got back or know how to turn it on. What if he broke the radio, foreclosing whatever marginal chance we had of getting help? There were lots of ways to screw this up, Dave realized. More occurred to him as he ran.

He found the radio. He turned it on. Then, having solved these problems, he encountered another he hadn't anticipated: *What is the appropriate thing you're supposed to say?* he asked himself. On TV, you see a lot of people saying "Mayday." And so, Dave faced the open water and started broadcasting into the fog: "Mayday, Mayday." Even in that moment, though, alone on a beach in the middle of nowhere, he felt slightly self-conscious about it. *This is so goddamn cliché*, he thought.

Back in the woods, kneeling over Jon, I was having the same problem: I didn't know what to say. He was lying near a log on his injured side, his beard and glasses flecked with dirt and tendrils of moss. He seemed to be on the brink of losing consciousness. At no time would the possibility of Jon's dying surface concretely in any of our minds. Still, I knew I was supposed to keep talking to him, to tether him to the world with my voice somehow.

I started vamping platitudes: We were going to get out of here soon, and so forth. But I could feel myself treading water, even blundering at one point into a long-winded apology, worried I had overstayed my welcome that one Christmas with his family. I was afraid that the helplessness in my voice might be counterproductive, unsettling Jon instead of steadying him. It was a tremendous silence to fill.

What can a person say? I had two literature professors in college who made us memorize poems. You never knew when some lines of verse would come in handy, they claimed. One liked to brag that, while traveling through Ireland, he found that if he spat out some Yeats at a pub, he could drink for free. This is how I wound up reciting a love poem to Jon.

It was "The Shampoo," by Elizabeth Bishop, a lyric poem about the enormity of time, which turns startlingly intimate at the end, when Bishop offers to shampoo her lover's silvering hair: "Come, let me wash it in this big tin basin, / battered and shiny like the moon."

After that, I imagine I also did some W. H. Auden; I knew a fair amount of Auden back then. The stuff in rhyme and meter was always easiest to memorize—"Looking up at the stars, I know quite well / That, for all they care, I can go to hell"—which is why I had a lot of Robert Frost at my disposal as well: "Stopping by Woods on a Snowy Evening," "The Road Not Taken." For the most part, I trafficked in hits.

Jon and I would spend about an hour and a half together alone on the forest floor. I ran through everything in my quiver— Kay Ryan, A. R. Ammons, Michael Donaghy—padding each poem with little prefatory remarks, while Jon said nothing, just signaled with his eyes or produced a sound whenever I checked in. I felt like a radio DJ playing records in the middle of the night, unsure if anyone was listening. And here's one about owls by Richard Wilbur, I would tell Jon, and off we would go.

I must have also done at least one by Hayden Carruth, my curmudgeonly pen pal at the literary magazine. Carruth's poems didn't lend themselves to memorization, but I'd worked hard to nail one of my favorites, in which he describes stopping to notice a deer standing in an apple thicket, then realizing the northern lights are flaring overhead. Hayden and the animal pass a moment in stillness together. "We are proud to be afraid," he writes, "proud to share / the silent magnetic storm that destroys the stars." Relative to that boundless violence above them, he and the deer are momentarily allied, though still not entirely connected: "a glimpse, an acknowledgment / it is enough and never enough."

That's what I said to my friend, powerlessly, tenting my jacket over his face when it started to rain. The title of the poem is: "I Know, I Remember, But How Can I Help You."

The Coast Guard cutter Mustang wasn't where it was supposed to be. The 110-foot patrol boat normally spent its time coursing through the Gulf of Alaska, inspecting halibut-fishing vessels, or circulating, as a terrorist deterrent, near the oil terminals at Valdez. It was home-ported in Seward, hundreds of miles from Glacier Bay. But the crew was transiting to Juneau for a training when, a few days earlier, they were smacked by the same storm that later poured inland, over us. "We had gotten absolutely pummeled," John Roberts, a petty officer on the Mustang, told me recently. For two days, the boat swished around in fifteen-foot-plus seas. Many on the crew had been hunkered in the mess deck, vomiting, while Roberts and a couple of his shipmates did their best to cover everyone's watches. Finally, the Mustang slipped into Glacier Bay to find some protection. The weather started to ease. That afternoon, as Roberts piloted the Mustang east, toward Dundas Bay, his pallid crewmates were finally staggering back up to the bridge, asking where the hell they were.

That was when Dave's Mayday call came through. The signal on the Mustang's radio was thin and faint, barely edging into range. Another of the ship's petty officers, Eamon McCormack, explained to me that in retrospect the connection feels "mind-boggling." Glacier Bay National Park extends over more than five thousand square miles. Our signal would have covered two or three miles at most. And yet, a boat—a Coast Guard boat, no less—happened to be passing through that exceedingly small window at precisely the right time. "I don't know if, nine times out of ten, you play that over again and the outcome would be the same," McCormack said. A moment earlier or later—seconds, potentially—and we might have slipped out of alignment. The moving boat would have cruised out of range, uncoupling from us forever.

It was 1:25 p.m. when the Mustang received Dave's call, according to one of the subsequent Coast Guard reports. Roberts couldn't believe it. "Come on, man, I'm tired," he said aloud, wearily, to the receiver in front of him. Roberts waited for a moment, per protocol, on the off chance that the Coast Guard's central communications center in Juneau would pick up the call instead. Then, after nothing more happened, he turned and asked his watch commander to pull out all the standardized search-and-rescue paperwork. He was steeling himself, resummoning his professionalism. "I guess we're doing this," he said.

Roberts was the crew member on the Mustang with the most current medical training; he would complete his EMT certification the following month. As he started firing questions at Dave on the radio, he didn't like the answers that he heard coming back: the shallowness of Jon's breathing, the likelihood of a punctured lung. More fundamental, Roberts remembered: "Any time a tree falls on somebody, it's not good." He was also unsettled to learn that Dave and I both lived in New York City—a red flag, he had found, when someone winds up in trouble in the wilderness.

We were a hundred nautical miles from the nearest hospital; a half-day trip, even in ideal conditions. The Mustang requested that the Coast Guard Air Station in Sitka send a helicopter, but the immediate plan was for Roberts and three crewmates to peel toward shore in the ship's Zodiac and track us down. Dave had found the flare in Jon's emergency kit and now, at 2:20, with the Zodiac underway, the Coast Guard asked him to fire it. He was still in front of our campsite, facing the water. He'd never shot off a flare before. He aimed straight up, but then watched as the bright tracer rose and arced somewhere far behind him, deep in the woods. He was uncertain whether this counted as a success.

He started scanning the fog in front of him, but the Zodiac never appeared.

Someone on the Mustang caught sight of the flare near the end of its arc and immediately directed the crew on the Zodiac toward it, steering them far away from Dave to the opposite side of the little peninsula we'd camped on. And yet, this was lucky: They wound up coming ashore much closer to where I was waiting in the woods with Jon. Soon, whatever poem I was reciting was interrupted by whistles blowing and voices calling, and eventually three shapes, wearing hard hats and heavy orange rain gear, rushed toward us out of the trees.

Roberts was especially impressive, a reassuringly large Boston-area native with a booming voice. He knelt and took Jon's vitals. The information was troubling: His pulse was sixty beats per minute; his breathing, fast and shallow. They put his neck in a brace and eased him onto a kind of truncated backboard, called a Miller Board, to move him out to the beach. Dave had returned by then. He and I crouched at one end of the board, near Jon's feet, as someone—presumably Roberts—bellowed a count of three to lift.

Later that night, lying down to sleep in a bed-and-breakfast in Gustavus—stunned and depleted, but dry and warm—Dave and I would talk and talk, reviewing the entire ordeal. We had drooped into a long silence, coasting toward sleep, when Dave spoke up with one last observation. When we were getting ready to lift Jon on the backboard, he said, it occurred to him that this was one of those crisis moments you hear about, like when mothers are suddenly able to lift a car off their baby. Dave expected we were going to have superhuman strength.

We did not have superhuman strength. On Roberts's command, the men raised Jon to waist height, swiftly and seemingly perfectly level, as though their arms and deltoids were hydraulic.

Then, in one motion, they took off downhill, with negligible help from us. This can't be accurate, but I remember the sensation of being almost dragged, like children in a sled.

A National Geographic television crew was embedded at the Coast Guard's air station in Sitka, filming an installment of a thrill-ride reality series. The network had sent crews to other Coast Guard stations around the country, too, though this assignment appeared to hold the most dramatic potential. Air Station Sitka was unique: Its pilots were responsible for twelve thousand miles of coastline, a sprawling, treacherous wilderness riven with fjords, inlets, and glaciers, often buffeted by implacably horrible weather. People who went into the backcountry in Alaska had a way of getting themselves into a different magnitude of trouble, too; as Roberts put it, "When stuff happens in Alaska, it's big." Still, this was the television crew's eighth day in Sitka, and as the show's producer later explained: "I was having calls with my bosses at headquarters saying, 'Nothing is happening!' We were scrambling to come up with Plan B." Then the Mustang's call came in at 1:42.

"What type of injuries are we looking at?" asked the dispatcher. She was taking the call from behind a semicircular counter, like the reception desk at a midlevel corporate branch office. She had a framed snapshot of a parakeet to brighten her work space, and a photograph of a dog with a heart that said, I WOOF YOU. A cameraman stood conspicuously beside her, holding a tense, tight shot.

"Probable broken ribs, a definite broken arm," said the man on the other end. Then his voice faltered, seemed to give up: "And whatever else would happen to you if a tree fell on you," he added.

The dispatcher retrieved the appropriate paperwork and scribbled "Tree fell on person" on one line. She read the current weather aloud: "thirty knots wind, three hundred ceiling, heavy rain, and one-mile vis." That would soon be revised: the ceiling had dropped to a hundred feet. Entering the weather conditions on one of the Coast Guard incident reports, someone would write, in a kind of nihilistic catchall: "Extremely terrible."

The Coast Guard's policy was to deploy a helicopter within thirty minutes of the initial request, but the air station's operations officer, Commander Karl Baldessari, informed everyone that this mission would take longer to plan. Baldessari was a twenty-five-year veteran of the Coast Guard, a fast-moving, sinewy man in a blousy flight suit, with a tidy mustache and spiky hair. His role at the air station was that of a firehouse chief. He was responsible for the safety of everyone working there, which meant making judicious decisions about what warranted sending them hurtling through the sky.

That calculus got knotty in conditions like these, though there was a baseline volatility to flying in Alaska at any time. The Coast Guard didn't let its helicopter pilots fly lead out of Sitka, no matter how much experience they had at other air stations, until they practiced difficult landings at specific locations in the region and got their egos battered a little by logging a full winter in the state. Visibility in Alaska was frequently poor; conditions changed quickly. One pilot told me about blindly tunneling through fog in the dark when his co-pilot got "caged": The man lifted his eyes momentarily from his instruments and, without any visual references or a horizon to latch on to, found it impossible to reorient himself, lost all sense of direction, and was felled by vertigo.

During much of the year it was also cold enough, with sufficient moisture in the air, that ascending to clear the region's many minor mountains or even just flying through a cloud risked the aircraft's icing up. To mitigate this, the Coast Guard had laid out virtual "track lines" across the entirety of their range: a grid of GPS points and a network of paths connecting them, along which pilots could chart a course and fly at a relatively low altitude, confident they weren't going to smash into a mountain. The system wasn't comprehensive; the track lines got the pilots close to their destination, but ultimately they had to diverge from this GPS superhighway and fly the remaining distance the old-fashioned way, with their radar and eyes. It was like taking an exit off the interstate, except there might be a granite wall in front of you wherever you chose to get off. It was possible the pilots would travel very far—a half-mile away from whoever needed their help—only to discover that the last leg was too risky and be forced to turn back.

Baldessari gathered the two pilots on duty that afternoon and the air station's flight surgeon, then unrolled a large paper map. He pointed to our location, explaining: "That's probably one of the lousiest places we fly in and out of. This Inian Pass, right here, is the worst place we could possibly go."

Inian Pass is a slim channel near the center of the Icy Strait, the long, interconnected system of waterways stretching through Glacier Bay. Conditions in the Icy Strait can be bad three hundred days of the year, Baldessari recently told me; wind, rain, and storm surges all push through it fast from the open ocean. But Inian Pass is a narrow keyhole at the center of the strait—a mile-wide opening between a few uninhabited islands and a rocky point—where all that weather speeds up. The only way for the pilots to reach us would be to fly straight through it.

Nothing in the National Geographic footage, at this point, feels reassuring. The flight surgeon holds his hand over his mouth and bites his lip. The co-pilot, Chris Ferguson, only a few months into his posting in Alaska, mills around and fidgets with his ear. It's obvious Baldessari needs convincing. He wasn't eager to send his men up if he didn't have to and wasn't certain they would make it all the way there if he did.

"It's kind of funny," he told the pilots, pointing at the map. "You've got a boat right here."

Lying on his backboard like a driftwood burl, Jon was conscious and cognizant of his pain, but he had started to feel somehow buffered from his body, uninterested in connecting with the world beyond it. He would later describe himself as a "thinking blob. It was a very passive experience." He didn't know what was happening but could tell our momentum had stalled. He was confused and felt impatient. In his mind, the three of us had solved the impossible problem: We'd managed to get help. This was supposed to be the simple part, when everyone rushed him to the hospital. Instead, his condition deteriorated. Within ten minutes of reaching the beach, Jon threw up. I'd never seen anything like it, a kind of dark purple gristle. I took out my wool cap to wipe his face, and he retched a second time, straight into my hat.

"I got that all over me," John Roberts told me recently. He'd seen vomit like that before; it meant Jon had ingested a fair amount of blood and signaled internal injuries. It made Roberts anxious. He had been on the Mustang for two and a half years at that point but had spent the previous four years in Palm Beach, a busy but less extreme posting that often involved rescuing weekend boaters from relatively close to shore—and where, Roberts pointed out, the water is warm and won't necessarily kill you if you go in. Moreover, the bulk of the Coast Guard's training is for maritime rescues, not rescues on land. Counterintuitive as it sounds, Roberts's comfort level and confidence had dropped significantly once he hopped off the Zodiac and set foot on the beach.

He reported back to the Mustang that Jon had thrown up, then soon radioed again, explaining that Jon was going into shock. He kept giving and requesting updates, trying to gauge how long this might take, and eventually started erecting a make-shift shelter out of plastic sheeting and medical tape, hoping to keep Jon out of the rain. Out of earshot of us, Roberts explained to his crewmate Eamon McCormack what the vomit meant: The possibility of Jon dying, here under their care, was real. At one point in the National Geographic footage, as Roberts's calls are relayed to the air station in Sitka, you can see where the dispatcher writes on her form: "E.M.T. does not feel comfortable."

By this time, the air station's flight surgeon had received enough information to be alarmed. "It sounds like he's got a pretty significant chest injury," he told Baldessari. Baldessari understood they would need to launch a helicopter but warned the Mustang that the aircraft might not make it through the weather; ultimately it would be the pilots' call, once they veered off their last track line and tried to shoot through Inian Pass.

They would go and give it a look, Baldessari explained over the radio, but the outlook was iffy. He explained that the guys on the beach must be prepared to get Jon back on their cutter and haul him to a hospital themselves, as fast as they could.

One evening this winter, my phone rang, and it was Karl Baldessari. Long retired from the Coast Guard, he was teaching aviation at a community college in Oregon, where I'd left a voicemail message earlier that day. I meanwhile had metamorphosed into a forty-year-old father of two and fumbled to explain to Baldessari that, as thrilled as I was to have tracked him down, I was, at the moment, racing to finish a risotto for my daughters before gymnastics practice and would have to call him back. Without missing a beat, Baldessari blared orders at me, joking, but still sounding as instinctually in charge as he did in the National Geographic footage: "OK," he said, "you want to stir it constantly, but slowly!"

I didn't expect any of the Coast Guardsmen I was cold-calling to remember that day. However dramatic it remained for me, I assumed the event would have been obscured in a yearslong wash of more sensational incidents. But everyone I spoke to did remember it, immediately and in detail. Baldessari had been involved in hundreds of rescue operations during his thirty-year career, and yet, as I stood at the stove on the phone that evening, he told me: "The moment I listened to your voicemail, I knew exactly the case! It was almost like it was yesterday."

There was something about the supreme freakishness of the accident that had left a lasting impression. For those who came ashore, the experience was also marked by a feeling of subtly escalating chaos and the pressure to surmount it. McCormack told me that ours was a story he retold endlessly, often to the younger Coast Guardsmen he was eventually tasked with training. In it was a lesson about "not taking situations that look impossible at face value," he said. "When things start to go wrong, don't panic or lose sight of what resources you've got." Keep working the problem until its absolute end—even, McCormack added, if it means deviating from official policy.

McCormack was not supposed to be landing an inflatable boat on an unforgivably rocky Alaskan shoreline, for example. But there he was, anyway, beaching the Zodiac as gingerly as he could, so that Roberts and the other men could load Jon aboard. They slid him in on his side "like a folder into a filing cabinet," as

Jon put it, and started motoring through the chop, very cautiously, back to the Mustang, about a mile away.

As relieved as Jon had been when the Coast Guard first arrived, he also felt instantaneously more vulnerable. Strapped to the backboard, his neck in the collar, he surrendered control of his body, however imperfect that control had been. He was being hauled around as an object now, with no ability to wriggle or shift positions, to manage his pain, or even to turn his head and see what was happening. He was helpless, entirely dependent on the upright people operating around him, those voices he could hear discussing him on the far side of some gauzy divide. About ten minutes into the trip on the Zodiac, Jon heard one of those voices say, "Oh, shit, we're losing air."

A section of the Zodiac's sponson—the inflatable fender that wraps around the boat—had punctured. One side was completely deflated. "It's a big deal," McCormack recently explained to me, sounding surprised that I had to ask. The sponson increases the boat's buoyancy and stability, as well as keeping water from cresting over the side; under normal conditions, a Zodiac with a broken sponson would have been taken out of service automatically. Instead, McCormack found the puncture and wedged the nozzle of a small pump inside. Then—steering the boat with one hand, operating the throttle with the other—he started working the pump with his foot, essentially doing leg presses, to keep the fender partly inflated. The ride was already bumpy in four-foot seas. Now McCormack began tracing a slow, zigzagging course, doing what he could to tamp down the turbulence and the violence to Jon's spine, as well as to guard against the possibility of the injured man's suddenly bounding over the side on his backboard.

Roberts and the other Coast Guardsmen on the Zodiac leaned over Jon to shield him from the splash. The pain was heinous;

Jon seemed to be passing out. Roberts talked to him, held his hand. Roberts felt crushed, he told me; he was torturing this guy in order to save him. When they finally reached the Mustang, rather than hoist Jon off the Zodiac, they swung the ship's crane around and simply lifted the entire boat out of the water, level with the deck, and then carried him aboard, to keep from joggling him any more.

McCormack eventually returned for me and Dave, and a half hour later we were reunited with Jon in the Mustang's athwartship passageway, a cramped steel hallway like the space between two cars of a train. Jon was still battened to the backboard, wedged up to keep the weight of his body on his less-painful side. They had cut off his clothes, though he'd murmured a plea not to—he was wearing a brand-new Patagonia jacket that he had borrowed from a friend—then swaddled him in a hypothermia blanket. Dave and I knelt and rubbed his feet.

The helicopter was going to make it. I don't remember there being a grand announcement. I'm not sure we were ever made aware of the possibility that it wouldn't. Now the crew got busy below: tying down anything that could be blown off by the rotor wash or stashing it in the mess. I also don't remember hearing the helicopter when it finally arrived.

Instead, I remember only a heavy door to our left swinging open to reveal, like a scene from an action movie, the silhouette of a man in a blue flight suit, feet planted shoulder-width apart to steady himself as the ship rocked sideways. The cable he'd been lowered on drew back into the ocean spray and fog behind him. "I'm flight surgeon Russ Bowman," he announced and stepped inside.

Bowman took Jon's vitals and gave him several successive shots of morphine. Soon, everyone was working to squeeze him back through the narrow doorway and onto the deck where the helicopter, an MH-60 Jayhawk, was idling overhead.

Until recently, the story I told about the accident unfolded in two basic acts: The tree fell, instantaneously unleashing a kind of unfathomable chaos; then the Coast Guard appeared and, just as swiftly, regathered that chaos into order. It was like watching footage of an exploding object, then watching it run in reverse. The maneuver the Coast Guard was readying to execute now, on the deck of the Mustang, would be the climax of that progression.

The helicopter hovered thirty or forty feet over the boat, mirroring its speed and trajectory, while both vehicles moved slowly forward. "Looks like you're heading for a rain squall," the co-pilot, Chris Ferguson, radioed the Mustang at one point, and asked the ship to adjust its course, to keep them in as forgiving weather as possible. Soon the flight mechanic was calling out instructions to tuck the aircraft into alignment: "Forward and right thirty. Forward and right twenty. Forward and right ten." Then finally—speaking, in the flight recordings, with an almost galling air of imperturbability—the lead helicopter pilot, Rich McIntyre, radioed the flight mechanic to begin the hoist.

The whole procedure, from our vantage point, seemed seamless and routine. In a way, it was: After the agonized deliberation at the air station, the pilots exited off their GPS route into fairly manageable conditions around Inian Pass. The winds were workable; the water wasn't excessively choppy. Ultimately, scooping Jon off the deck of the Mustang would resemble a standard exercise that the pilots drilled in their trainings. "Not to dumb it down," Chris Ferguson told me—plucking someone with a spinal injury off a moving boat and hoisting them into a moving helicopter is a pretty insane thing to do. "But we normalize what isn't normal."

A few moments earlier, as the men scurried around Jon on his backboard, packaging and fastening him for the hoist, Jon worried that the second he got airborne he would start twirling uncontrollably, like the feathery end of a cat toy, and potentially thwack his head on the equipment on deck. But now, he was levitating smoothly—a solitary, swaddled bale of a man, perfectly parallel to the ground. Dave and I watched it happen: our friend rising steadily away from us, improbably, to safety. As Jon floated higher, he could hear the Coast Guardsmen on the Mustang beneath him begin to cheer. He felt it was safe to open his eyes. When he did, he saw someone, hunched in the open cargo door of the helicopter, pointing a television camera at him.

Jon was rushed into surgery at the hospital in Sitka that evening. He'd punctured both lungs, one to the point of collapse, sustained multiple fractures on eight of his ribs, broken several vertebrae, shattered his left shoulder blade, and snapped his brachial plexus nerves. His spleen had been macerated into countless flecks. After awakening from surgery, Jon was disappointed that the doctors had swept those shards into a bag and thrown his spleen in the trash; he wanted to get a look at it, maybe even keep it preserved in a jar, alongside his cyborg-banana.

Once back in Gustavus, Dave and I realized that we would need to call Jon's parents in Switzerland. I didn't have to push the job on Dave this time; he was adamant. He felt he would need to face conversations like these if he was going to be a doctor. It was Jon's father who picked up, and after absorbing the news, he paused and caught Dave off guard. "Thank you," he said solemnly. "You guys saved my son's life."

Dave's stomach dropped. "I remember thinking about it," he

told me recently, "and realizing, Yeah. I guess, logistically, we did." I had the same reaction when Dave hung up the phone and, clearly shaken, relayed his conversation to me. Until that moment, the idea that we saved Jon's life had never occurred to us, possibly because the idea that Jon might have died still hadn't occurred to us. We had zero sense of accomplishment, or even agency. In our minds, all we did was avoid screwing up until the real help could arrive and save him.

But Jon hadn't absorbed the story that way. From the instant he willed himself out of the water, he felt all of us locking into that same seamless flow of order steadily displacing chaos that Dave and I only experienced once the Coast Guard arrived. It was amazing to him how the three of us managed to generate solutions for each successive problem. Even my reciting those poems, which to me had always felt like a moment of utter helplessness, became, in Jon's telling, a perfect emblem of that streak of serendipitous problem-solving. "You conveyed a calmness," he told me recently. "I remember it being this nice moment." He added that if he ever had to spend two hours dying on a remote forest floor again, having me there to recite poetry would be one of his top ways to do it.

The feeling of inevitability that day became only more pronounced for Jon as time passed and the entire story of our rescue receded into a prologue to the rest of his life. The surgery in Sitka was only the first of half a dozen, and it would take several years for him to regain 60 percent of the use of his arm, wrist, and hand, as the nerves gradually regrew along his injured side. He was in good enough shape to go back to Alaska the summer after the accident—repairing boats in the company's warehouse and occasionally helping out at the bed-and-breakfast—but he struggled. He could repair kayaks but needed help lifting them. He was unable to wrestle the mattress corners into the fitted sheets when he made the beds. After that, he started working at a recording studio in Portland, just as he envisioned while stuck in the water, and he now runs his own audio-mastering company: Spleenless Mastering.

Eventually Jon seemed to have recovered from the accident without any conspicuous disabilities. But his life has been quietly corroded by chronic pain and, almost equally, by the stresses of navigating the doctors and medications (and their side effects) to manage it. About two years after the accident, he learned he had PTSD. The trauma wasn't the falling tree, but his experience of powerlessness as a perpetual patient in the American medical system. It manifested as a kind of unbearable empathy for anyone who was suffering. Jon found himself shouting at doctors, on his own behalf but also on behalf of strangers in waiting rooms who weren't being seen. He would hear interviews with natural-disaster victims or people without homes on NPR and have to pull his car over. There continued to be other tribulations, too—more mundane ones. A few times a year, he still rebreaks a rib out of nowhere; once or twice, Jon told me, all it has taken is an especially affectionate hug from his wife.

Jon found early on that he could cordon off this suffering, both in his own mind and in conversation, by making jokes about the accident itself and sticking to the happy ending of our rescue, a trick that got much easier after the National Geographic show aired later that year. "Mission Rescue: Final Frontier," the program was called. The soundtrack was all heart-thwacking synth drums and shredding guitar. A foreboding, Ken Burns–effected snapshot of Dave and Jon looking joyful before the trip gave way to a whirring reenactment of someone else's legs, cast in the role of Dave's legs, sprinting through the blurry woods for our radio. A melodramatic narrator pondered the fate of "Kayaker Jon Cohrs."

Initially, the schlockiness of the production felt like a blessing. The show depersonalized the accident, giving us all a shorthand to convey how dramatic that day had been, without confronting how destabilizing and senseless it might have felt. At a party, you could lay out the basics—a tree fell on Jon—then say, "National Geographic even made a TV special about it," and everyone would go wide-eyed but then move on, figuring you would un-spool the real story some other time.

But we never realized the degree to which that kitschy short-hand started to obscure the real story—then, gradually, to re-place it. I'm embarrassed to admit that, though Jon and I have remained close, I did not know the extent to which he has con-tinued to suffer for the last seventeen years until talking to him for several hours in order to write this account.

The morning after the accident, Dave and I traveled back to Dundas Bay to pack up our campsite and collect the kayaks we abandoned the previous evening. We were shuttled there from Gustavus by the same boat captain who dropped us off three days earlier, a forbiddingly taciturn commercial fisherman named Doug Ogilvy.

The tide in the cove was way out when we arrived; it was, as Ogilvy put it, "a suck-ass beach." The approach was so shallow that he had to drop anchor a hundred yards or more from shore. He asked if we had waders. We did not. So Ogilvy put on his, climbed down the ladder, and told Dave to get on his back. Then stoically, like an ox or an old-timey strongman hauling a safe, he trudged through the thigh-high water, dropped Dave on the gravel beach, then lurched back and hauled me the same way, as if I were a man-size infant in a papoose.

Dave told me he'd had a strange feeling on the ride out, as if we would discover that an even more massive tree had fallen on our tent since we last slept there and that all three of us would have been crushed and killed if we'd spent another night in Dundas Bay, as planned. That is, he half-expected to find evidence that the accident had been fortuitous somehow, that there was a reason, or redemptive value, behind it. My mother had the same instinct when I called her the night before. On the phone I strained to emphasize for her—she was only two years into her cruelly premature widowhood, and I was new at being the over-protective son of a widow—that Jon was going to be all right, and that Dave and I were safe. She told me that my dad must have been up there looking out for us somehow.

I resented all the supernatural thinking. If it comforted other people, fine, but I'd somehow known right away that I didn't need a reason for the accident. It was senseless, but straightfor-ward, as unequivocal a fact as my father's death had been. A tree fell in the woods. It might not have, but it did. Jon could have died, but he didn't. Other possibilities spiraled infinitely out-ward from there, though apparently I wasn't too interested in contemplating them. As strange as it sounds, it was years before I realized that the tree could have hit me—and only after a friend pointed this out, as I told the story around a fire one night. And it was only a few weeks ago, while on the phone with Jon, that it occurred to me that the tree could have hit all three of us—we were standing in a single-file line, after all, waiting to cross the creek—and that we all might have wound up clob-bered and scattered in that river, dying slowly and watching each other die.

It's also probably true that I helped preclude these possibili-ties by being so feverishly paranoid about bears, wheeling around at the sound of the snapping roots. That's what allowed me to see the tree coming, just barely, and scream that infinitesimal heads-up for Dave. And so, the real meaning of the accident, if I felt compelled to find one, might be that it had validated my most exaggerated fears. But instead, it somehow helped cleanse me of them. There was comfort for me in accepting the arbitrariness of what happened, in regarding it as a spasm of random damage in time and space that, just as randomly, a small number of human beings got the opportunity to repair. We were more capable than I had understood. We were also far more helpless.

On the ride back to Gustavus with our gear, I pictured myself, again, as a small blip in empty space. The ride was rough and jumpy as Ogilvy impatiently pounded his boat through the last vestigial wave energy of the storm; Dave and I had to hold on, to plant ourselves on the bench behind him. But there was a moment when I felt so safe that I loosened my grip, leaned slightly into the motion of the boat, and, closing my eyes, felt myself lift off the seat.

This Is My Serious Face

| 2022 |

One night, many years ago, two friends spotted something extraordinary hanging on the wall of a restaurant in Granada, Spain, and both knew, right away, that they'd need to email me a picture of it.

It was an old photograph, a hazy black-and-white portrait of a young matador sitting on a bench. The bullfighter was slender and long-limbed. He wore a pale, heavily ornamented jacket with oversized epaulets, matching pants, and white knee socks, and sat with one hand formally fixed to his hip while the other flaccidly clasped the nub of a cigarette between his knees. His posture suggested that he'd done his best on short notice to snap his body into a dignified pose for the camera but only got halfway there.

The man's head was tilted, and his dark eyes rose just slightly to meet the lens. His long nose was misaligned. His expression was loaded but elusive. He looked tired, crestfallen, or maybe just bored. My friends hadn't bothered writing anything when they emailed a picture of this photograph to me, but I was hammered by its significance right away: That bullfighter looked exactly like me.

I remember physically jittering back in my seat when I clicked open the image. The likeness was chilling, but also exhilarating—just as it had apparently been for my friends. Apparently, they'd both simultaneously jerked to a stop in front of the photo on their way out of the restaurant, deliriously loaded down with oxtail stew. After a dopey beat of silence, one finally said, "Why is there a picture of Jon on the wall?"

Of course, I understand how exasperatingly subjective these things can be—how a resemblance that feels uncanny and self-evident to one person can bounce off everyone else. Sometimes all you get is a lot of skepticism and squinting, people searching for any sliver of correspondence between the two alleged doppelgängers—*Maybe around the lips, I guess*—just to be polite.

But this photo of the matador was different. For years, I'd show that picture to people at parties without a word and, every time, the shock of recognition was spontaneous and profound. It smacked people with an eerie jolt, joggled them into befuddled swearing or laughter, or downright creeped them out. Even my mother recognized instantly that I and this anonymous Spaniard looked identical, which clearly seemed to rattle the poor woman's core belief that, in all the universe, her boychick was unique and special.

Eventually, I learned who the man in the photograph was. He was known as Manolete, and he is almost invariably described as the best bullfighter of the 1940s and among the greatest of all time. When Manolete died, his funeral took four hours, and a military plane flew low overhead, showering the ten thousand mourners in attendance with a monsoon of red carnations. An American reporter wrote: "Manolete's death carries for his followers the impact that the death of the entire Brooklyn Dodger team would produce in Flatbush."

I ordered an obscure biography of the man, written by an American named Barnaby Conrad, who'd lived in Spain in the '40s and fought bulls himself. The book was slim but filled with photographs, and flipping through it the night it arrived, I was astonished to see my own face everywhere, from every angle. There I was: doting on my fat Spanish mother, eating paella, lancing bulls. There I was: suiting up in my bedazzled jacket at the height of my fame, or caught candidly at close range, looking goofy and agog. And there I was at the end of the book, hewn from marble—eyes shut, unmistakable in profile—resting on top of my tomb.

Before long, I had absentmindedly lowered myself onto my kitchen floor and pressed the spine of the paperback open to a random page, to start reading the book in earnest. And this— I swear—was the very first sentence that I read:

"He has a face that's as dreary as a third-class funeral on a rainy day."

Manolete was ugly. He was *remarkably* ugly—by which I mean, people could not stop remarking about how ugly he was. They just kept taking swipe after swipe at the glum-looking, contorted hideousness of his face. It only took reading a handful of pages of the biography to understand that Manolete's conspicuous ugliness seemed to be a defining feature of his persona. He was ugly the way that Einstein was a genius, the way Gandhi was nonviolent, the way Jeff Bezos is rich.

The peculiarity of his appearance preoccupied everyone. Even people who adored Manolete, even in the middle of praising his talents in the ring, always managed to tack on some gratuitous cheap shot about the unpleasantness of his face. Writers called him "tired-looking" or a "pop-eyed, chinless, badly bodied, painfully and barely dignified man," or the "the mournful-faced, hawk-nosed Manolete." Another went with "Old Big Nose."

The more I read about Manolete, the more it started to feel like this man's face triggered some kind of involuntary slur-reflex in other human beings. One morning, I left the biography on my coffee table, and my six-year-old daughter—who knew nothing about the book, or why I was reading it—happened to catch sight of the portrait on the cover as she trundled by and, out of nowhere, stiffened up and announced: "I can't believe they made a book about someone so ugly!"

Weirder still, Manolete's ugliness appeared to be a very specific strain of ugliness, one that communicated unmistakable sadness and dejection. His long, bowed face was described as "tragic-looking." *The New York Times* wrote that he possessed "such a solemn, gaunt, deadpan face that he sometimes seems twice his age," and another observer noted that "his wide, sad, heavy-lidded eyes hinted at knowledge of terrors the rest of us could only imagine." And yet, this aura of despondency was actually part of Manolete's aesthetic appeal. Over time, he had arrived at a style of bullfighting that was unconventionally minimal and almost apathetic-seeming. He would shuffle into the arena without flair or grace, then repeatedly wave the bull by him with his cape while standing straight as a toothpick, without any facial expression at all, except the brooding and indifferent one with which his face was perpetually fixed. But as Norman Mailer put it, the crowds were "so stirred by the deeps of sorrow in the man that the smallest move produced the largest emotion." Somehow, the dissonance between Manolete's affect and the great feats he was executing created a kind of alchemic beauty. His style hinged on this contrast—this "beautiful ugliness," as one writer put it. "He was by nature a melancholy man, and this sadness was plainly reflected in his art," another explained. "But it was the sadness of an artist, a sadness tinged with languor, and a sadness against which his artistry stood out in high relief in a manner that was quite extraordinary."

I knew almost nothing about bullfighting when I got that first Manolete book, and, to be honest, I've resisted learning any more than necessary about the sport because I find it cruel. Still, here was a man going about his job without any of the clichéd, invincible bravado that I'd associated with matadors, but instead with a look of unease, resignation, vulnerability—even victimhood: a second animal sent into that ring for the trivial enjoyment of a paying audience, trapped all alone behind the unknowable buffer of his own face. Apparently, at the beginning of every bullfighting season, Manolete felt pricks of pain behind his eyes, as though he'd walked into a dusty room. But "there's certainly no dust in this room," he pointed out before one match, grasping for an explanation, "so it must be fear."

I thought about this as I made eye contact with myself in all those old pictures. I couldn't help wondering why this random matador had hurtled out of history, through that portal on a restaurant wall, to reach me here in the present—what inscrutable information he might be carrying, whether his life and his face had anything to do with mine.

Manuel Laureano Rodríguez Sánchez was born in Cordova on July 4, 1917, and nearly died of pneumonia at age two. His father passed away when he was six. He would spend his childhood clinging to his mother, who spoiled him, and seldom played with other kids.

Little Manolete was aloof, morose, and wandered through Cordova lost in thought. He liked to read. He liked to paint. Occasionally, he ventured to the movie theater but was too shy to buy a ticket. And he did not care about bullfighting at all.

The one corrida Manolete had gone to as a small child made no impression on him, and when kids at school pretended to be bulls and matadors, play-fighting with one another, Manolete kept to himself, off to the side. This confused his classmates: They knew Manolete came from a family of bullfighters and assumed he'd inevitably follow in his relatives' footsteps. They didn't understand why he was wasting his time at school in the first place.

It was true: Manolete's grandfather and two of his uncles had been bullfighters, and so had his father, who'd fought under the name Manolete as well. But this first Manolete had developed a degenerative eye condition as a relatively young man, and though he kept trying to perform, even when he saw two blurry animals running at him instead of one, he eventually gave up the sport. ("The sight of a matador with spectacles was too ridiculous for the crowd to take," Conrad writes in his biography.) At that point, Manolete's father took a job as a butcher, carving up immobilized bovines instead. When he died, he was broke and virtually blind.

Manolete's great-uncle was apparently the most successful torero in the family: a titanic, immaculately confident man known as Pepete. "Rather than ever having to conquer any fear," one writer explained, Pepete "simply did not recognize what the emotion was." He'd become a somewhat legendary figure, after rushing to help an injured friend during a bullfight in Madrid in 1862, only to be stabbed by the animal himself. Pepete stood up immediately, dusted the sand off his pants, walked to the edge of the ring, and, regarding his wound with some curiosity, asked,

"Is it anything?" Then blood started surging out of him, and he was dead three minutes later. The bull had harpooned Pepete straight through the heart.

This family history of suffering and gore explained why Manolete's mother, Angustias, sheltered him so vigorously when he was a boy. Even before marrying Manolete's father, she'd been widowed by a different matador husband. And recognizing this tragic compulsion of the men in her orbit to throw themselves at bulls, she "sedulously kept from [Manolete] everything that even most remotely might turn his mind towards a passion that in her own eyes was the most fatal of all obsessions," an acquaintance of Manolete's wrote. This included giving away or selling her two husbands' costumes and other artifacts from their careers, to get them out of the house. The descriptions of Manolete's mother are more potently misogynistic in some accounts than others, but she is generally caricatured as a woman who is both pathetic and overbearing, who labors, out of her own panic and terror, to keep her little boy swaddled in a kind of perpetual, guilt-ridden infanthood. "You wouldn't want to make your mother unhappy—desperately unhappy—would you, my little one?" she purportedly asked young Manolete when he once expressed a glint of interest in bullfighting. She ordered him to learn a nice trade and get an office job instead.

The events of Manolete's early life tend to be fluid in different tellings, and are often irreconcilable; almost everything I read relayed his story in a kind of old-fangled, florid prose. To some unknowable degree, the truth was being embellished and smeared into folklore. Manolete's story, as I was able to absorb it, read almost like a parable, the story of a man being swept, almost passively, toward his destiny as a matador. No matter what his mother did, there was only one future for her son.

That narrative turns on a kind of mythic conversion story. One afternoon, when Manolete is around eleven years old, he is wandering past the bullfighting arena in Cordova exactly at the moment when matadors from all over Spain are filing in for an event from the hotel next door. A crowd has gathered to cheer and ogle the bullfighters, but when a particularly famous one passes by, a man heckles him, barking that he's nothing compared to the matadors the city of Cordova has produced. And when the heckler lists off a couple of these local heroes, Manolete is astonished to hear his own father's name.

Manolete looks around, stiffens up with pride; all at once, he sees the magnificent respect these matadors command, the fervor of this huge crowd that's converged outside the arena just to slap them on the back, or reach out a hand and feel the fabric of their jackets. And, more than the prestige, he recognizes the money involved: the measure of security that this sport might provide for himself and his mother. "Now it had happened," Conrad writes, "happened suddenly and irrevocably": Manolete wanted to fight bulls.

He tore off for home as fast as he could and managed to find an old matador's tunic in a cupboard in the attic—the one bullfighting accessory that his mother had apparently overlooked in her purge. The Spanish journalist Antonio Díaz-Cañabate, an acquaintance of Manolete's, describes Manolete furtively lifting the garment out, surprised by its weight, and admiring "its gilded splendor . . . tarnished and dull with age." The boy clumsily slips it over his shoulders—and, miraculously, the tunic fits. And suddenly, as soon as Manolete has it on, "some innate instinct" compels his arms forward; he begins swinging them around to execute a fit of imaginary cape work, as though, there in his attic, he is enchanting and commanding an invisible bull. It is precisely at this moment that Manolete's mother walks into the room, crying: "Alas!" she tells him. "The poison is already in your veins!"

From then on, Manolete would spend his adolescence hanging out with bullfighters, never saying much, just silently absorbing their craft. He hadn't ever wanted to fight, but as Conrad puts it, "He was starting to become a man and had just begun to realize that fighting bulls was simply what men in his family were supposed to do." He was surrendering to the sport more than pursuing it, letting it drag him out like a tide. He was like the human inverse of Ferdinand the Bull.

The same kids who'd been confused when Manolete didn't want to play bullfighter with them at school now excluded and mocked him. When he announced that he intended to fight bulls, one said, "You? You want to be a torero? With a thin and miserable face like that?"

By the time Manolete was twenty-seven years old, in 1944, he was appearing in ninety-two bullfights a year. He was described as "indisputably Spain's greatest hero" and "almost unanimously regarded as the greatest matador of all time." He was mobbed in the streets, was the subject of a bestselling book and a popular song, and the namesake of a new liquor called Anís Manolete. After each bullfighting season in Spain, he'd spend the winter touring Latin America. His Mexican fans, known as Manoletistas, wore lapel pins of his face—his "elongated, dolorous profile," as one reporter described it.

Soon, Manolete was said to be worth the equivalent of $36 million today and to command fees equivalent to $175,000 for a single afternoon. Already, he had dispatched over a thousand bulls in the course of his career. He always killed them swiftly and coldly, with a forceful, old-fashioned technique that had largely been abandoned since it left the matador momentarily exposed: He would lance the animal head-on, straight over its right horn—without smiling, without waving, seemingly without any recognition of his audience at all.

Every facet of his performances was similarly somber and machine-like. (One reporter described him as a "cool, punctilious technician.") Early in his career, Conrad writes, "The stiffness of the lanky boy's body and the sadness of his face . . . just caused audiences to laugh." But Manolete's manager had urged him away from mimicking the garish, balletic style of bullfighting that was popular at the time and taught him, instead, to leverage his rail-thin build and natural demeanor into something more stately and composed. Even Manolete's signature flourish, known as the Manoletina, was really an *anti*-flourish: he would wave the furious bull forward with his cape, then pivot only slightly, usually without even moving his feet, to let it rush by. It gave the impression that Manolete was barely bothering, committing to a minimum of strain.

He brought the same asceticism to his life outside the ring. "Unlike most matadors," one newspaper wrote, "his name is associated with neither liquor or women." He had few genuine friends, and his fame made him wary of meeting new people. He spoke very little at cocktail parties; it seemed he had nothing to say. If a woman flirted with him, he responded in halting and timorous monosyllables. Asked by a reporter why he didn't smile more, Manolete replied: "This business of the bulls is a very serious thing." In fact, his relationship to his trade was so stoic that it felt fatalistic at times. Once, during a fight in Mexico City, he was gored in the leg and, as the medics carried Manolete away to stitch him up, someone asked him why he'd stood his ground for so long, when even some people in the crowd recognized how erratically the bull was behaving and yelled for him to fall back. "It's why I'm Manolete," Manolete answered. "For that, I charge what I charge."

But when the 1947 season got underway, Manolete announced that it would be his last. Though he was only thirty years old, he planned to retire. He was done with bullfighting. He wanted to exit the sport while he was still healthy—still alive—and spend his days hunting and riding horses on a ranch he'd purchased outside his hometown. He wanted serenity. He wanted to stop putting himself in the path of angry monsters and just barely sliding out of the way.

Manolete's fans wouldn't hear of it, though; his announcement provoked "a wave of fury and anger," one reporter wrote. The public started to turn on Manolete and accused him of cowardice, suspecting that he was actually retiring because he was intimidated by an upstart, loudmouthed matador who'd burst onto the scene as his rival. Manolete wasn't augustly transcending the sport at the end of a prestigious career, they insisted; he was just running away.

Luis Miguel Dominguín was twenty-one years old in 1947 and comes off, in written accounts, as an almost cartoonish distillation of every matador cliché the American imagination can conjure. Dominguín was suave, cocky, ambitious, defiant, theatrical—a man of "indomitable self-esteem" and physical vigor who was always surrounded by "company that was completely joyous and happy" and whose life seemed to pour over him in a warm, never-ending bath of eager women and delicious wine. ("If only you knew how difficult I find it to refuse," he said of his womanizing. "I just let myself drift.") Also—this is worth saying directly—he was stupefyingly handsome. His face was perfect, appealing in a completely symmetrical, proportional way.

Like Manolete, Domínguín came from a family of matadors, but whereas Manolete's mother fought to shield Manolete from the profession, Domínguín's bullfighter-father was like a stage parent, grooming and propelling his son, since toddlerhood, toward his predestined career. The writer Antonio Díaz-Cañabate, who befriended Domínguín when the matador was a teenager, described him at that age as a precocious phenom with an impossibly outsized persona. "He already had the maturity of a man of fifty," Díaz-Cañabate wrote, because even at nineteen years old he'd "lived far more intensely than I or many of my contemporaries, poor withered old sticks, who had hardly lived at all."

Manolete had always been known for his understatement in the ring. Domínguín dealt in cheap flash. He'd run the bull into the ground, toy with the animal until it was dazed and panting, then cuddle up to it, kiss the bull on the forehead, and pose with one of its horns stuck close to his own ear—a move known as the "telephone call." He was motivated almost exclusively by pride and claimed to fear humiliation more than death. He needed to turn every bullfight into an audacious expression of his supremacy over the other bullfighters appearing that afternoon, as much as over the animal itself.

Domínguín began ascending professionally in 1943, just as Manolete's fame was exploding. But then, his career plateaued. He was having trouble breaking into the biggest and most prestigious corridas, colliding with some unbudgeable barrier that he couldn't comprehend. Everyone who Domínguín met, in person, absolutely loved him; he was perplexed why bullfighting fans weren't going similarly wild.

Then, early in the 1947 season, Dominguín was forced to miss several fights because of an injury. Recuperating in bed, with no outlet for his ambition, he was both bored and consumed by his frustrations. One day, he called a Madrid radio station and asked for some time on the air; he had a lot of incendiary opinions that he felt compelled to share, he said. The next day, a reporter arrived at Dominguín's bedside with a recorder, and the station aired his tirade that same afternoon.

Dominguín railed about how unfairly the bullfighting world was treating him, how the powers that be wouldn't allow him to compete against their golden prince, Manolete. "I am anxious to furnish proof that I am a better torero than he, and that I can unseat him from the pedestal on which public opinion has placed him," Dominguín insisted. "It is my intention to prove my superiority in the only way open to me"—in the ring. "The moment I am given the chance," he said, "I will prove that I am the best of them all."

The speech had allegedly been Dominguín's father's idea. As his son's manager and promoter, he had pushed Dominguín's career far but not far enough, and now saw instigating a feud as a shortcut to the sport's last, most elite, tier. Dominguín's discouragement with bullfighting had already become apparent in the ring; some afternoons, he seemed to smolder with a kind of nihilistic resentment, and the only thing that could re-energize him was when the public picked up on this moodiness and hit him back with booing. "The atmosphere created by a hostile public, which paralyzes most toreros, far from worrying Luis Miguel, was, in fact, a source of constant incentive," Díaz-Cañabate writes. He loved the moment in a bullfight when he could feel the crowd's distaste for him giving way to respect, when he'd proven that the audience was just another apoplectic animal he could dazzle into the ground. Psyching himself up before one particular fight, Dominguín explained to a friend that he wasn't even thinking about the bull. Instead, he said, "I'm thinking of all those people who can't stick the sight of me . . . all those idiots, bores and importunates."

Now, his challenge to Manolete on the radio was an escalation of this antagonistic persona. He was transforming himself into a heel. And right away, the stunt seemed to be working. Dominguín's appearance on the radio as a deliciously swaggering narcissist suddenly gave fans permission to feel bored with the comparably bland, dour-faced man who'd dominated bullfighting for years. In truth, the excitement around Manolete had already begun to peter out. Spain's dictator, Francisco Franco, had recently banned Mexican bullfighters from competing in the country, sidelining Manolete's only credible rival. And bullfighting overall seemed to be losing some of its drama, too. The bulls were said to be smaller and less ferocious now, and doctors were better able to treat matadors' injuries and save their lives. Manolete, with his delicate style and enormous fees, was a natural target for disillusioned fans who missed the wickedness and peril of the earlier era. The more he was paid for every fight, the more the crowd expected of him and the harsher its impatience and disappointment would be with yet another one of his subtle and refined performances. "Manolete was doing his utmost to satisfy his public, but the latter demanded superhuman exhibitions, and Manolete was only mortal—not a god," Díaz-Cañabate writes.

At first, Manolete tried to ignore Dominguín's trash-talking. He considered this loud young man a nuisance; this whole manufactured rivalry, repellent and un-classy. He was content to soldier through the rest of his contracts for the season, then vanish into retirement. He was done—done with bulls, but also done with the fickle, petulant fans for whom he fought them. "They are asking more than I can give," Manolete told the press. "Always more and more. All I can say is that I wish the bullfighting season was over."

But Dominguín kept hounding Manolete, and the public piled on. An old friend described the backlash as sadistic: Manolete's fans had become "infuriated by perfection," he said. "Out of boredom, they now want to destroy their beloved idol."

It began to take a toll. Another bullfighter described Manolete "as too sincere an artist not to suffer under this treatment." As the summer wore on, he started drinking heavily, and seemed even more troubled and sadder than his face usually made him look. "To tell the truth, I was shocked by his physical state," his manager would recall.

One afternoon, between engagements that July, Manolete went to visit his mother.

"Manolo, you look very run-down," she told him.

"Mother," Manolete said, "I am not the child I once was. I have to fight bulls."

He decided to accept Dominguín's challenge.

Recently, I was passing through a metal detector at the entrance to a museum when a security guard sprang off his stool, shaking his head, and waved at me to stop. He had a look on his face like, *Give me a break.* "Guy," he said. "You gotta lose the chew."

I'd been lost in thought, but did a quick inventory of my mouth. Was I chewing something? Then I realized that he meant chewing tobacco: my jaw skews so severely to one side that he thought there was something wadded in my cheek.

"No," I heard myself explaining to this security guard, this stranger: "This is my face. This is just what my face looks like."

My face is a conversation piece. People can't help noticing

that it's there and often want to talk about it, ask about it, or even, once in a while (especially in high school), feel entitled to offer an unsolicited critical take. By now, I can tell when someone I'm talking to has gotten momentarily distracted by my face—scrutinizing its angles, considering it as an object. Mostly, they want to know why it's so conspicuously crooked, to hear the story of the presumably outlandish accident that fractured my large, bumpy nose in ōne direction and wrenched my long jaw in the other so that, no matter which way I incline my head, it never quite feels like I'm looking straight at you.

But the truth is, I never broke any bones; my face just grew that way. At some point when I was a kid, things started drifting, just slightly. And, like a spacecraft that's been infinitesimally poked off course, that lopsidedness kept escalating as I hurtled through the vacuum of adolescence. Like Manolete's face, something about this arrangement seems to project gloominess, loneliness, or woe. Not long after my friend emailed me that photo of the matador, I appeared on a late-night television show to talk about a magazine story I'd written and, looking online afterward, found one commenter asserting that I had the face of "a depressed pervert." More recently, when a right-wing website criticized a *New York Times* story I wrote as liberal propaganda, a commenter named "AnonymousCoward" urged the writer to post a picture of me along with his critique, to show "how deeply weird Jon Mooallem looks, and how his feelings of alienation probably help him identify with the fringe." From there, other anonymous cowards joined in, all marshaling different levels of literary talent to delight in my warped appearance. "Whoah! [*sic*]" one guy wrote. "What the *Hell* is up with his rubbery jaw!!?" Another compared my face to something Salvador Dalí would paint: "Like a smirking camembert melting in the sun."

No one appreciates my face with more uncontrollable gusto

than dentists, though. More than once, I've endured one calling in a colleague from the other room to come have a look. They peer at my X-rays with giddy concentration, as though pressing open a fresh book of sudoku, and sometimes ask me to get out of the chair and stand against the wall, so they can get a few shots with a regular camera, too. (I was in my mid-thirties before I realized that these demoralizing portrait sessions weren't a standard part of a dental exam.) Every time I see a new dentist, it's the same: they get like archaeologists before a dig, eager to know what sort of ruined structure is hidden under there, imagining all the physical dysfunction and pain I must be living with, and the many diagnostic tools and specialists that might be gathered behind the project of setting it all right.

They aren't wrong. My jaw is so misshapen that I can feel it wriggle out of joint whenever I open wide enough for a hamburger or a yawn, and then bonk back into place. And the gums on the left side of my mouth are wearing away at a distressing rate, since those teeth apparently clamp together long before the ones on the other side can connect, and therefore do most of the chewing. But my only serious complaint has been the headaches, a small genus of pains that have racked me periodically since childhood. There's a particular kind of dull headache that sprouts under and above my eyes like mold. There's one that presses and holds its weight against my face from inside, like a tantrumming toddler squatting against her bedroom door to keep the world out. There's the throbbing one that hangs around diffusely for hours and only produces pain when I focus on it, like a pang of guilt.

Maybe none of this makes sense: These headaches molder at the periphery of language, in a nonsensical cloud of synesthesia and memories—purple pain, newsprint-colored pain; pain that has the turgid heft of Greek yogurt or smells like the inside of an umbrella; pain that funnels me back to one gloomy Sunday afternoon from my childhood, splayed on the carpet, watching Steve Martin in *The Jerk* on Channel 11.

Does anyone truly comprehend the pressures roiling inside their own head? As far as I understand it, the source of my headaches is probably my sinuses, which over time were narrowed and crushed like a plastic straw, as the bones of my jaw and nose grew into them, out of alignment. But I can't say for sure. At a couple of different points in my life, I've gotten motivated to better diagnose and even fix these problems, shuttling around for exploratory scans and consultations. Doctors have proposed plastic surgery to straighten out my nose, or surgically breaking my jaw and resetting it. After walking me through the complete cartography of the human face in an anatomy textbook, one postulated that perhaps my flattened sinuses could be bored open wider with lasers. But to be honest, I've never earnestly considered pursuing any of these doctors' recommendations, just nodded along inertly with my misshapen face as they spoke. Somehow, every intervention has felt so pointlessly ambitious, so laborious, so dramatic. For better or worse, these problems feel normal to me. And the truth is, I started to identify so deeply with the peculiarities of my face that the idea of "correcting" those imperfections eventually became unthinkable. Looking in the mirror, I'd try to imagine every part of me pointing flawlessly forward and wonder: *Who would I be then?*

When I was younger, I worried I was ugly. But by the time I turned thirty, there was even a measure of perverse vanity involved: I'd come to appreciate my face so much that I was willing to live with the pain of having it attached to my head. And that's why, reading that first Manolete biography on my kitchen

floor the night it arrived, it didn't upset me to learn how allegedly grotesque my doppelgänger was, how unrepentantly and
universally this face we shared was ridiculed.

I was able to brush it off, even wrest some wry amusement
from the discovery. And that felt good—good to feel unthreat-
ened, good to recognize that a kind of genuine acceptance and
equanimity had apparently been growing inside me, from an
odd angle, all those years. In short, that night I felt myself freely
loving who I am, and was proud.

But then I read the rest of the Manolete biography.

Manolete was still asleep on the morning of August 27, 1947,
when his manager slipped into his room at the Hotel Cervantes
in Linares to check on him.

"How are they?" Manolete asked. He meant the bulls.

"Fine. Not too big, not too small," his manager told him. Then
Manolete went back to sleep.

He woke a few hours later, at noon, ate a steak and some
grapes and drank a cup of coffee, then went to wash and shave.
A writer and photographer from *LIFE* magazine came to his
room, but Manolete asked them to leave and return after the
fight. He didn't look like himself, he said: "Fear puts a mask on
us now."

Later, Manolete's manager, José Flores González, known as
Camará, would describe Manolete essentially sleepwalking
through the previous several days. Now the maestro prayed to
the portrait of the Virgen de la Macarena on his night table—
"Don't let them catch me today; protect me once more, I beg of
you"—got dressed in a rose-colored costume embellished with
golden thread, folded his lucky cape under his arm, and left for

the fight a little after five o'clock. In a room down the hall, Dominguín was still taking his time getting dressed.

The two men had already faced off twice in the preceding weeks, and both times Manolete found himself at odds with a disinterested or even virulent public, as the crowds thronged behind Dominguín instead. Walking off after slaying yet another bull at one of these matches, but receiving no sign of adulation or even appreciation for it, Manolete murmured to another matador, "I know very well what they want, and one of these afternoons I just might give it to them to keep the bastards happy." Now, nearly nine thousand people had come to watch their third showdown in Linares. One of Manolete's sword boys would remember walking through town before the match, eavesdropping on people bad-mouthing and betting against his boss.

Each matador would face three different bulls that afternoon. Dominguín played to the crowd with ostentatious stunts, dropping to his knees in the sand and windmilling his cape as the bull leapt by. But Manolete's first animal was not particularly aggressive, and he had to labor to manufacture an interesting performance before killing it with a quick, straight lunge of his sword. A few people applauded, but many more booed. "They keep demanding more and more of me, and I have no more to give," Manolete told an onlooker as they dragged the carcass away.

His second time out, Manolete drew a bull named Islero, bred on a ranch outside Seville notorious for the nastiness of its animals. The writer from *LIFE* magazine would describe the bull as "an unusually ugly customer"; it weighed more than a thousand pounds and was aggravated from the get-go, jerking itself headlong out of the gate and careening around the arena, as though hunting. Then eventually it steadied itself, inscrutably, at the center of the ring.

Manolete stepped forward. He flared his cape, but the bull was unresponsive. A couple of times, the animal started to charge but seemed to short-circuit and stutter to a stop. Eventually, the picadors were sent in to poke at the bull, to get it more riled up. Islero barreled into the side of one of their horses and knocked the man off.

Camará didn't like the look of the animal; he shouted at Manolete to walk away. But Manolete coaxed the bull into a fierce, flagrant charge, then swiveled almost imperceptibly, so that its horns scraped the air close to his body. The crowd erupted and, after that, a genuine fight was underway. Manolete was wringing Islero through pass after pass, absolutely dominating the animal, until he was comfortable enough to turn his back on the bull, step away, and make a dainty performance of tidying his cape. He seemed to be allowing for a beat of anticipation, before the kill. But just as Manolete speared the bull between its shoulder blades, Islero jerked suddenly to the right and planted a horn in Manolete's groin. The bull shoved the man upward, into the air. And when Manolete hit the ground, the bull skewered him again. Then it stomped on him.

People rushed in from different directions to help, swarming the bull like a flurry of flies. Some grabbed at parts of the animal and some grabbed for Manolete, to drag him out from under the heavy pistons of its hind legs. As they hauled the matador out the door, the bull, still with Manolete's sword in its withers, crinkled in on itself, dead. Everyone in the arena had abruptly turned silent, left to stare at the two pools of blood in the sand.

The tear at the top of Manolete's right leg was six inches long. He was losing a tremendous amount of blood and going into shock. At 8:00 p.m., shortly before he was transferred to a proper hospital for surgery, he regained consciousness briefly and moaned about the pain. He would die just before sunrise the following morning. Camará stared numbly at the empty, crooked face of his protégé as someone slipped a crucifix into the dead man's hands and folded his fingers around it.

And that was it: the end of the allegory into which the story of this real man's life was always molded. But the more I scrutinized that story, the more ungraspable its moral became. Was Manolete meant to be dignified? Pitiful? A hero, or a kind of passive human sacrifice? Was it too much integrity that killed him, or not enough?

The whole thing struck me as baffling and disturbing. Even at the end, in his hospital bed, one of the last things Manolete had apparently said was: "Did the bull die?"

A sinus is literally nothing: an absence, a perfect puddle of air nestled into bone. The human paranasal sinuses are arrayed behind our faces in four sets of two: one mirror-imaged pair of air pockets above the eyes; two pairs around the bridge of our noses; and a fourth set of much larger sinuses that sprawl open alongside the nose, under each eye. All mammals have sinuses. Dinosaurs had sinuses. But we, presumably, are the only species that's wondered why: What reason could there be for these empty spaces in the otherwise labyrinthine technology of our heads?

Anatomists in the Middle Ages speculated that the sinuses were storehouses of oil that lubricated our eyeballs to keep them moving smoothly. Others wondered if they helped produce our voices. Leonardo da Vinci believed that sinuses held an elixir that nourished our teeth. One sixteenth-century Spanish physician believed they were a kind of rectum of the brain—"la cloaca del cerebro"—a spillway through which its "malignant spirits" were pushed out.

After centuries of speculation and investigation, the current scientific understanding, as one recent study put it, is that our sinuses "are simply functionless structures." Or, as an anthropologist named Nathan Holton told me: "In most cases, I'd guess they don't do a heck of a lot. The reason humans have sinuses is that we've inherited them. We had ancestors that had sinuses, and their ancestors had sinuses, and their ancestors had sinuses." A sinus is nothing, and it does nothing, too.

Our sinuses also appear to do nothing *badly*. They are works of lavishly dysfunctional engineering. We all know that mucus drains through the sinuses, but while it whisks down the upper sinuses, into the nose and on through the throat, our largest set of sinuses—the maxillary sinuses, under the eyes—must somehow push that sludgy, viscous garbage *upward*, heaving it into the nose against the force of gravity, toward a small opening at the top known as an ostia. (One writer has described these sinuses as "evolutionary errors." In plumbing terms, the drain was installed in exactly the wrong place; it's like we're trying to flush a toilet upside down.) For this reason, it's the maxillary sinuses that most often clog, and where most sinus infections first take hold. It's also where my own headaches tend to start, as that backlog of snot stacks up and pressurizes. That is, my own helter-skelter anatomy appears to have piled extra dysfunction onto a baseline of dysfunction that all humans share.

After one doctor I visited explained this cockamamie arrangement to me, I wondered if I'd misunderstood him, and started doing research, reading about the science and mechanics of human sinuses with a similar compulsion with which I'd read about Manolete—a strange, somewhat narcissistic hope that this body of knowledge would contain some cosmic information to help me better understand myself. (At one point, I even read a study of bull sinuses, which claimed to be "the broadest and most comprehensive quantitative analysis of sinus morphology ever attempted.") Finally, there in Volume 40, Issue 1, of the *Journal of Otolaryngology—Head & Neck Surgery*, I found something approaching an answer.

The study was disgusting; it involved pumping salt water into the decapitated heads of five human cadavers and the decapitated heads of five dead goats. In the experiment, led by a researcher named Rebecca L. Ford, at the King's College London, one person would hold the head on a metal tray, while another injected saline solution into its maxillary sinus. The team measured how much liquid accumulated inside the sinus before the fluid level reached the ostia—the opening at the top—and the sinus started to drain.

The scientists did this with each head positioned straight up and down, then did it again a few more times, tilting the head forward every time, until it had bent ninety degrees. (That is, the human head started in its natural position and finished facing down, while the goat head started with its snout high in the air, as if it were groaning at the moon, and ended with its head in its own natural position.) Ford and her colleagues found that both species' sinuses drained far better when they were positioned at ninety degrees. And these improvements were significant; it wasn't even close. That is, the study revealed that our sinuses would work much better if we crawled around on all fours and looked down at the ground, like goats.

"These findings support the theory that the position of the human maxillary sinus is an example of the evolutionary lag phenomenon," the paper concludes. "Sinus anatomy may have become established early in human evolution, and adaptation of the sinus ostia to an upright position may have lagged behind as bipedal humans evolved from their quadrupedal primate ancestors." Meaning, the problem isn't that these openings in our sinuses are in the wrong place—they're positioned perfectly relative to how we held our heads when we were apes. The problem is, they stayed that way. Cognitively, as a species, we may have been ready to stand up and evolve and flourish into the sophisticated creatures we are now. But our sinuses weren't ready, and never changed.

The study suggests that from a certain perspective, then—a sinus-centric perspective—we're all walking around in a condition that's against our very nature. Unless, in fact, our actual nature is to stand up and attempt to *transcend* our nature: to struggle perpetually to do the difficult thing for which we are not perfectly built. And when I held that conundrum in my head alongside the story of Manolete, I couldn't discern what the answer might be. Frankly, the whole situation felt like a mindfuck of the highest order.

It's been fifteen years since my friends spotted that photograph in Spain, and I'm now a dozen years older than Manolete was when he died. I've lost my wavy black hair since then, and sometimes, when I look quickly at pictures of myself, I see a hollowness under my eyes that wasn't always there. Still, the resemblance seems to be intact; if I show someone that photograph of the beleaguered-looking matador, they are still startled, still perplexed, and they laugh just as hard. And it still feels uncanny to me, as well, though it's now just as eerie to mark the differences materializing between our two faces: the crow's-feet and fissures spreading through this one, and all the other ways it's diverging from the one that never got to age.

Recently, after years of deflecting doctors' concerns and putting it off, I got a skin-graft procedure to reinforce the weakened portion of my gums—a minor bit of maintenance that will buy my teeth some time, until I need another. But evidently, I'm still idly committed to living with the headaches and everything else; the last time I went to see a new dentist, I didn't even do her the politeness of hearing out her spiel about nose jobs and jaw surgeries. Instead, I affected a kind of amiable world-weariness about the whole predicament, then smiled crookedly, leaned back in the chair, and wrenched open my handsome, ramshackle jaw as wide as I could manage so that she'd just get on with the exam.

Surely all of us, at certain moments in our lives, have felt ourselves in conflict with some deeper and more essential self: addled by insecurity or shame about who we are, or exhausted by our restless attempts to change it. And we all know that it takes courage to instead make peace with who you really are. Except, of course, if who you *really* are is a prisoner of inertia or fear or self-destructiveness or apathy or depression—in which case, we all know that making peace with *that* self would just be giving up, and that the courageous thing to do would be to fight *against* your essential self, to transform yourself into someone stronger.

The problem is, it can be impossible to tell the two scenarios apart; to know at any given moment, facing any given impediment or injustice, which self we're supposed to be; to understand when acceptance is Zen-like and healthy, and when it's just going to get you gored by a bull.

Maybe this is what I really look like: spun around and confused, charging determinedly toward one illusory ideal only to skid to a stop and double back to chase the other. Maybe you've had the same fight with yourself. Maybe I look like you, too.

Can You Even Believe This Is Happening?

(A Monk Seal Murder Mystery)

| 2013 |

The Hawaiian monk seal has wiry whiskers and the deep, round eyes of an apologetic child. The animals will eat a variety of fish and shellfish, or turn over rocks for eel and octopus, then haul out on the beach and lie there most of the day, digesting. On the south side of Kauai one afternoon, I saw one sneeze in its sleep: its convex body shuddered, then spilled again over the sand the way a raw, boneless chicken breast will settle on a cutting board. The seals can grow to seven feet long and weigh 450 pounds. They are adorable, but also a little gross: the Zach Galifianakises of marine mammals.

Monk seals are easy targets. After the Polynesians landed in Hawaii, about 1,500 years ago, the animals mostly vanished, slaughtered for meat or oil, or scared off by the settlers' dogs. But the species quietly survived in the Leeward Islands, northwest of the main Hawaiian chain—a remote archipelago, including Laysan Island, Midway, and French Frigate Shoals, which, for the most part, only Victorian guano barons and the military have seen fit to settle. There are now about nine hundred monk seals in the Leewards, and the population has been shrinking for twenty-five years, making the seal among the world's most imperiled marine mammals. The monk seal was designated an endangered species in 1976. Around that time, however, a few monk seals began trekking back into the main Hawaiian Islands—"the mains"—and started having pups. These pioneers came on their own, oblivious to the sprawling federal project just getting underway to help them. Even now, recovering the species is projected to cost $378 million and take fifty-four years.

As monk seals dispersed through the mains and flourished there, they became tourist attractions and entourage-encircled celebrities. Now when a seal appears on a busy beach, volunteers with the federal government's "Monk Seal Response Network" hustle out with stakes and fluorescent tape to erect an exclusionary "SPZ" around the snoozing animal—a "seal protection zone." Then those human beings stand watch in the heat for hours to keep the seal from being disrupted while beachgoers gush and point.

But the seals' appearance has not been universally appreciated. The animals have been met by many residents with a convoluted mix of resentment and spite. This fury has led to what the government is calling a string of "suspicious deaths." But spend a little time in Hawaii, and you come to recognize these deaths for what they are—something loaded and forbidding. The word that came to my mind was "assassination."

The most recent wave of Hawaiian monk seal murders began on the island of Molokai in November 2011. An eight-year-old male seal was found slain on a secluded beach. A month later, the body of a female, not yet two years old, turned up in the same area. Then, in early January, a third victim was found on Kauai.

The government tries to keep the details of such killings secret, though it is known that some monk seals have been beaten to death and some have been shot. (In 2009, on Kauai, a man was charged with shooting a female seal twice with a .22; one round lodged in the fetus she was carrying.) In the incident on Kauai last January, the killer was said to have left a "suspicious object" lodged in the animal's head.

Killing an endangered species in Hawaii is both a state and federal offense. Quickly, the State of Hawaii and the Humane Society of the United States put up a reward for information. "We're all in agreement that somebody knows who did this," one Humane Society official told me. The islands are close-knit but also loyal, particularly the Native Hawaiian communities. In January, when I met with the state wildlife agency's chief law-enforcement officer for Kauai—a man named Bully Mission—he confessed that, after a year, Kauai's tip line hadn't received a single call. In fact, there was still a reward out from a separate seal killing in 2009.

A quick aside about Bully Mission: I went to Hawaii thinking I'd write a straight-up police procedural—you know, *CSI: Monk Seal*. When I heard that Kauai's top wildlife cop was named Bully Mission, I figured I'd found my hard-boiled protagonist. But for one thing, Bully Mission isn't anything like the detectives on TV. He's a small, wide-smiling man, who seems to inner-tube through life on currents of joy and amusement. (His real name is Francis.) And wildlife crime–solving doesn't fit the network-drama formula, either. The wilderness is a big, unwatched place. The ocean is a violent environment. Sometimes it's tough even to determine a cause of death. A seal with skull fractures may have been beaten, or it may have died miles out at sea of natural causes, then knocked around in the surf. Plus, when your victim is a seal, one federal agent points out, "you can't interview the seal; you can't interview its friends." Often, you can only pile up a reward and wait.

And so, as the seal deaths kept coming after that initial murder on Molokai, environmental groups chipped in more money, bringing the total reward to $30,000, or $10,000 per seal. Then, in April 2012, a fourth seal was killed on the east side of Kauai. This particular seal was well known in the neighborhood; it frequented an inlet under a scenic walking path. Locals nicknamed it Noho, Hawaiian for "homebody."

Mary Frances Miyashiro, a retired teacher and social worker who patrols that coastline as a volunteer monk seal responder, had arrived on the scene first. She sat with Noho's body for an hour, waiting for others to come and heft the seal into an insulated body bag so it could be driven into town for a necropsy, or animal autopsy. "My heart sank," Miyashiro told me. "I didn't know what to do with those feelings, so I picked up trash." It felt hopeless, like the killings might go on forever.

Two days later, a uniformed law-enforcement officer from the National Oceanic and Atmospheric Administration (NOAA), the federal agency responsible for monk seals, flew to Kauai from Honolulu to open the U.S. government's investigation. This officer's name was Paul Newman.

Newman went to the crime scene—the beach—and photographed whatever seemed notable. Not much, really. There was one lead—someone had overheard a man bad-mouthing the monk seal—but it went nowhere. So that night, Newman hopped a commercial flight back to Honolulu. He had a cooler with him, packed with ice, sealed with official tape. Inside was Noho's wounded head. The head was the only evidence.

The reward ticked up to $40,000.

We live in a country, and an age, with extraordinary empathy for endangered species. We also live at a time when alarming numbers of protected animals are being shot in the head, cudgeled to death, or worse.

In North Carolina, for example, hundreds of brown pelicans have recently been washing ashore dead with broken wings. The birds, nearly wiped out by DDT in the 1970s, are now plentiful and often become semi-tame; they're known to land on fishing boats and swipe at the catch. One theory is that irritated fishermen are simply reaching out and cracking their wings in half with their hands. In March, in Florida, someone shoved a pelican's head through a beer can.

Around the country, at any given time, small towers of reward money sit waiting for whistleblowers to come forward. This winter four bald eagles were gunned down and left floating in a Washington lake (reward: $20,250); three were shot in Mississippi ($7,500); and two in Arkansas ($3,500). Someone drove through a flock of dunlins—brittle-legged little shorebirds—on a beach in Washington, killing ninety-three of them ($5,500). In Arizona, a javelina was shot and dragged down a street with an extension cord strung through its mouth ($500), and in North Carolina, eight of only a hundred red wolves left in the wild were shot within a few weeks around Christmas ($2,500). Seven dolphins died suspiciously on the Gulf Coast last year; one was found with a screwdriver in its head ($10,000). Sometimes, these incidents are just "thrill kills"—fits of ugliness without logic or meaning. But often they read as retaliation, a disturbing corollary to how successful the conservation of those animals has been.

Since the passage of the Endangered Species Act forty years ago, so much wildlife conservation has been defensive at its core, striving only to keep animals from disappearing forever. But now that America has recovered many of those species, we don't quite know how to coexist with them. We suddenly remember why many people didn't want them around in the first place. Gray wolves, sandhill cranes, sea otters: Species like these, once nearly exterminated, are now rising up to cause ranchers, farmers, and fishermen some of the same frustrations all over again. These animals can feel like illegitimate parts of the landscape to people who, for generations, have lived without any of them around—for whom their absence seems, in a word, *natural*. As Holly Doremus, an environmental legal scholar at the University of California, Berkeley, writes, America has saved so much without ever asking "how much wild nature society needs, and how much society can accept."

The monk seal is not one of these success stories. The species, as a whole, is still skating toward extinction. But the situation in Hawaii follows the same script: There used to be zero monk seals living around the main Hawaiian Islands; there are now between 150 and 200. And I heard story after story from fishermen about galling seals stealing fish from their nets or hooks, or lurking at favorite fishing spots and scaring away everything else. A lot of fishing in Hawaii is done for subsistence—a way for working-class people to eat better food than they can afford to buy. The monk seals are perceived as direct competition, or at least an unnecessary inconvenience. "They're troublemakers," a young spear fisherman told me one morning at Kauai's Port Allen pier.

Also, as often happens with endangered species, many of the people asked to coexist with the monk seal see the animal less as an autonomous wild creature than as an extension of the government working to save it. There has been frustration with the federal government among fishermen and other "ocean users" in Hawaii since at least 2006, when President George W. Bush

turned the water around the Leewards into the Papahānaumo-
kuākea Marine National Monument, barring the small number
of fishermen who had permits to work there from 140,000 square
miles of the Pacific, an area larger than all of America's national
parks combined. Now various agencies are bandying about so
many other proposals—to protect corals, humpback whales, sea
turtles—that several people I met on Kauai seemed compelled
to make second careers of attending the government's informa-
tional meetings to keep watch over their rights. It's unclear if
these proposals might lead to new fishing regulations, but the
sheer volume of environmental strategizing, and the bureaucrats' sometimes inelegant ways of communicating their plans,
have led some people to presume that it's all one big, aquatic
land grab. A commercial fisherman named John Hurd told me
that he believed the feds wanted to make the ocean "a fishbowl."
"Divers can't go in there, fishermen can't go in there," he said.
"It's going to be an aquarium."

That skepticism is compounded for Native Hawaiians. After
all, they now walk beaches that their families have used for centuries and find tracts of sand literally roped off by NOAA monk
seal responders—men and women who, on Kauai, are almost
exclusively white, wealthy retirees from the mainland. (It's these
haole, as Hawaiians call white outsiders, who have the luxury of
standing watch over a sleeping monk seal all day.) Even the idea
that a wild animal needs such coddling strikes some locals as
absurd. "The seal needs to rest!" one man, Kekane Pa, told me
sarcastically. "The seal needs to rest because it's been swimming
in the water."

Pa is forty-nine years old and gigantic, with a voice that's
somehow both hoarse and totally overpowering. He'd picked me
up at my hotel, found a nice spot to park his truck at Waimea
Beach, and proceeded to shout his side of the story at me for

nearly two hours, popping a Heineken at one point and rolling down his window whenever he fogged the windshield.

Pa works construction and is also the speaker of the house of the Reinstated Hawaiian Government, a parallel, grass-roots government working to reclaim Hawaii from the United States, which, it maintains, annexed the islands unlawfully in 1898. Like others I met, Pa saw the monk seal controversy within this historical context. He brought documents to show me and delivered a scathing people's history of the islands, from the overthrow of the Kingdom of Hawaii in 1893 to the "Apology Resolution" signed by President Clinton in 1993. He felt the same imperial indifference coming from the government now: Hawaiians are second-class citizens, he said; the tourists come first. Now Hawaiians were being skipped over again—for a seal. "There's issues here that have never been resolved since the time they stole Hawaii," Pa told me.

He shouted all of this with a mix of exasperation and righteousness; his eyes never stopped saying, *Can you even believe this is happening?* He was asking for recognition for his people, who were being treated like afterthoughts, who so-called civilization had long ago pushed aside. It was the same cry the monk seal, or any endangered species, might make if it had a voice. And yet the seal was just an animal, and it was now getting all the help and money it needed without ever having to ask.

I asked Pa if more seals would be killed. "I hope not," he said. "But I can tell you this: It's just starting to heat up, brah."

As monk seals became more visible in recent years, this umbrage and suspicion stacked up like kindling. Then, in September 2011, when NOAA officials toured the islands to hold a series of public meetings, it ignited.

A meeting was required by law to hear public comments about NOAA's new "programmatic environmental-impact statement," or PEIS, for Hawaiian monk seals. As a hundred or so locals arrived at an elementary school on Kauai one Saturday evening, they were offered USB drives loaded with the document. It was 462 pages long, not including appendices.

The PEIS outlined new ideas for helping the monk seal, which, despite how things looked around Kauai, was in a dismal tailspin as a species. Young seals in the Leewards seem to be having trouble getting enough to eat. Pups are being picked off by sharks, which have learned to slither toward them while they're nursing, in as little as six inches of water. Also, for a long time, there have been more male seals than females on some of the Leewards, and pups had been bitten or drowned by sexually frustrated males trying to get to their mothers, or crushed when those rippling bulls tried to have sex with them instead. Females have been smothered when multiple males tried to mate with them simultaneously in so-called mobbing attacks.

The scientists working in the Leewards were trying everything they could to protect the female pups especially—the future breeders. They used wooden shields called "crowding boards" to break up fights, or swatted the belligerent bulls away with palm fronds, or ran down the beach screaming at them. Now the PEIS was proposing an elegant workaround to the problem: NOAA wanted to move a number of young female monk seals out of the Leewards every year and into the friendlier waters around the mains. They would mature there for a few years, then be captured and moved back once they were able to fend for themselves. NOAA called this process "translocation." Ecologically speaking, the idea made sense; it bordered on ingenious, even. But sociologically—if you focused on Hawaiian people, and not just Hawaiian monk seals—it was hopelessly tone-deaf.

For one thing, many in Hawaii were already convinced that, as one attendee put it at the elementary school, the entire "history of the monk seal is based on a lie." Because the species was eradicated in the mains so long ago, people had lived on Kauai their entire lives without seeing a single monk seal until recently. Traditional Hawaiian knowledge carries great authority on the islands, and in every cranny of the culture where you'd expect to see monk seals, people saw none: no mention of the seals in traditional chants, no wood carvings. People often point out that they don't even know of a Hawaiian word for the animal. (NOAA believes the ancient word *ilioholoikauaua*, "dog running in rough water," refers to the seal, though that has been resisted; at one public forum, a man called applying that word to monk seals a "defamation of my language and my culture.") The logical explanation, for many, was that the seal wasn't actually native to Hawaii, that the government had brought the animals, in secret, to create jobs for scientists and push its environmentalist agenda. (This conspiracy theory may have grown from a bit of misunderstood truth; in 1994, NOAA brought twenty-one monk seals to the mains from one Leeward Island in an earlier attempt to even out the genders there.) It seemed arrogant for NOAA to announce that it wanted to bring more now.

Another objection was rooted in an equally uncooperative set of coincidences: namely, the situation with the birds. It was Kauai's mayor, Bernard P. Carvalho Jr., who filled me in about the birds. A towering, debonair man in an earth-toned aloha shirt, Carvalho met me in his office to talk monk seals. But it was obvious that, as far as he was concerned, I was asking about the wrong animal. He explained how seabirds called Newell's shearwaters come to Kauai to mate and nest every spring. In the fall, the fledglings leave the nest and become disoriented by bright lights. They will freeze up and drop from the sky. For as long as Carvalho can remember, he said, when you find a dazed shearwater, you simply pick it up and bring it to the firehouse, where it's tucked in a pigeon box and tended to until it recovers.

The shearwater fledgling season happens to coincide with the high-school football season. One local described how little kids have always raced around the sidelines, under the Friday-night lights, collecting the paralyzed birds. But the Newell's shearwater is a federally protected species. In 2010, the U.S. Fish and Wildlife Service informed the County of Kauai that each downed shearwater would be considered a violation of federal law. Fines, the mayor was told, could reach $25,000 per bird. "So that was kind of a big . . . *what?*" he said.

Friday-night football became Friday-afternoon football. Working parents had trouble seeing their kids play, and the island lost one of its central forms of entertainment. There was anger, incredulity, and T-shirts that read BUCK THE FIRDS. The mayor, who happened to be a former high-school football star on Kauai, told me: "Friday night is football night. Don't even go there!" Now, more than two years later, the county was still working with the federal government to retrofit the lights and get in compliance. In part, the mayor explained, this involved keeping track of the relative brightness of the phases of the moon.

There were other birds, too, he went on: like the Hawaiian nene goose, which was once within a few dozen birds of extinction. Now many congregate on a golf course next to the airport, where the mayor worries—"God forbid"—that one might bring down a flight. Conservation is important, he said, "but where does it end? How far does it go?"

A version of this question was raised at the elementary-school hearing again and again. As one man put it, "Nowadays, it seems that wildlife has more support than the people." The government was focused so narrowly on helping monk seals survive an immediate threat, but it wasn't communicating any cohesive vision of the future. How many monk seals in the water around Kauai would be enough? What would coexistence with that many seals look like? One speaker asked, for example, whether he'd be fined for striking a seal if the animal threatened his little cousins while they were swimming. But the NOAA officials holding the meeting couldn't answer his question—or anybody's. There had been town-hall meetings held throughout the year, but federal law required that this hearing be a "listening session" only. The panelists were barred from speaking to anyone who testified. It was meant to be respectful—*we're all ears*—but it came off as insulting. ("Silence," one participant, a construction worker named Kimo Rosa, told me. "Silence!") And so, one by one, people rose to delineate their conspiracy theories or plead for respect, until a timekeeper flashed a red sign and their three minutes were up.

Near the end of the hearing, a man named Kalani Kapuniai noted that if the government were here to ask for the community's input on translocation, then "from what I gathered over here, you guys, the answer is no. . . . So put [this] down in your notes," Kapuniai said. People are getting fed up with the monk seals, and "they're going to kill them. Bottom line."

There was applause. All the moderator could do—all she was allowed to do—was say, "Thank you." Eight weeks later, a beach-goer found the eight-year-old seal slaughtered on the Molokai beach, the first of the four killings that winter.

Many of the monk seals slipping back into the main Hawaiian Islands in the early '70s landed first on the shores of Niihau, the island closest to the Leewards. Niihau is plainly visible from the west coast of Kauai but also, in a sense, completely invisible, since it has been privately owned since 1864, when a white family named Sinclair bought the island from King Kamehameha V for $10,000 in gold.

Niihau is seventy-two square miles—the size of Brooklyn, roughly, or one and a half San Franciscos. While the twentieth century was happening to the other Hawaiian Islands, the Sinclairs' heirs, the Robinsons, pugnaciously kept outsiders away from theirs, preserving it, like a diorama, for the family's old-fashioned ranching operation and a small community of natives to the island who still live in a village at one end. Even after a two-way radio was installed on Niihau in 1959, information was still regularly relayed to Kauai by messenger pigeon—when information was relayed at all. Mostly, the Robinsons and the Niihau people wanted to be left alone. An irresistible scrim of secrecy still hangs around the island. In 1957, a journalist seemingly went so far as to crash-land a small airplane on Niihau so he could look around.

Pristine and mostly empty, Niihau has been a perfect gateway for Hawaiian monk seals as they have flowed out of the Leewards and recolonized their species' ancestral habitat on the mains. It's no secret that lately the federal government's recovery effort has been mired in a fair amount of desperation. And so the scientists involved can get a little breathless when they speculate about the fantastic number of monk seals that must be living happily on Niihau. But no one knows for sure: Keith and Bruce Robinson, the aging brothers who, along with their mother, inherited control of Niihau in 1969, haven't given the government the kind of access or data it would like. Jeff Walters,

NOAA's monk seal recovery coordinator, described the island as both one of the real "hopes for monk seals in the main Hawaiian Islands" and as a giant "black box" at the center of the story.

"What a horrible-looking sow!" Keith Robinson bellowed as a scraggly black hog materialized from the bushes and scampered alongside our truck. Robinson seemed somehow uplifted by its hideousness. It was the jolliest I'd see him all day.

I'd managed to talk Robinson into giving me a tour of his family's island. He is seventy-one and bracingly direct. He lives on Kauai—neither Robinson brother has ever lived on Niihau for longer than a few months at a time—and within seconds of our meeting there, he handed me a copy of his self-published book, *Approach to Armageddon: One Christian's Speculation About the End of the Age*. The cover showed a wasteland of mushroom clouds and twisting pillars of smoke. At the bottom, standing like a solitary figure in a Japanese landscape painting, was an old white man in work clothes and a green hard hat, carrying a rifle. The man in the hard hat was Keith Robinson. He was wearing the same outfit, including the hat, when I met him in the doorway of his office.

The Robinson brothers have, in recent years, made Niihau a marginally more open place than it once was. They started allowing a small number of tourists, though they barely advertise, don't run tours on any discernible schedule, and permit outsiders to visit only certain parts of the island. Keith Robinson presented himself and his brother as wretchedly cash-poor—he spent the twenty-minute helicopter flight over from Kauai badgering the pilot to fly in a straight line, so as not to waste fuel—and the island as like a cherished grandparent who they're devoted to keeping alive, no matter the cost or aggravation. The

Robinsons have been able to afford this largely through partner-
ships with the U.S. Navy, which operates tracking stations on the
island for aircraft and missile testing offshore. The Navy also
holds exercises in the channel between Niihau and Kauai—
which, Robinson explained, can be used as a proxy for the Strait
of Hormuz, the link between the Persian Gulf and the Arabian
Sea, off the coast of Iran. Years ago, the Navy also ran downed-
pilot drills on Niihau's interior. A pilot would be tasked with finding his way off Niihau, as if after a crash, while bands of Niihau
people pursued him on foot. The Niihau tend to be solidly built
and fast; one of the few women there who I was able to talk
with described how they hunt hogs on the island: by running
down the animals and grabbing an ankle. They apparently took
to the downed-pilot drills enthusiastically—their only extramu-
ral sport. The poor pilots never had a chance, Robinson explained.

We trundled around the northwestern portion of the island,
looking for monk seals in a battered, Korean War–era weapons
carrier, a kind of truck, with wooden planks for benches. Our
chauffeur was a silent, barrel-chested Niihau man. He pushed
the truck over the sand, or on primitive dirt trails, while Robinson issued him quick, clipped instructions in Hawaiian. (The
Niihau may be the last surviving community of native Hawaiian
speakers.) The scenery was spectacular, in an illicit, *Jurassic
Park* kind of way. The beaches looked like screen-saver beaches.
Every so often, we saw a monk seal and stopped, rising from our
seats in the truck to observe the animal doing nothing. Robinson
had not been on Niihau for many months, and was disturbed by
how few seals we were spotting. "There are no monk seals here!"
he kept saying. He blamed fishermen from Kauai who've been
turning up to fish Niihau's pristine reefs. He claimed these fishermen are disturbing, and even occasionally shooting, the monk

seals. I sensed that these "marauders," as Robinson called them, were also an affront to the isolation and privacy that his family has always cherished. Robinson described these Kauai fishermen the way the fishermen described the monk seals: as an invasive species, barging in to threaten the natives' survival.

"Darn it, this is not good," Robinson huffed as we crossed another empty beach. "This is a catastrophe. This is disastrous." His shock and concern were quickly phasing into sulking.

Relatively speaking, Niihau is actually packed with monk seals. At its peak, about a decade ago, the population there may have reached two hundred—about a fifth of the world's current total. Returning from their millennium-long exile in the Leeward Islands, the seals found, in Niihau, a landscape that not only looked remarkably the way it did when they left it behind but that was also governed by two eccentrics willing to make room for them.

It turns out that the Robinson brothers are devout conservationists. "I'm a right-wing extremist," Keith told me, and this means feeling an obligation to use the earth wisely and replenish it, just as God instructed in the Bible. "If they want to shoot monk seals on the other islands, that's fine," he said. "But Bruce and I like having them around."

For decades, the brothers have done their best to foster and protect the seals on Niihau, organizing the Niihau people to monitor them along the coastline. That is, they've cultivated acceptance of the seals among the Niihau people—exactly what NOAA has failed to do with people elsewhere. Robinson told me that, in the early days, he heard the same kind of grumbling about monk seals from the Niihau people that I encountered on Kauai. "But Bruce and I just said: 'Look, let's tolerate these seals. You may have to work a little harder for your fish, but the fish will still be there, and the seals will have a chance.'" When I asked how they managed to pull this off, Robinson noted that, for one thing, there truly are more fish to go around on Niihau. But also, he added, "well, we're the nasty, old feudal landlords." The Niihau people are the Robinsons' tenants and their employees. No messy public hearings on his island.

Robinson told me that he would happily host as many more monk seals as NOAA wanted to relocate from the Leewards, as long as he could manage the animals his way. He has no stomach for the tyrannical regulations and egregious spending that he feels the government uses endangered species to justify. As we drove, he laid out his case against America's "eco-Nazis," an epithet he uses tirelessly and, I would learn, without any intended hyperbole. (Robinson later gave me writings outlining his belief that environmentalism is a deliberate conspiracy to install totalitarian government in America while distracting its citizens with cuddly, vanishing animals, just as Hitler's rise to power in Germany was cloaked by nationalism.) But look at Niihau, he said: "We've done all this quietly, on our own, and with our own money. It didn't cost the government a cent." On the other Hawaiian Islands, people were sticking it to the government by murdering the seals it was working to save; Robinson was sticking it to the government by actually saving them.

Robinson has always imagined his conservation work as this sort of principled, guerrilla resistance to the eco-Nazi regime. A gifted horticulturist, he started growing many imperiled native Hawaiian plants on his family's land on Kauai in the 1980s. This included a particular subspecies of *Caesalpinia kavaiensis*, a Hawaiian hardwood, which was coming close to extinction in the wild; Robinson managed to produce a single tree from surviving seeds. But in the mid-1990s, he discovered a draft document from the U.S. Fish and Wildlife Service expressing the agency's wish to "secure" and "manage" the tree on his land. He jumped to the conclusion that this meant seizure by eminent domain. (John Fay, a former botanist for Fish and Wildlife, told me, "Basically, it was a misunderstanding." Deeper in the document, the agency asserted that Robinson's work should be "supported and assisted.") Robinson called the agency in a rage. He recounted the phone call to me several times, always in a single, Homeric run-on: "I also stated that if they wanted to take my reserve over, they would probably have to engage in a gun battle with me, and kill me, and I said that coming after the debacle at Ruby Ridge and the debacle at Waco, which had just happened a few months before, if the government's next heroic exploit was to attack and murder a conservation worker in his own reserve to take over work that the government was too lazy and incompetent to do itself, that might look a little strange to the public." Seventy-two hours after he hung up the phone, Robinson told me, his *Caesalpinia kavaiensis* tree was dead. The implication was, he killed it. He felt sick about it, he added, but freedom comes first.

Now, Robinson explained, he and his brother were being threatened again. With monk seals flourishing in the main Hawaiian Islands, environmental groups are pressuring the federal government to designate the water around Kauai and Niihau "critical habitat" for monk seals under the Endangered Species Act. It's an abstruse legal move that wouldn't directly affect most fishermen, but would subject the Navy to a review process that could ultimately force it to alter or even abandon its work there. This would cut off the income that has allowed the Robinsons to protect the seals' habitat in the first place. And so recently, in an uncharacteristic move, the brothers approached NOAA about including Niihau's coastline and near-shore waters in a national marine sanctuary instead. One of the Robinsons' central conditions would be to ban the Kauai fishermen.

As Robinson explained all this to me as we toured Niihau, his sporadic bleats of indignation and alarm began to sound more nuanced. In his eyes at least, our difficulty finding monk seals that day was the appalling proof of the damage those Kauai fishermen were doing, of how urgent the sanctuary deal had become. His panic was genuine, but I wondered whether this was why he'd allowed a journalist on his family's so-called Forbidden Island in the first place: not to see monk seals, but to *not* see monk seals.

"This place should be crawling with monk seals!" Robinson said as we got out to explore one bluff. "Something's awfully wrong here. Awfully wrong."

Dana Rosendal, the pilot for the family's helicopter company, was unfazed. We'd covered only a quarter of the island, he told Robinson, and we'd already seen ten seals.

"Dana," Robinson cut in, "we've only seen five or six, plus one lousy turtle."

Rosendal ticked off each sighting, then counted up his fingers. Ten, exactly.

"Well, whoop-dee-do!" Robinson shot back. "Ten seals!" Then he stepped into the shallow tide, in his work boots and hard hat, and walked down the beach by himself. Suddenly, his island must have felt too crowded.

I spent my last morning in Hawaii at a coffee shop on Molokai, waiting for an anonymous monk seal murderer to show up, or not show up, for an interview.

Molokai is the small island just to the west of Maui. It's a poor and rural place, with a higher percentage of Native Hawaiians than any other island except Niihau, and defiantly resistant to large-scale tourism. (The island has a single hotel.) Monk seal politics have been particularly fierce on Molokai, where unemployment is high and the rights of subsistence fishermen feel even more vital and sacred. A local activist, Walter Ritte, described how elders on Molokai have fostered a feeling among the island's youth that monk seals are not actually Hawaiian and should be gotten rid of.

I'd met Ritte the previous week in Honolulu, where he'd been spending the day. He is soft-spoken and slight with a knotty beard and a fearsome reputation as an organizer. (Lately, he has been battling Monsanto, which grows genetically modified crops on Molokai.) On the monk seal issue, however, Ritte has tried to be a voice of tolerance for the seals—a native voice that can carry that message with more credibility than the government. Everyone knows him as "Uncle" Walter, a Hawaiian term of respect.

In Honolulu, Ritte had disclosed to me that he knew who killed the first of the four monk seals in 2011, the big male on Molokai's southwestern shore. When he heard the news, he said, he made a point of finding out—Ritte commands that sort of unofficial mayoral power on Molokai—and went to speak with the person. By the time they were done talking, he said, "I don't think that person was really happy with what they did. The remorse was really, really deep."

I kept after Ritte while I was on Kauai the following week. The people I was meeting there were so angry and entrenched. It was comforting to know that at least one person—"the Kid," as Ritte referred to him—seemed to have changed his mind on the issue. Eventually, Ritte called to say that the Kid had agreed to have breakfast with me the following morning on Molokai. I flew over. But minutes before our meeting, the Kid called Ritte to back out.

I told Ritte I'd be at Coffees of Hawaii, reading a book, if the Kid changed his mind. Three hours later, for reasons I couldn't have imagined, he did.

The Kid was nothing like what I expected. He's in his mid-thirties but projected such bashfulness that he seemed ten or even fifteen years younger. He'd asked to meet on the porch of a more private location and, with Ritte looking on for support, he explained how, one day shortly after the incident, Uncle Walter simply knocked on his door unannounced and said, "I want to talk to you about the seal."

The Kid had initially mustered an enthusiastic defense. He told Ritte that he believed what the elders said: that monk seals didn't belong here and were upsetting the natural balance Hawaiians depended on. Ritte listened, then told him about his own first experience with monk seals.

This had been back in 2006, while Ritte was campaigning to stop a developer from building luxury housing on a remote Molokai coastline called Laau Point. Laau Point is a prime fishing and hunting ground, and Ritte and his troops believed that losing access to it would degrade Hawaiians' ability to provide for themselves, driving them and their traditions even closer to extinction. Hundreds of protesters occupied the point for three months, sleeping on the beach. And there, in the quiet, monk seals began to appear on the sand—the first that some protesters had ever seen. Ritte told me that, sleeping side by side—Hawaiians and Hawaiian monk seals—it was just so clear to him: "I was there for survival, and the seals were there for the same reason. I saw myself in the seals."

"Uncle Walt is a well-respected man," the Kid now explained to me. He knew that Ritte's appearance on his doorstep that day was itself a rebuke. So the Kid had kept listening as Ritte explained how monk seals had actually lived in Hawaii long before Hawaiians did, and that Hawaiians—a people who know displacement and disregard—should feel kinship with the animals, rather than resentment. The seal was here first, and we have no right to push it out, Ritte told him. This way of framing it had hit the Kid hard; as he recounted it now, he still sounded crushed under the weight of this truth: "I actually killed another Hawaiian," he told me.

Outside the Kid's house that day, Ritte hadn't actually asked him for any details about his murder of the seal. He didn't need to hear: the two sides of the monk seal debate had become so predictable that it was easy for him to fill in the story for himself. When we first met, Ritte had told me that the Kid was presumably "doing what the elders had said. It was like killing a mongoose that ate his mother's chickens. I mean, he thought nothing of it." And now, I caught myself making the same assumptions. Until I asked.

The Kid seemed relieved to walk me through the story. He and his friends had hiked out to fish but kept finding monk seals at all their favorite spots, he said. Finally, at one location, they encountered the eight-year-old bull, a huge animal with a deformed jaw, sprawled out as though it were waiting for them. One of the Kid's friends was fuming by now—they'd walked so far—and he goaded the Kid to do something. "I guess it was out of anger, frustration," the Kid told me, "and kind of like peer pressure." In retrospect, so much about what happened next surprised him: how impulsively he reached for a rock and threw it; how, though he only intended to scare the animal off and was standing a fair distance away, the rock somehow struck the seal squarely in the head, and how—once it did—some force inside the monk seal instantaneously shut off.

His friends clammed up. The Kid was the smallest, gentlest guy in the group, and "that was the first time I ever did something like that," he said. At first, they assumed he only knocked the animal out, unconscious. But eventually it sank in that the seal was dead, and they steeled themselves and turned to walk home. "Already," the Kid told me, "it was eating me up."

Later, a federal investigator told me that key details of the Kid's story were consistent with the necropsy report. ("The animal was hit on the head," he said. "It was a blunt trauma to the head.") A government scientist familiar with the case was more circumspect; he explained that it would be possible to kill a resting monk seal by throwing a very heavy rock—maybe on impact, or more likely by causing internal bleeding—but extremely difficult. Frankly, I don't know what happened. The Kid seemed so vulnerable that I believed his story on the spot. I've had moments of skepticism since then—moments when I've wondered if, say, the Kid hadn't actually stood over the animal and dropped a twenty-pound boulder on its head, and was now trying to distance himself from the ugliness of that act. But either way, he acted impulsively and now regretted what he had done.

It was only a few weeks after the incident that the second murdered monk seal was found on Molokai. "Then, after the second one," the Kid said, "they had the one on Kauai, and I was thinking like, *Oh, no, what did I start?* Even Uncle Walter told me that it might have set off some kind of chain reaction." The Kid had never really been a churchgoer, he said, but recently his wife decided they ought to start. And a couple of weeks ago, he prayed about the monk seal for the first time. "I kind of just prayed and asked for forgiveness," he explained. He wanted to come clean but worried his family would suffer if he did. "I know what I had done was wrong, and I just basically asked Him for guidance," he said—a safe way to confess. "And lo and behold," the Kid told me, "here you are."

It was sad—every bit of it, and in so many freakish ways. NOAA was focused on saving an endangered species by repairing the ecology around it. But more and more, the success of conservation projects relies on a shadow ecology of human emotion and perception and luck, variables that do not operate in any scientifically predictable way. Looking back, I was astonished by how the pieces of this story just kept snapping together, and stubbornly locking in place, in precisely the worst way: how, at the public hearings, the government's attempts to show respect and empathy were read as just more imperiousness; how reasonable the conspiracy theory about the monk seal's origins actually seemed in context; how the one safe place the monk seals *had* found was inaccessible, under erratic Robinsonian rule. There was so much terrible serendipity.

And now, here was the Kid: not the angry, muscle-bound fisherman that environmentalists tended to imagine when they pictured the monk seal killers—not even really a fisherman, it turned out. He'd gone fishing only twice that year, and the second time, when his companion started threatening a monk seal in the vicinity, the Kid de-escalated the situation by telling his friend that NOAA now implanted tiny security cameras in the animals' eyes and would be watching them. He flashed a hang-loose sign at the seal's eyes and urged his friend to do the same—to tell the bureaucrats hi. "You should have seen the face on that one guy," he told me on the porch. "So gullible." Then he paused a second and said, "I wish I could be there for everybody, and tell them the same thing."

The Kid wasn't technically a kid at all, and yet what he'd described felt like a classic coming-of-age story—something out of a novel you'd read in middle school about a boy who, in a moment of recklessness, shoots a robin with his BB gun to impress his friends, then weeps over the little corpse. Except it wasn't a robin; it was a federally endangered Hawaiian monk seal at the center of a blazing controversy, and so, the Kid worried, his transgression had set off a killing spree. In fact, the night before he and I met on Molokai, news had broken that another monk seal—a seven-month-old female—was found speared on an island off Oahu. It survived, and in a photograph that NOAA released, the animal stared into the camera with narrowing eyes, one prong of the metal fishing implement still stuck through her forehead. She looked like a guileless horse that had been ridden into battle and lanced.

In Hawaii, so many circumstances had knotted together to snare this species. In a way, they had snared the Kid, too. But he wouldn't allow himself to see it that way. At one point, he mentioned again, plaintively, that he only wanted to scare the monk seal away, not kill it, and I tried to say something sympathetic, lamenting his bad luck. He was quick to correct me: "Mostly, bad decision," he said. "*Stupid* decision. You got to accept what you did."

The Outsiders

| 2015 |

Two men were sitting in a parked car, waiting to pick someone up. Carlos Cervantes was in the driver's seat. He was thirty, with glassy green eyes—quiet by nature, but with a loaded, restrained intensity about him. He had picked up Roby So at home in Los Angeles around three o'clock that morning, and they'd made it here, to this empty parking lot in front of the Richard J. Donovan Correctional Facility, on the outskirts of San Diego, just after six. Now the sun was rising over the bare, brown mountains in the windshield. A hummingbird zipped around an air-conditioning unit outside. Already, they'd been waiting close to an hour.

Roby was three years older than Carlos but carried himself like a large and joyful child. He was hungry. He wanted biscuits and gravy and was still laughing about how, earlier, he caught himself telling Carlos that, unfortunately, he'd have to wait until tomorrow for biscuits and gravy, because today was Monday, and Monday was pancakes day, and biscuits and gravy day wasn't until Tuesday. Part of his brain still tracked his old prison breakfast menu. "Why do I still know these things, man?" Roby said. "It's been four years. I was supposed to . . ." His voice trailed off, so Carlos finished his sentence: "Delete."

Roby started reciting the weekly prison menu, to see if he could still do it. When he got to Thursday—peanut butter and jelly, four slices of bread, Kool-Aid—Carlos, without turning to look at him, chimed in with "sugar-free gum."

Roby went on. (Roby tends to do most of the talking.) The trick, he said, is to save those packets of peanut butter and spread it on your pancakes, the next time there are pancakes. It sounds gross, but it's not. "The only way I eat my pancakes now is with peanut butter—because that's the way I ate them in there," Roby explained.

Carlos understood. He still put peanut butter on his pancakes, too. "It does have a different flavor," he said.

"Yeah! And you can put it in your oatmeal!"

"Oatmeal is real good with peanut butter," Carlos said.

"I still do that, too!" Roby blurted.

He continued with the menu. After Sunday—eggs, ham, hash browns—he looked at Carlos and said, "You put it all together?" to make sure Carlos knew to heap the whole thing between two slices of toast and squeeze jelly over it. Carlos knew. "That's a pretty fat sandwich, right?" Roby said.

"Yeah," Carlos said emphatically.

Roby still puts jelly on his egg sandwiches, too, he explained. Strawberry, grape—he doesn't care. "People look at me like I'm crazy!"

"People don't even know," Carlos said. They were laughing at themselves now. Carlos had done almost eleven years; Roby, close to twelve. Now they were free men, sitting outside a prison, waxing nostalgic about prison food.

They waited some more. Waiting came easily to them; incarceration makes you patient. Finally, after three and a half hours, a white corrections-department van pulled into the parking lot. It was going backward, fairly fast, then made a wide turn—still in reverse—to roll in beside Carlos and Roby, who jumped out of their car to meet it. As the van turned, the prison guard driving it leaned his head through the window and, as a kind of manic explanation for the backward driving, hollered, "I'm doing it on a dare!" He sprang out of the van, grinning and chuckling—he seemed overstimulated, as if he couldn't believe they were letting him drive the van today—and went to open the back door. But then he stopped short: All the backward driving had confused him about which side his passenger was on.

Eventually, Dale Hammock stepped out of the van. Hammock was sixty-five, white, his head shaved completely bald, both arms wrapped in black tattoos. He wore sweat shorts, a white T-shirt, canvas slip-ons, and white socks pulled up near his knees. All his clothes were bright and brand-new. As he approached Carlos and Roby, he thrust his chest toward them as far as it would go. Inside, this might have signaled strength and authority, but out here, it looked bizarre, as if he had some kind of back deformity.

Carlos shouted, "Welcome home, Mr. Hammock!"' Roby shouted, "How are you feeling, Mr. Hammock?" They introduced themselves and hurried to collect his few possessions from the guard—a brown paper bag and a pair of work boots— moving as if they'd done this exchange dozens of times, which they had, while Hammock stood between them, looking stunned.

Carlos handed Hammock the key and asked if he wanted to pop the trunk. But the key wasn't a key; it was a button. After squinting at it for a second, Hammock handed it back and said, "I wouldn't know what to do with that."

He'd been in prison for twenty-one years.

Hammock was sent away in 1994, at a time when new, stiffer sentencing requirements around the country were piling more people into prison for longer amounts of time. These included California's "three-strikes law," which took effect just months before Hammock was arrested. The law imposed life sentences for almost any crime if the offender had two previous "serious" or "violent" convictions. (The definitions of "serious" and "violent" in California's penal code are broad; attempting to steal a bicycle from someone's garage is "serious.") Similar laws proliferated in other states and in the 1994 federal crime bill, becoming signatures of that decade's tough-on-crime policies and helping to catapult the country into the modern era of mass incarceration. But as the criminologist Jeremy Travis, then head of the Justice Department's research agency, later pointed out, America had failed to recognize the "iron law of imprisonment": Each of the 2.4 million people we've locked up, if he or she doesn't die in prison, will one day come out.

It wasn't until the mid-2000s that this looming "prisoner reentry crisis" became a fixation of sociologists and policy makers, generating a torrent of research, government programs, task forces, nonprofit initiatives, and conferences now known as the "reentry movement." The movement tends to focus on solving structural problems, like providing housing, job training, or drug treatment, but easily loses sight of the profound disorientation of the individual people being released. Often, the psychological turbulence of those first days or weeks is so debilitating that recently incarcerated people can't even navigate public transportation; they're too frightened of crowds, too intimidated or mystified by the transit cards that have replaced cash and tokens. In a recent study, the Harvard sociologist Bruce Western describes a woman who "frequently forgot to eat breakfast or lunch for several months because she was used to being called to meals in prison." I met one man who explained that, after serving fifteen years, he found himself convinced that parked cars would somehow switch on and run him over. So many years inside can leave people vulnerable in almost incomprehensibly idiosyncratic ways, sometimes bordering on helplessness: "Like that little bird, getting his wings" is how one man described himself on Day One. Many spill out of prison in no condition to take advantage of the helpful bureaucracies the reentry movement has been busily putting in place.

This became clear in 2012, after California voted to overhaul its three-strikes law and a criminal-justice group at Stanford Law School, the Stanford Three Strikes Project, started filing petitions to have roughly 3,000 prisoners serving life sentences set free with time served. (So far, close to 2,300 have been released.) Many were serial offenders who were sent away for life after one last witless screwup, like Lester Wallace, who was caught trying to steal a car radio on the first morning the law went into effect, or Curtis Wilkerson, who did sixteen years of his life sentence after shoplifting a pair of socks from a department store called Mervyn's. When Wilkerson got out, he sounded as if he couldn't believe the whole thing: "Ordinary white socks," he said. "Didn't even have any stripes."

Unlike typical parolees, third-strikers are often notified of their release just before it happens, sometimes only a day in advance. (It can take months for a judge to rule after papers are filed.) They're usually sent out the door with two hundred dollars, a not-insubstantial share of which they often pay back to the prison for a lift to the nearest Greyhound station: An inmate might be released from a prison outside Sacramento and expected to find his way to a parole officer in San Diego, five hundred miles away, within forty-eight hours. Stanford's Three Strikes Project was setting up transitional housing for its clients, but initially, a lot of the third-strikers weren't making it there—they were just blowing away in the wind. Then Carlos and Roby started driving around the state and waiting outside to catch them.

The job started as a simple delivery service, to carry some of these discombobulated bodies from one place to another. In late 2013, the director of the Three Strikes Project, Michael Romano, contacted a nonprofit called the Anti-Recidivism Coalition, which has built up a close community of formerly incarcerated people in Los Angeles. Romano asked if ARC could dispatch one of its members to pick up third-strikers and drive them to their housing near the Staples Center in Los Angeles. ARC recommended Carlos, a dependable young man just three years out of prison himself, who—most important—also had his own car and a credit card to front money for gas. Carlos was hired, for twelve dollars an hour, to fetch an old man named Terry Critton from a prison in Chino. On the way back, Critton asked if Carlos wouldn't mind stopping at Amoeba Records, so he could look at jazz LPs—he'd been a big collector. They wound up spending almost two hours in the store, just looking. Then Critton wanted a patty melt, so Carlos found a place called Flooky's, where they ordered two and caught the end of a Dodgers game on TV. It was extraordinary: All day, Carlos could see this man coming back to life. He wanted to do more pickups, and he wanted to get his friend Roby involved. He told his bosses he needed a partner.

By now, Carlos and Roby—officially, ARC's Ride Home Program—have done about three dozen pickups, either together or individually, waking up long before dawn and driving for hours toward prison towns deep in the desert or up the coast.

Then they spend all day with the guy (so far they've picked up only men), taking him to eat, buying him some clothes, advising him, swapping stories, dialing his family on their cell phones, or astonishing him by magically calling up Facebook pictures of nieces and nephews he's never met—or just sitting quietly, to let him depressurize. The conversation with those shell-shocked total strangers doesn't always flow, Roby told me. It helps to have a wingman.

"The first day is everything," Carlos says—a barrage of insignificant-seeming experiences with potentially big consequences. Consider, for example, a friend of his and Roby's: Julio Acosta, who was paroled in 2013 after twenty-three years inside. Acosta describes stopping for breakfast near the prison that first morning as if it were a horrifying fever dream: He kept looking around the restaurant for a sniper, as in the chow hall in prison, and couldn't stop gawking at the metal knives and forks, "like an Aztec looking at Cortés's helmet," he says. It wasn't until he got up from the booth and walked to the men's room, and a man came out the door and said, "How you doin'?" and Acosta said, "Fine," that Acosta began to feel, even slightly, like a legitimate part of the environment around him. He'd accomplished something. He'd made a treacherous trip across an International House of Pancakes. He'd peed.

But what if Acosta had accidentally bumped into a waitress, knocking over her tray and shattering dishes? What if that man had glared at him, instead of greeting him, or snapped at him to get the hell out of the way? Ann Jacobs, director of the Prisoner Reentry Institute at New York's John Jay College of Criminal Justice, told me that even the smallest bungled interactions on the outside leave recently incarcerated people feeling "like they're being exposed, like they're incompetent. It's feeding into their worst fear, their perception of themselves as an impostor who's incapable of living a normal life." Carlos and Roby have learned to steer their guys through that perilous newness—and to be nonchalant about it, to make the sudden enormity of life feel unthreatening, even fun. On one ride home, I watched a third-striker venture inside a convenience store, alone, to buy a candy bar while Roby pumped gas. The man seemed emboldened after a few hours of freedom, actually hopping a bit as he walked. But then he tripped over the curb and tumbled forward, arms thrashing, nearly face-planting in front of the door. Roby just shrugged and said, "Well, you've got to get that one out of the way."

"Been a long time since I looked at a menu," Dale Hammock said. He was sheltered in a corner of a booth at a Denny's near the prison. The restaurant was overcrowded, loud and full of the kind of hyperdifferentiated nonsense that ordinary Americans swim through every day, never assuming it can or should be fully understood. But Hammock was having trouble sorting the breakfast menu from the lunch menu, and the regular Denny's menu from the Denny's Skillets Across America limited-time menu. There were two kinds of hot sauce and four different sweeteners on the table. On the Heinz ketchup bottle, it said: "Up for a Game? Trivial Pursuit Tomato Ketchup."

The first meal after a long prison sentence is an ostensible celebration laced with stress. The food tastes incredible. (Roby gained sixty pounds after his release, desperate to try the Outback Steakhouse Bloomin' Onion and other fast-casual delicacies he'd seen commercials for on TV.) But ordering—making any choice—can be unnerving. Waiters are intimidating; waitresses, especially pretty ones, can be petrifying. So at Denny's, Roby started things off, ordering a chocolate milk. Hammock ordered a chocolate milk, too. Then he reconsidered and said: "I want a milkshake! I'll just have that!" He ordered a Grand Slam. Then he changed it to a Lumberjack Slam. And when the waiter shot back with "Toast: white, wheat, or sourdough?" Hammock went stiff momentarily, then answered: "Toast, I guess."

One morning twenty-one years ago, Hammock was pulled over for not wearing a seat belt, and the cop found a half pound of methamphetamine under the passenger seat. (Hammock was driving a friend's car and claims he didn't know the drugs were there, but the police report also notes that he had a small amount of meth in his pocket and was carrying close to a thousand dollars.) He'd been an addict most of his life, flying in and out of prison, with some thirty arrests and a dozen other drug or drug-related charges behind him. In 1973, he shot and injured a man while trying to rob him, and in 1978, he snatched a nineteen-year-old woman's purse. (There was two dollars inside.) Those two charges both counted as "strikes." The meth in the car was Hammock's third. He was given a sentence of thirty-one years to life.

He moved through ten different prisons and watched first-hand as the age of mass incarceration took hold. In the forty-two years between his first strike and his release, the state's prison population had quintupled. Facilities started running at 135 percent capacity, gyms were converted into dorms, all kinds of privileges were discontinued (some prisons even outlawed fresh fruit, to crack down on homemade alcohol) and everyone, Hammock said—the inmates and the guards—started walking around with more abrasive attitudes. Hammock, meanwhile, had mellowed somewhat, become an old man. For the last five or six years, he'd been the prison barber, which required him to shuttle among the different housing units and stay on good terms with everyone; a supervisor's report praised him as an "asset" who mentored younger, more volatile inmates. He was too worn out to be menacing anymore. Gabbing with Carlos and Roby while they waited for their table, he explained wearily that, years ago, "I stabbed two guys in Soledad. But you know how that goes, those situations arise sometimes"—either them or you.

Freedom hadn't instantly re-energized him. From the moment he hopped into Carlos and Roby's car that morning, he'd seemed less gung-ho than accepting—a good sport. "Oh boy, it's going to be different," he kept saying, or, "It's going to be an experience, brother, I swear to God." Several times, he told them: "I was thinking about trying to get into barber college," latching on to that phrase like a handrail on a shaky train. This was the one thing Dale Hammock knew right now: "I've been thinking about barber college, if I could get enrolled in barber college."

His milkshake came. He took a tentative sip, then removed the straw and started gulping. Roby took a picture on his phone, showed it to Hammock, then zapped it off to the team at Stanford. Hammock was amazed. "Everything now, you just touch it, and it shows you things?" he asked. It was like having breakfast with a time traveler. Was he correct in noticing that men didn't wear their hair long anymore? Was it true that everyone had stopped using cash? Later, in the restroom, he wrenched the front of the automatic soap dispenser off its base instead of waving his hand under it.

Carlos and Roby had been careful so far not to overwhelm Hammock, but with his milkshake in place, they eased into discussing some practicalities. They talked about cell phone plans and how to get two forms of ID, so Hammock could register for welfare and other assistance. This was the beginning of Carlos and Roby's signature reentry crash course, rooted in their own experiences coming home, which they casually threaded through the duration of every ride. Hammock seemed determined to figure it all out. He didn't see an alternative. "I'm too tired of prison," he told them. "I know that."

If he was serious about cutting hair, Carlos said, there was a government program that might pay for his licensure classes. Roby offered to buy him a set of clippers so he could get a little business going right away, giving haircuts to the other third-strikers at the housing facility where they were heading. In fact, Carlos added, he commuted past there every day. "I was thinking you could hook me up, and I'll pay you to cut my hair."

"No problem, no problem at all," Hammock said, tilting his head to size up Carlos's fade. "You keep it short like that?" He sounded just like a barber.

Carlos encouraged him: He'd have to hustle and find a niche, just as prisoners are accustomed to doing inside. "You already have the tools," Carlos explained. "It's just about applying them now to a different environment. You know how to dictate how people treat you. You know how to tell who's going to scam you and who's not. Using that same psychology, you're going to be all right."

Hammock nodded. This seemed to make sense to him in a way that nothing else had so far. "I'll be all right—it's just going to take a minute, that's all," he said. "Looks like it's time to eat."

His breakfast took up three separate plates. He ate inelegantly and quickly, working the food over with his half-set of dentures and toothless lower gums. When he was done, he bellowed, "Well, I'm not hungry no more!" Then, with that out of the way, he looked across the table at Carlos and asked, "How long you been out?"

The first ride home Carlos and Roby did together was in February 2014. They were dispatched for an early-morning pickup at

San Quentin, seven hours from Los Angeles in Marin County, and Michael Romano, the director of the Three Strikes Project, suggested they drive up the day before and stay at his house in San Francisco. He expected to take them out to dinner—get to know them, spoil them a bit. Instead, Carlos and Roby rolled in after midnight and unceremoniously bedded down on a couple of couches.

Lying there, it hit them how unusual this was: They were both still on parole at the time, but here they were, welcomed into this white lawyer's home in the middle of the night, while his wife and two little children slept upstairs. "That really changed everything," Carlos remembers. "It changed our perspective of how people actually viewed us." He and Roby had been locked up so young that they'd never lived as regular, trustworthy adults. This, they told each other before falling asleep, must be what it feels like.

Carlos grew up in the San Gabriel Valley, east of downtown LA. His father walked out on his mother while she was still pregnant with him, and Carlos had the misfortune of reminding her of his dad, he says, which made her resentful and abusive. Soon she remarried, but while her new husband bought his own two sons new clothes and Super Nintendos, Carlos and his older brother got none of that. Once, when Carlos was eleven, his father mailed him fifty dollars—a hundred actually, but his mother took a cut—and Carlos immediately picked up the phone and ordered a medium pizza. When the doorbell rang, he paid the delivery guy, took the pizza inside, and ate it out of the box, very methodically, in front of his family. He remembers the scene clearly—how shocked everyone was that he had something of his own and wasn't giving any of it to them. "And I was like: 'Yeah, but it's *my* pizza. I'm going to sit here and enjoy this pizza.'" He liked the feeling of satisfaction money brought. So he started stealing bikes and breaking into houses. "After that, my life was thieving," Carlos says. "I was a thief, for sure."

His childhood turned even more formless and reckless. He had started smoking pot at nine, and by fifteen he was a heavy meth user who spent all day in the street. His mother warned him he would end up in jail—sort of. "She said, 'I hope you fucking end up in jail,'" Carlos remembers. "And in Spanish, trust me, it sounds even worse. Two weeks later, I was arrested."

One afternoon, some older gang members jumped Carlos, knocking him off his bike and beating him, and Carlos enlisted two friends to drive around with him, looking to retaliate. One of them wound up shooting at a young man from the car, injuring him; Carlos was the only one arrested. After waiting in a county jail for nearly two years, he says, he was finally offered a deal: He could plead guilty to attempted murder and be sentenced as an adult to twelve years, or he could fight the charge and get thirty-five to life if he lost. Carlos took the deal. He was sixteen.

Carlos floundered in prison but found a mentor after a few years—an older cellmate, also named Carlos. Under the older Carlos's influence, he began willing his way into adulthood: studying, reading, examining his anger. A girl from his neighborhood started driving out to see him, and they eventually married. After a few conjugal visits, they had a baby, a daughter Carlos met one Saturday morning in the prison visiting room. Over the years, Carlos saw inmates go home and then wind up back inside; the system seemed to offer little preparation for release, setting them up for failure. He started mailing away for details about advocacy groups, housing, Social Security, driver's licenses—not just in Los Angeles, where he'd be living when he got out, but in counties around California, so he could share what he learned with other inmates. He made packets of information and put a notice on the prison bulletin board, next to the day's menu: If you're getting out and need any "resources," as he called them, come talk to Carlos in Bunk 28 Low. The prison's chaplain told me, "He was basically a social worker behind bars."

By that point, Carlos was housed at the California Rehabilitation Center, not far outside LA. He was part of a small circle of more mature inmates who, having done time at high-security prisons, were taking college classes, looking for calm in the last years of their sentences. Among them was a wisecracking Asian guy whom everyone knew as Big Head. His real name was Roby So.

Roby's story was less gothic than Carlos's, but it had led him to the same dismal place. His parents escaped the killing fields in Cambodia and opened a Laundromat and a bargain store in Los Angeles. He grew up in Echo Park, near Dodger Stadium, a dangerous neighborhood in the 1980s, where he fell in with a gang of other Cambodian kids called the Oriental Boys. Roby was seven years into a thirteen-year sentence when he met Carlos, having pleaded guilty to second-degree attempted murder in 1998. (Roby had driven four friends to a party in San Diego, and one fired a handgun at a rival there and missed; the gun was still in Roby's trunk when they were all arrested at a gas station the next day.)

Prison society is usually strictly segregated, so it was no small thing when Carlos, a Mexican, and Roby, an Asian guy, struck up a friendship. Roby would walk across the dorm to Carlos's bunk and sit down on the other bed—oblivious to, or uninterested in, whether he was welcome on it—and they'd fall into long conversations about books and life. Breaking bread with someone of a different race or ethnicity is especially taboo, but Carlos and Roby frequently cooked meals for each other anyway, improvising with ingredients pocketed in the dining hall or bought from the commissary. Roby made the first one for Carlos on the floor of his bunk, cooking rice, canned mackerel, and rehydrated bean soup in a bucket of water, which he heated with a "stinger"— a metal rod resembling a curling iron. Then he puréed all of it, piled it in an egg-roll wrapper, and topped it with sriracha. (In retrospect, the dish was symbolic: an Asian-fusion burrito.) On Saturdays, Carlos and Roby would sit side by side watching a block of cooking shows on PBS: *Yan Can Cook, Simply Ming, Mexico—One Plate at a Time* with Rick Bayless. They picked up techniques and gathered ideas. "Like, instead of onions, let's try a little more ginger," Roby explains.

"Once we started talking, it was like I knew this guy already," Carlos remembers. "He had the same energy, the same mentality." They discovered they were scheduled to be paroled one day apart, and plotted their reentry into Los Angeles together. Then, once they were out, they started executing the plans they'd assembled on Carlos's bunk. They went to file for government relief payments together. They waited at the DMV together, wondering why everyone else there seemed so impatient and aggravated. And they held each other accountable to their respective to-do lists. Eventually, Carlos found a job as a contractor, and he now works for a nonprofit that guides kids through the juvenile justice system. Roby started fiddling with a GoPro and taught himself video editing. Last year, he lucked into a post-production job on a streaming show called *Sin City Saints*.

Waiting outside the prison for Hammock that morning, Roby got an email on his phone that *The New York Times* had just published the first review of the show online. He started reading it out loud to Carlos. But the knocks came pretty quickly— "a disjointed and not particularly funny series"—and his excitement curdled. "Blah, blah, blah. You're just giving your opinion," Roby finally said to his phone. "Let's let the viewers decide."

Then he put the thing away and started digging idly through the glove box.

The opening riff of "Good Times, Bad Times" kicked in on the stereo as they hit Los Angeles County, just before 2:00 p.m. Carlos bobbed his head in the back seat. The mood in the car was up—for a minute or two. Then construction work narrowed Route 101, and Roby grumbled as they slowed nearly to a stop. "See that, Dale?" he asked Hammock. "I'm complaining about traffic. You know what that's called?"

"No," Hammock said.

"That's called 'free-man problems,'" Roby said.

They fought through the congestion to their next stop, a Target in downtown LA, where Roby put Hammock in charge of the big red shopping cart. "There you go, pushing a cart!" he shouted as they set off into the aisles. "Who would've thunk it!"

Every ride home includes a stop to get the third-striker out of his sweats and buy him some real clothes and basic toiletries. It's typically the last thing Carlos and Roby do; walking into a crowded big-box store asks a lot of these guys. Roby was released on Presidents' Day weekend, and his father and cousins took him straight to an outlet mall. The swarm of bargain-seeking humanity overwhelmed him. In prison, people move slowly, drag their feet, and keep their distance; all of a sudden, Roby was being jostled and bumped. And after twelve years in the same state-issued clothing, he had no idea what to buy. When his father asked him what size he wore, Roby told him: "I don't have a size."

Now, Roby tends to take the lead at Target, working as a kind of unflappable personal shopper for the third-strikers, like a kid eager to do tricks on a piece of playground equipment that once scared him. "You look like a 34," he told Hammock. He led him to a dismayingly large wall of jeans: several different brands; slim, boot cut, carpenter. When Hammock finally reached for a pair, Roby told him to gauge the waistline by stretching it around his neck.

"Around my neck?" Hammock asked.

"Yeah," Roby told him. "I learned it from Oprah."

Soon, they moved on to shirts. Then underwear. Then socks. It was like marching Hammock through the stations of some consumerist cross. He peered into the racks of razors with names like military fighter jets: Schick Xtreme, BIC Hybrid Advance 3. He confronted the toothbrushes: Colgate 2X Whitening Action, Colgate 360 Degree Whole Mouth Clean, Oral-B Indicator Contour Clean. In the deodorant aisle, there was an entire section of Old Spices named after wild animals. Carlos always likes to recommend AXE—he believes in the company's products—and this time, he gasped slightly when he noticed the apparently rare AXE White Label antiperspirant on a high shelf. He took off the cap to smell it—Forest Scent—then extended it to Hammock. "Are you an AXE man?" Carlos asked. When Hammock decided to go another way, Carlos seemed hurt.

They got toothpaste. They got soap. Roby upsold Hammock on a reversible belt. Often, as they arrived in front of the next expanse of products, Roby and Carlos would shoot each other glances, eager to see what Hammock would do. Their policy was to throw the third-strikers into these challenges, rather than coddle them. This was ordinary life. It was safe; it was fun. "Take this and slide it," Roby now told Hammock, handing him his credit card at the register. Hammock dragged the card through the slot methodically, formally, turning to face Roby's camera, as though at a ribbon-cutting ceremony. But it didn't catch. "I think you gotta go faster," Roby said. And so Hammock slid it again. The machine gave off a satisfying beep: success.

There was one more thing, though. Carlos was already in line at the Starbucks kiosk near the entrance, ordering Hammock what he described to him as a "Cadillac"—prison slang for sweet, milky coffee. Soon came the announcement: "Grande caramel macchiato for Dale!"

Hammock took a sip. He looked nearly as stunned as he had the moment they met him that morning, when he was driven out of prison backward after twenty-one years. "Wow," he said. Carlos and Roby burst out laughing. But Hammock was not laughing. He was very serious. "Wow," he said again. "Coffee's come a long way! This here's the Rolls-Royce of Cadillacs!"

He took another sip. He shook his head and peered down, through the sip hole in the lid, trying to understand what this stuff was and how it came to be his. Someone had even written his name, "Dale," with a marker on the side of the cup.

It was a short drive through downtown from Target to their final destination. Everyone seemed drained. Carlos said almost nothing, while Roby crammed a few last bits of acclimating information into the conversation, seemingly as they occurred to him. (Some parking spots downtown cost $192 a month. "There's this thing called a Keurig.") He turned to Hammock and asked, "How you feel so far?"

Hammock didn't know what to say, so Roby rephrased the question: "Are you free yet?"

"I'm getting there," Hammock told him.

Soon they were all climbing out of the car in front of the Amity Foundation, the housing and rehabilitation center where

Carlos and Roby have been delivering most of their third-strikers for the last year and a half. One of them, Stanley Bailey, was meeting them downstairs to help Hammock get settled.

All day, Carlos and Roby had been slipping inspirational details about Bailey into their conversations with Hammock. He was a solid role model: a fifty-three-year-old longtime heroin addict who had been locked up for twenty-five years. Carlos had picked him up at Ironwood State Prison in October. Now, five months later, he was doing public speaking at criminal-justice nonprofits and universities and working doggedly to get his truck driver's license. Recently, he'd run the Los Angeles Marathon. "He's the story I always tell," Carlos said.

Bailey met them at Amity's registration desk, dispensing big, wholehearted bro hugs. "Hey, Running Man!" Roby shouted. Like Hammock, Bailey had zero hair on his head and a full black sleeve of indecipherable tattoos on each arm. But he was slimmer, healthier-looking—glowing, comparatively, in a light blue polo shirt. When he introduced himself to Hammock, it was like watching him shake hands with some wrinkled and diminished alternate self.

The two third-strikers sidled into an easy back-and-forth, comparing which prisons they'd been in, finding some overlap. Hammock took another sip of his Starbucks drink—he was still nursing it—and lifted the cup to show Bailey. "This thing here," he said, and made a whistling sound. He still couldn't put it into words. Then, after a while, Carlos and Roby wrote their phone numbers on a slip of paper for Hammock and said goodbye—nothing dramatic; they'd stay in close touch. They always did. Hammock corralled each of them into a hug, one at a time. "Thank you, brother," he told Carlos.

Bailey followed Carlos and Roby into the hall. He wanted a word, in private. He'd called Carlos earlier that day to ask for advice and wanted to finish the conversation. (They still texted and spoke frequently; whenever Carlos was downtown, he'd take Bailey out for tacos.) The truth was, Bailey was struggling and frustrated; he was being presented as a reentry success story, but his situation was precarious. He seemed to be hustling in all the right ways, volunteering at several nonprofits and now at a trucking company down the street, too—sweeping up, or doing odd chores, just so he could sit in their truck cabs with his driver's manual and study. But things still weren't coming together. He'd gotten stalled for months, trying to track down a copy of his birth certificate, without which he couldn't get other forms of ID, access to government aid, or his learner's permit. All the celebrated speaking gigs he did were unpaid, and his funding to stay at Amity was almost up. He wasn't sure where he'd go. Though he'd reconnected with a woman in Colorado, one condition of his release was that he wasn't allowed to leave the state. It was as if Bailey were swimming determinedly away from some monstrous undertow, trying to keep the distance he'd put between himself and his past from closing. "To be honest, I'm not looking for a big, big life," he said. "I just want to be remembered for more than what I was."

Carlos slipped some money into Bailey's hand as he shook it and said goodbye. (That night, he'd start emailing people on Bailey's behalf, even asking if Stanford and ARC would consider hiring Bailey to ride along with him and Roby sometimes as an assistant.) Down the hall, meanwhile, Hammock was finishing his intake interview and getting to know a couple of former lifers in the building. An older man who was paroled last Christmas Day after thirty-one years asked Hammock how his day had gone. "You been inside a store yet?" the man said.

"Yeah," Hammock told him. It sounded like nothing, but it wasn't. He'd made it all the way here, to the beginning.

At the Precise Center of a Dream

| 2014 |

Jacques-André Istel woke up at his home in Felicity, California, did 100 push-ups and 125 squats, swam in his elegantly lit lap pool, then returned upstairs, where he took a light breakfast in bed, as has been his custom since his boyhood in Paris. After breakfast, he dressed in a blue shirt and ascot and walked to his office at 1 Center of the World Plaza. It was Istel's birthday. He was turning eighty-five years old.

Istel is the founder of Felicity and the town's longtime mayor, having been elected, almost thirty years ago, to an apparent lifetime term. The vote was unanimous: Istel voted for himself and so did Felicity's other resident, Istel's wife, Felicia. The town, established in 1986, consists of the Istels' home and a half dozen other buildings that the couple built on 2,600 acres in the middle of the desert near Yuma, Arizona, just off Interstate 8. At the north end, up an imposing staircase, sits the Church on the Hill at Felicity—inspired by a little white chapel in Brittany—that Istel built in 2007. The church is gorgeous and serene and looks almost spectral and out of place, though less out of place than the twenty-one-foot-tall stone-and-glass pyramid on the opposite end of town. The pyramid is there to mark the exact center of the world.

Any point on the surface of the globe could be considered the center of the world—the globe being almost a perfect sphere—and Istel doesn't argue with that. "The center of the world could be in your pocket!" he told me. And yet, he has managed to make his center of the world the Official Center of the World: In May of 1985, Istel cajoled the Imperial County Board of Supervisors to join in his absurdist joke and designate that point in Felicity as the middle of everything. A plaque now marks the spot.

Between the pyramid and the hill, in the bizarre heart of Felicity, is an array of triangular monuments. Most are one hundred feet long, about forehead high, and comprise sixty-two granite panels. Each panel weighs 477 pounds. Twenty-five years ago, Istel had a simple thought: *Wouldn't it be nice to engrave the names of some loved ones on a "Wall of Remembrance"?* ("If you love people, you want to remember them," he explained.) So he hired an engraver and then, as that project begat other projects, a young artist to etch portraits and historical scenes into the granite alongside the text. There are now monuments chronicling, for example, the histories of French aviation, the French Foreign Legion, California, Arizona, and the United States. It is an encyclopedic and sophisticated form of cave art. The monuments are anchored three feet into the ground with reinforced concrete. Istel specified to his engineers that they should last four thousand years.

Very quickly, Istel could feel his so-called Museum of History in Granite consuming his life. He researches and writes all the text, sometimes moving through fifty or sixty drafts of a single panel; Felicia, a former researcher and reporter at *Sports Illustrated*, proofs his copy. But in 2004, he figured he could take on more. He began a set of eight monuments—461 panels total, arranged in a compass rose, with a multilingual Rosetta Stone at its center. On them, he would record the "History of Humanity." He's about a quarter of the way through: the story begins with an etching of the Big Bang and cuts off after a summary of Viking death rituals.

What's embedded at the center of Felicity amounts to a stupefying and unsummarizable catalog of human triumph, folly, idiosyncrasy, and violence. Here is Van Gogh's *Starry Night*. Here is Sandra Day O'Connor. The first recorded game of polo in 600 B.C. The expansion of Islam. H. G. Wells. Lao-tzu. The hamburger. A nineteenth-century political cartoon mocking Thomas Jefferson as a prairie dog, buckled over and vomiting money. The Ancient Greeks' belief that diamonds were splinters of fallen stars. Advice from Julia Child: "If you are afraid of butter, use cream." And because Istel can't predict who or what his audience will be in four millennia, he has developed a gift for conveying fundamental truths as though they're being considered for the first time: "Beautiful and romantic, our moon profoundly influences humans."

I arrived in Felicity on Istel's birthday and was invited to stay in one of the twelve motel-style apartments that the couple built on the east side of the museum and were lately having trouble renting out. (One was occupied by an Ocean Spray produce inspector, who was visiting vegetable-processing plants in the area; in another was a former employee for the California Highway Patrol who had agreed to a monthlong lease and has so far stayed eleven years.) On the desk in my apartment was a formal letter, handwritten on mayoral stationery, inviting me for a birthday toast at a dive bar in Yuma called Jimmie Dee's, then dinner at a casino. "We will leave Felicity at 5:30 p.m. on Tuesday, January 28, 2014," it said.

Also in town were a strait-laced, retired private-school head-master named Donn Gaebelein and his wife, Norma Gaebelein. Donn is Istel's oldest friend. They met almost seventy-five years ago, in eighth grade. On first glance, Gaebelein said, Felicity makes no sense: Why is any of it here? Why does this frenetic Frenchman keep compulsively building more of it? Take the church, Gaebelein said. Not only is Istel not religious; his mother was Jewish. And yet, he went through significant trouble to build this magnificent little chapel on a hill; in fact, he built the hill, too, hiring heavy machinery to push earth out of the flat desert and into a scrupulously engineered, seismically fit trapezoid thirty-five feet high. Istel can articulate exactly why he felt obligated to build that hill for the church—"I'm a traditionalist, and I believe in protocol and courtesy; if you build a house for a higher power, for God, it should be the highest thing," he would tell me—but he can't explain why he built the church in the first place.

"Jacques will die not knowing why he built that chapel," Gaebelein explained, "but also knowing that he *had* to." Honestly, he added, you could say that about everything here. This was Gaebelein's fifteenth stay in Felicity, he said—it's how he and Norma dodge winters in New York. And at some point, for him, what looked like absurdity had tipped into profundity. "You have to live with this place, you have to sleep on this, to get the feel of its power," he said.

Istel is handsome and fit, with a square jaw, olive skin, and a sweep of slightly graying black hair that gets matted on his forehead by midday if he doesn't keep an eye on it. He was sitting at his computer, ascot knotted, yellow sweater tied primly over his shoulders, when I came by his office the next morning. (The office is next to Felicity's combination gift shop and post office and upstairs from the "brasserie," where a woman named Debbie makes pretty good sandwiches.) Istel began relaying his life story, which, even before the part about starting a town in the middle of the desert, reads like a magical-realist novel.

He was born in Paris in 1929, the third of four children. His father, André Istel, was a distinguished financier, a partner in a couple of brokerage firms who served as an adviser to Charles de Gaulle and French delegate to the Bretton Woods conference, which established the International Monetary Fund and the World Bank. André was a stern parent; Jacques characterizes much of his childhood as moldering boredom interrupted by corporal punishment. When he misbehaved, he would get whacked—first by his governess, then his mother, then his father. "It would go right up the chain of command," he said. Of all the siblings, he was the most defiant. (Jacques-André's younger brother, Yves-André, lived up to their father's vision. He was a managing director at Lehman Brothers and now serves as a senior adviser at Rothschild.)

Jacques was eleven when the Nazis occupied Paris. "It was absolutely catastrophic," he told me. His father got the family out on diplomatic passports and, after fleeing through Spain and Portugal, they arrived in New York in August 1940. "We assumed we had lost everything," he said. But his mother, who had taught Jacques and several neighbors' children at home while living in Paris, eventually returned to find that the parents of these students had clandestinely rescued all of the Istels' furniture during the war, then returned it. Even their laundry was washed and folded.

In New York, Istel felt uprooted and lost. He was sent to the Stony Brook School, a Christian boarding school on Long Island, where, despite not speaking a word of English, he was thrown into the eighth grade. One teacher gave him comic books instead of textbooks. Every night, he lay in bed weeping.

Then, in 1943, the summer after he turned fourteen, Istel rode his bicycle two hundred miles to Vermont, sleeping in barns and picking up a job mixing concrete. That went well, so the following summer, he decided he ought to hitchhike across the United States. He'd saved up seven dollars, after all. He was struck by the openness and generosity of people he met; he was falling in love with America.

Soon, he fell in love with parachuting, too—one of many sharp turns in Istel's life with a cinematic backstory. In short, it involves a twenty-year-old Istel making an impulsive solo flight across North America, from Vancouver to New York, in a single-engine airplane that he had just barely learned to fly. After a handful of perilous and comic mishaps, covered in local papers along the way, which embarrassed his parents, he finally touched down at LaGuardia with a broken radio. (He landed elsewhere first and called the tower from a pay phone to let them know he was coming.)

By the 1950s, after working as a stock analyst on Wall Street and being miserable there, Istel was leaping out of airplanes quite frequently. He loved the feeling of free fall; he loved being alone in the sky. Before then, parachutes were used almost exclusively by the military. The primitive devices opened with an excruciating jolt, blew wherever the wind took them, and landed violently. But in 1957, Istel started a company, Parachutes Inc., and, with an employee, designed steerable, more user-friendly chutes. This helped tame and democratize parachuting. Civilians were empowered to make jumps after only a couple of hours

of training. Istel founded three profitable parachuting schools—
Sports Illustrated called the one in Orange, Massachusetts, "the
Sorbonne of American sport parachuting"—and became an
evangelizer for the new sport. He took out a full-page ad in *Time*.
He was pictured in a business suit beside the caption: "I invite
you to jump out of an airplane."

In 1956, Istel led the first-ever American team to the World
Parachuting Championships in Moscow. Then, in 1962, he
brought the competition to the United States. It took years of
maneuvering. When Istel had trouble raising money to stage the
event, he talked the Massachusetts governor, John A. Volpe, into
letting him address the state legislature in Boston. Istel arrived
by parachute, slipping through a narrow clearance between the
crowns of two trees and touching down next to Volpe on Boston
Common. (Actually, he says, he sort of clipped the governor's
arm on the way down.) A photograph of Istel, a split second before landing, now hangs in his office in Felicity.

Istel bought the acreage that became Felicity in the 1950s.
He has a lifelong habit of buying land—in Ireland, Bimini, New
Hampshire, the Hamptons—that, even if it looks crummy to
others, he judges to be either undervalued or unbearably beautiful. He claims to have made a few million dollars this way. He
also started buying up farmland surrounding his parachuting
schools, to preempt noise complaints, and watched it appreciate
significantly.

Felicity, Istel recognized, sat on a good aquifer and was potentially well situated in the long term: eight miles from Yuma,
and almost exactly midway between the growing cities of San
Diego and Phoenix. Still, for decades, Istel rarely thought about
the property. But in the 1980s, when he began selling off his

parachuting business, his imagination turned to that dusty blank canvas. It seemed like an exciting challenge. "I told Felicia, 'We're going to sit in the desert,'" he said.

"I thought it would be fun to start a little village," he told me. As a young man, Istel's father had fantasized about founding a town in Canada with a friend. They imagined calling it "Barrière," French for "barrier." To Jacques, this seemed like a terribly unwelcoming name for a new town. He would choose something friendlier, happier: "Felicity," after his wife. He also thought it would be fun to get his little village officially recognized as the center of the world. ("Why not the center of the world?" Istel said when I asked him to elaborate.) The first step seemed obvious: He needed to write a children's book.

Children's books carry a strange authority, Istel reasoned: No one can argue that Little Red Riding Hood's cloak was actually blue. Creating a picture book of Felicity might make his vision for the town feel more accessible—more legitimate—when it materialized in real life. The book, which Istel self-published in 1985 and titled *Coe: The Good Dragon at the Center of the World*, is about a dragon who loves children. Coe discovers the exact center of the globe in a desert town called Felicity. A pyramid stands over the spot. And there to welcome him is the dragon species' debonair ambassador to humanity, a man in white tie and tails named JAI (Jacques-André Istel).

In May of that year, Istel appeared at a meeting of the Imperial County Board of Supervisors. He arrived in white tie and tails, preceded by three high-school trumpeters playing a fanfare. Istel introduced himself as the "ambassador of all good dragons" and requested that the board officially recognize Felicity as the center of the world. "The idea had no logic!" Istel told me. Clearly, this was what made it beautiful to him.

Felicity was officially established as a town the following year.

For a time, Istel imagined growing it into a community of 30,000 or 50,000 people, a haven of charm and clean air. But a development plan drew opposition from the nearby Quechan tribe, and Istel realized, he told me, that "the idea of development is absolutely foreign to my soul." He was enjoying Felicity as it was. He had already built the pyramid and a house for himself and Felicia. He staged a grand opening for his new post office. (For operating the post office, the Istels receive an annual payment of one dollar; instead of cashing the government's checks, they frame them and hang them in their office.) Istel says several hundred people attended to collect the inaugural stamp cancellations. The office processed more than 2,300 pieces of mail that first day. The Chinese consulate in San Francisco sent a diplomat, who delivered a speech in Mandarin. (Felicia is Chinese American.) Istel wore what he always does to official town functions: a dark suit and satin mayoral sash, hung with various medals.

"The early days of Felicity were great fun," Istel told me. "The problem was, this was all whimsy. When we started doing serious stuff, nobody took us seriously."

The first afternoon that Istel walked me through the monuments, six or seven other people were ambling around, too. This was high season for tourists. Istel does not advertise and almost never approaches the media. His attitude is: There will be plenty of time for humanity to appreciate what he built. But every winter, retirees from frigid places like Edmonton and Idaho take up residence on tracts of nearby land and sometimes wander in. From the highway, you can see their white RVs clustered in the emptiness, like desert blooms.

Istel was glad to have guests. "Welcome to Felicity," he said, bowing and clasping the ladies' hands to pantomime a kiss. "What do you think of this?" he kept asking. Their responses did not seem very satisfying—nearly everyone said, "It's very interesting"—but Istel seemed genuinely touched. "What do you think of this?" Istel asked a large man from Missouri in jean shorts. The man was wheezing a little—it was hot. After a beat of silence, his wife said, "A lot of engraving!"

As an editor of all human experience, Istel has a sly aesthetic—an eye for offbeat detail and pointed juxtapositions. On the American-history monument, for example, a panel describing the nation's "pioneering initiative" doesn't just include the invention of the safety pin alongside the airplane, the computer, and sending a man to the moon; it lists the safety pin first. George Washington, in addition to all the famous, foundational accomplishments, is remembered for his taste in beer. Simple, ageless truths mingle with antiquated boneheadedness. The museum made me feel extraordinarily small. One defining thing about humanity, it seemed clear, is how right we always assume we are and how urgent the present always feels, but how bad we are at appreciating the irony of that later. "You'll see, for instance, we engraved a sign that says, 'No Irish Need Apply,'" Istel said. "A few years later, we elect an Irish president. You see how we amputated runaway slaves, and decades later we elect a black president."

But Istel could explain the impulse behind his work in only the simplest terms. "I think it's very human to hope for continuity of one kind or another," he said. Mostly, he just kept saying, "Look at that panel!" and waiting patiently while I read whatever had caught his eye: Avicenna's "diseases of the mind" ("I find that panel quite interesting, don't you?"); Eratosthenes measuring the circumference of Earth ("Look at this guy!"). It took courage for an amateur historian to take this on. He frequently reached out to professors at Harvard and other universities for advice, but they brushed him off. Once, he claimed, the Indian Institute for Advanced Study in Shimla refused his request for help with a Hindi translation, so he booked a trip to India with Felicia and knocked on their door. "I do have a sense of responsibility," he said. "You're talking to a fellow who has a great possibility of looking like an idiot for the next several thousand years. But we're doing the best we can." He had made his peace, in other words, and preferred not to reflect on the risks.

Really, he preferred not to reflect at all. It was as if the entire town had sprouted from some preverbal place in his imagination—some need for beauty and meaning. (Even my asking why he stopped skydiving seemed to paralyze, then annoy him. He didn't stop skydiving, he finally insisted, he simply hasn't made a jump since 1973.) I kept at him, though. Finally, one evening during drinks on the Istels' balcony, he seemed to lose patience and told me: "Basically, Feli and I are pretty simple people. Don't make us complicated. If I were more introspective, I wouldn't have done this."

What does it feel like to walk around in another person's dream? It felt dreamlike, actually. Just having those hulls of granite at the center of things, set to ride out the next four thousand years, had a way of encouraging contemplation, of lending even some mundane conversations in Felicity a strange weight.

Late one night, I spotted a light outside, near the center of the museum. It was Gene Britton, Istel's lead artist, hustling to meet a deadline. In three weeks, on February 22, Washington's Birthday, Istel would be hosting a dedication ceremony for the American-history monument. He had arranged for a Marine color guard to attend (Istel served in the Marines during the

Korean War); a skydiver to zip down carrying an American flag; and several children and thirteen adults—one to represent each of the original colonies—to ring a 250-pound, half-scale replica of the Liberty Bell, which sat on the ground beside us, waiting to be installed. Britton, however, still had seven illustrations to go. He had a work lamp and compressor set up, and the heavy power cord of his die grinder was slung over his shoulder. Little moths flickered around the ankles of his camouflage pants and hurled themselves at the illuminated granite.

By now, Britton had almost as much of his life invested in the museum as Istel did. He first came to Felicity thirteen years ago, when he was twenty-one, to assist another artist with etchings for the history of French aviation. Now he was thirty-five and a single father of three, forced to leave the boys at home in North Carolina with his parents for as many as five months at a time, so he could etch a portrait of Woodrow Wilson or reproduce Raphael's *Meeting of Leo the Great with Attila* in Felicity. Britton had taken to working at night because he worried that a growth above his thumb, exposed to the sun when he was holding his tool, was malignant. Some of the trickiest etchings had demanded a hundred or more hours of his time. His name did not appear anywhere on the monuments.

Britton's relationship with Istel seemed dysfunctionally familial: strained but affectionate; hopelessly codependent. Istel accepted that he needed Britton—the tiny, sometimes haunting detail that Britton could splinter into his illustrations was unreal. But he enjoyed complaining about Britton's lack of discipline and badgered him to pick up the pace. They argued frequently. ("I am reluctantly fond of him," Istel told me.) I assumed Britton kept taking the work only out of financial necessity, to support the children it tore him from. But he said that he could make an easy living etching angels into tombstones back home. The reality was that Britton was in Felicity because, like Istel, he couldn't *not* be—because he cared.

"I was very young when I first met Jacques, and I did not understand it, to be honest with you," Britton told me. But Istel showed him his plans for Felicity. He was imagining hundreds of monuments, ultimately—maybe more; the subjects worth remembering were infinite, and therefore construction could be endless. He had 2,600 acres, after all. "The fact that he had the vision to put this out here in the middle of nowhere blew my mind," Britton said. "He sold me on the idea. What can I say?" Istel had spent his life as a businessman, Britton said, while Britton was an artist; of course they would clash. "But he's always impressed me with his idea of what's beautiful," he said.

At one point, while we talked, red and blue lights suddenly swirled in the desert—Border Patrol SUVs chasing a migrant. (The Mexican border is a few miles away; when you stand at the door of Istel's hilltop chapel, you can see a $40 million fence.) I asked Britton what it's like to spend all night out here by himself. He said he likes to stare up into the cradle of stars and think about how negligible his existence is, and yet how long these pictures he's carving will last. He was working on an etching of a Daniel Chester French sculpture called *The Angel of Death and the Sculptor,* for a panel titled "Aspects of American Art." A winged angel reaches up with her left hand to block a young sculptor's chisel, ending his work and taking his life. Britton's tool resembled a dentist's drill. He was making the angel's robe ripple and flow.

Britton assumed that Istel understood more about the motivation behind all this and was less impulsive than he liked to let on. "He's far too intelligent not to consider it," he told me. And in fact, it was astonishing how shrewd Istel could be, even as he appeared to be consumed by the imagination of a child; how often, in his life, his fantasy had actually touched reality. Britton's theory was that there had always been an element of grandeur and surreality to Istel's life, and that Istel wanted to leave a gift to humanity—and also a personal legacy—that conveys the same feeling. It was impossible to guess how much money he was pouring into the project. ("More than a hot dog, less than a space shuttle" is all Istel ever says.) But he took every diplomat or government functionary he got to attend one of Felicity's many ceremonies as a validation.

At the same time, Britton said, the main audience for Istel's work has been the people who happen to dribble in from their RVs. "He hasn't had too many intelligent eyes on what he's doing," Britton said. And, for a man who insists his museum is at the center of the world, he seems strangely reluctant to ask for more serious attention. "It's definitely born out of fear that it won't be accepted among people that he respects," Britton told me. "He doesn't want to be laughed at."

For decades, Istel has been soliciting short letters of endorsement from distinguished people, even though they never visited: Ed Koch, Paul Volcker, John C. Bogle, the former head of Vanguard. They were like little blurbs for the granite book he's writing. Earlier that evening, Istel had called them up on his computer for me, running his index finger under the text on the screen as I read. Then he printed out copies and stapled them together with a piece of a memoir that he wanted me to read.

Now, leaving Britton to work, I went inside and took a look at those pages. The memoir described Istel's first experience parachuting, in 1950. He'd hired a real estate salesman named Jack Holden to take him up in his little Piper Cub. "I will tell you when to jump," Holden bellowed as they climbed. Holden had zero experience with anything like this, Istel wrote, but radiated confidence; Istel could tell he was a good salesman.

At 1,500 feet, Holden finally said it: "Jump!" All of a sudden, catapulting himself out of an airplane seemed real to Istel in a way that it hadn't before. He stalled. He pretended not to hear Holden. He asked him to repeat himself. "Jump," Holden said again.

Istel was trapped and confused by his feelings. "Pride and honor were involved," he wrote. "I jumped."

We Have Fire Everywhere

| 2019 |

The fire was already growing at a rate of one football field per second when Tamra Fisher woke up on the edge of Paradise, California, feeling that her life was no longer insurmountably strenuous or unpleasant and that she might be up to the challenge of living it again.

She was forty-nine and had spent almost all of those years on the Ridge—the sweeping incline, in the foothills of California's Sierra Nevada, on which Paradise and several tinier, unincorporated communities sit. Tamra moved to the Ridge as a child, married at sixteen, then raised four children of her own, working seventy-hour-plus weeks caring for adults with disabilities and the elderly. Paradise had attracted working-class retirees from around California since the 1970s and was beginning to draw in younger families for the same reasons. The town was quiet and affordable, free of the big-box stores and traffic that addled the city of Chico in the valley below. It still brimmed with the towering pine trees that first made the community viable more than a century ago. The initial settlement was poor and minuscule—

"Poverty Ridge," some people called it—until a new logging railroad was built through the town in 1904 by a company felling timber farther uphill. This was the Diamond Match Company. The trees of Paradise made for perfect matchsticks.

Like many people who grow up in small communities, Tamra regarded her hometown with affection but also exhaustion. All her life, she dreamed of leaving and seeing other parts of the world, not to escape Paradise but so that she could return with renewed appreciation for it. But as the years wore on, she worried that she'd missed her chance. There had been too many tribulations and not enough money. She was trapped.

Then again, who knew? That fall, Tamra was suspended in a wide-open and recuperative limbo, having finally ended a five-year relationship with a man who, she said, conned her financially, isolated her from her family, and seized on her diagnoses of depression and a mood disorder to make her feel crazy and sick and insist that she go on disability. "What I thought was love," she said, "was me trying to buy love and him stealing from me." But now, a fuller, bigger life seemed possible. She'd tried community college for a semester. And just recently, she got together with Andy, a big-hearted baker for the Chico public school system, who had slipped out of her bed earlier that Thursday morning to drive down the hill to work. Tamra was feeling grounded again: happy. It was odd to say the word, but it must have been true because there she was, getting out of bed at 8:00 a.m.—early for her—energetically and without resentment, to take her two miniature schnauzers and Andy's lumbering old mutt into the yard to pee.

She stepped out in her slippers and the oversize sweatshirt she'd slept in. She smelled smoke. The sky overhead was still faintly blue in spots, but a brown fog, forced in by a hard wind, was rapidly smothering it. "I've been here so long, it didn't even faze me," Tamra remembered later—small wildfires erupted in the canyons on either side of Paradise every year. But then the wind gusted sharply and a three-inch piece of burnt, black bark floated lazily toward her through the air. Tamra opened her hand and caught it. Bits of it crumbled in her palm like charcoal. She took a picture and texted it to her sister Cindy. "WTF is happening," Tamra wrote.

Cindy knew about wildfires. In fact, she'd spent every summer and fall fixated on fire since the "fire siege" of 2008, when Paradise was threatened by two blazes, one in each of the canyons alongside it. On one particular morning, as the eastern fire approached, the town ordered more than nine thousand people to evacuate as a precaution, Cindy among them. But when Cindy pulled out of her neighborhood, she instantly hit gridlock. An investigation determined that it took nearly three hours for most residents to drive the eleven miles downhill.

Sitting in traffic that morning, Cindy had felt viscerally unsafe. And ever since, she obsessively tracked the daily indicators of high-fire danger on the TV weather reports and with apps on her phone. "It consumed me," Cindy said. She spent many nights, unable to sleep, listening to the wind plow out of the canyon and batter her roof. Many days, she refused to leave home, worried a fire might blow through her neighborhood before she could return for her pets. She didn't just sign up to get the county's emergency alerts on her phone; she bought her own police scanner.

It pained Tamra to see her sister fall apart every fire season. Cindy seemed irrational—possessed. It was hard to take her seriously. "That's just Cindy," Tamra would say. Now, standing with her phone in one hand and the charred bark in the other, Tamra needed Cindy to be Cindy. She needed Cindy to tell her what to do.

"Evacuate," Cindy wrote back.

"Answer me!!" Tamra texted again. "It's raining ash and bark." She hadn't gotten Cindy's text; neither woman realized that some messages weren't being received by the other. Then the power went out, and Tamra, who had dropped her cellular plan to save money and could only use her phone with Wi-Fi, was cut off from communicating with anyone.

"Leave, T. Paradise is on fire," Cindy was texting her. "Leave!!"

By then, Cindy was almost off the Ridge, bawling in her car from the stress and dread. Forty-five minutes earlier, she'd learned that a fire had sparked northeast of town, and she immediately didn't like the scenario taking shape. The relative humidity that morning, the wind speed and direction, which would propel the fire straight toward Paradise—it was all very bad. "In my mind, I pictured exactly what happened," she would explain. She'd spent years picturing it, in fact. She left right away.

This time, there was no traffic; Cindy says she saw only two other cars the whole way down. Later, she spotted her home in aerial footage of Paradise on the local news. Her aboveground swimming pool was unmistakable. Nearly everything else had burned into a ghostly black smudge.

By the time Tamra got in her yellow Volkswagen, the sky had transformed again: It was somehow both shrouded and glowing. Many other residents had learned to keep a "go bag" packed by the door, with water, medications, and copies of important documents; a woman from the local Fire Safe Council, a volunteer known affectionately as the Bag Lady, held frequent workshops demonstrating how to pack one. But Tamra was indecisive and moving inefficiently. It had taken her nearly forty minutes to commit to leaving, wrangle the dogs, and scramble haphazardly to grab a few possessions.

It was now 8:45. So many calls were being placed to 911 that a dispatcher interrupted one man reporting a fire alongside Skyway Road—the busiest street in Paradise and the town's primary evacuation route—with a terse "Yeah, sir, we have fire everywhere." Officials had started issuing evacuation orders about an hour earlier; Tamra's neighborhood was among those told to clear out first. Her street was plugged with cars. A thick line of them crept forward at the end of her driveway.

There are five routes out of Paradise. The three major ones spread south like the legs of a tripod, passing through the heart of town and continuing downhill toward Chico and the valley below. Tamra lived in the northern part of town, on the easternmost leg of the tripod, Pentz Road; she rented a bedroom from a woman who worked at a nursing home in town. It baffled her to see that all the cars in front of her house were heading north on Pentz, cramming themselves away from the center of Paradise, away from the valley, and further uphill. The opposite lane, meanwhile, was totally empty. It seemed obvious to Tamra that, if the fire was approaching from somewhere in the canyon behind her house, there would be plenty of Paradise left in which to safely wait it out. So she pushed across the traffic, into the empty lane. But she'd barely gone a hundred yards before a driver sitting in the jam alongside her rolled down his window and explained that Pentz was blocked up ahead.

"Great," Tamra muttered. As she turned around and took her place in line, she wished the man good luck.

"You, too," he said.

She was recording everything on her phone, compelled by some instinct she would strain to make sense of later. She wanted people to know what happened to her and presumed, nonsensically, that her phone would survive even if she didn't. Maybe, too, she wanted someone to be with her while it happened. Her phone created the illusion of an audience; it was the best she could do.

It was suddenly much darker. Everyone had their headlights on. The sky was blood red in places but waning into absolute black. The smoke column was collapsing on them: The plume from the wildfire had billowed upward until, at about 35,000 feet, it froze, became heavier, and fell earthward again. Outside Tamra's passenger-side window, the wind snapped an American flag in someone's yard so relentlessly that it seemed to be rippling under the force of some machine. Then a mammoth gust kicked up, spattering the street with pine needles. It sounded like a rainstorm and, when it subsided, bright orange embers appeared beside Tamra's car: trails of pinhole lights, like fairies, skittering low over the shoulder, chasing each other out of the dry leaves, then capering off and vanishing in front lawns.

Tamra noticed a minivan struggling to merge just ahead—people weren't letting the driver in. She stopped to let it through, then suddenly screamed: "Oh, my God! There's a fire!"

She yelled it again, out her window, as though she worried she were the only one seeing it: the tremendous box of bright, anarchic flame where there used to be a home.

It was 9:13 a.m. Tamra had been in her car for nearly half an hour and traveled altogether nowhere. The burning house was only a few doors down from her own. There was a second structure aflame now. The fires were multiplying rapidly.

"I don't want to die!" Tamra shouted. The mood had shifted. People started honking. Tamra honked, too. She began to sob and scream, to open her car door and lean her head out, asking what she should do. Later, she felt embarrassed. She would see so many YouTube videos of people calmly piloting their cars through the flames. There was one guy who went viral, singing to his three-year-old daughter as he honked and swerved, commenting on the encroaching inferno as though it were an inter-active exhibit at a science museum. ("Be careful with that fire!" the girl says adorably. The father replies, "I'm going to stay away from it, OK?") It didn't make sense to Tamra that she would be the only person screaming. Even the three dogs with her were silent, though two of them were deaf and mostly blind and the third was shivering, eyes locked open, too shocked to make a sound. "I'm scared!" Tamra shouted. "Somebody!"

"OK, calm down," a voice called. The person urged her to turn around again. She did and suddenly, still crying wildly, found herself shooting south again, through the other, wide-open lane of Pentz, following a white truck with a Butte County Fire Department decal on it. She tailed the fireman intently, coasting past one burning house after another. Some were being steadily, evenly devoured; others angrily disgorged flames straight up from their roofs. Tamra knew the people who lived in many of these houses—this was her neighborhood. "This is Pentz Road!" she yelled as she drove. "These are people's homes." Then added: "I'm sorry. I am so sorry!"

When she got to the corner of Pearson Road, a major east-west artery, she saw someone directing cars to take the right turn, where she and the fireman in front of her found they could accelerate even more, winding along S-curves through a wooded area that was almost entirely aflame. Fires speckled the slopes along Pearson so that, in the dark, the hillside looked like a lava flow. "It's so hot," Tamra said. "Keep going! Keep going!" But then, they shot around another curve and the fireman's brake lights came on. They had hit a wall of cars, across both lanes.

"No!" Tamra yowled. "What did I do?"

She was silent for a moment. Then something started beep-ing. It was the low-fuel alert. She was almost out of gas, though it ultimately wouldn't matter. Moments later, her car caught fire.

Afterward, you could feel your mind grinding against what happened, desperate to whittle it down into a simple explanation of what went wrong, who should be blamed, what could be learned. There were many credible answers, specific mistakes to call out. But it was easy to worry that, given the scale of this particular disaster, the principal takeaways might be only humility and terror.

From the start, the Camp Fire was driven by an almost vengeful-seeming confluence of circumstances, many of which had been nudged into alignment by climate change. Paradise had prepared for disasters. But it had prepared *merely* for disasters, and this was something else. In a matter of hours, the town's roads were swamped, its emergency plans outstripped. Nine of every ten homes were destroyed and at least eighty-five people were dead. Many were elderly, some were incinerated in their cars while trying to flee, and others apparently never made it that far.

It was all more evidence that the natural world was warping, outpacing our capacity to prepare for, or even conceive of, the magnitude of disaster that such a disordered earth can produce. We live with an unspoken assumption that the planet is generally survivable, that its tantrums are infrequent and can be plotted along some existentially tolerable bell curve. But the stability that American society was built around for generations appears to be eroding. That stability was always an illusion; wherever you live, you live with risk—just at some emotional and cognitive remove. Now, those risks are ratcheting up. Nature is increasingly finding a foothold in the unimaginable: what's not just unprecedented but hopelessly far beyond what we've seen. This is a realm beyond disaster, where catastrophes live. Tamra wasn't just trapped in a fire; she was trapped in the twenty-first century.

By way of analogy, Paradise's emergency-operations coordinator, Jim Broshears, later described giving fire-safety tutorials at elementary schools, back when he was the town's fire chief, teaching second and third graders that if there's fire at their bedroom door, they should go out the window, and vice versa. "Inevitably," Broshears told me, "there's the kid who goes, 'What if there's fire at the door *and* the window?'" And no matter what alternative Broshears would provide, that kid could always push the story line one step further.

"At some point, they've painted you into a corner and, well, do I tell an eight-year-old kid, 'In that case, you're going to die'? Do you tell a community, 'If this particular scenario hits, a bunch of you are going to die'? Is that appropriate? I don't know the answer." He added, "I think that people are going to conclude that now."

Tamra saw the first flames skitter in the depression where her windshield met the hood. She opened her car door again and leaned her head out. Embers burned tiny holes in her leggings. She was yelling, asking if anyone had water. A contractor in a pickup behind her hollered: "You don't need water. You need to get in my truck." He beckoned her and all her animals over.

Tamra wedged herself among the tools and paperwork scattered on the man's front seat, two dogs on top of her and the largest at her feet. As the vehicle inched forward, she took a picture of her burning car and was crushed to realize that she had just abandoned the few possessions she'd managed to save, including the ashes of her big brother, Larry, who, ten years earlier, had died suddenly in his sleep.

"I'm Tamra," she told the man driving.

"I'm Larry," he said.

The coincidence was too much: Tamra started crying again.

Larry Laczko wore sleek, black-rimmed glasses and a San Francisco Giants cap and seemed, to Tamra, almost preternaturally subdued, speaking with the slow resignation of a man enduring ordinary traffic on an ordinary Thursday morning. Larry and his wife had lived on the Ridge for fifteen years, then migrated to Chico in 2010, after raising their two kids. For years, Larry worked at Intel, managing sixty employees, traveling constantly. Then, one Saturday, his wife told him to clean the windows of their home in Paradise—and to clean them *well* this time. Larry did some research, geeked out a little, and wound up ordering a set of professional-grade tools from one of the oldest window-washing supply companies in the United States. His wife was pleased. Soon, he was washing windows every weekend, toddling around the Ridge with his tools, getting to know his neighbors and friends of friends. "I liked the work, the instant gratification of a dirty window turning clean," Larry explained, "but it was the interaction with people that I loved." That was sixteen years ago. He quit his job and had run his own window-washing company ever since.

Larry was on Pearson Road by chance—or because of his own stupidity. In retrospect, he conceded, either assessment was fair. His mother-in-law lived in Quail Trails Village, a nearby mobile-home and RV park. She was eighty-eight and used a walker. Larry's wife, who was nearby that morning, had already got her out. But Larry wanted to be helpful. He'd recently installed an automatic lift chair on his mother-in-law's stairs and remembered how, after the 2008 evacuation, many people wound up displaced from the Ridge for days; it would be nice for his mother-in-law to have that chair. So he drove up the hill and cut across on Pearson, only to be turned around by police. Backtracking, he smacked into the traffic that had formed behind him: a blockade of cars, barely moving and every so often, as with Tamra's Volkswagen, suddenly sprouting into flame.

When Tamra climbed into Larry's truck, the seriousness of his predicament was only beginning to catch up with him. What sounded to Tamra like extraordinary calmness was actually extraordinary focus: He was scanning his surroundings, updating his map of everything that was on fire around him—that tree; the plastic fender of that SUV—while also taking a mental inventory of the back of his pickup, gauging how likely each item was to catch.

"We're getting out of here," Larry told Tamra. He projected enough confidence that he reassured himself, just slightly, as well.

But clearly he and Tamra were stuck. Thousands of people were, on choked roadways all over the Ridge, each sealed in his or her own saga of agony, terror, courage, or despair. It was like the 2008 evacuations, but far more serious—the gridlock, cinched tighter; the danger, exponentially more acute—and also harder to stomach, given all the focus the town had put on avoiding those problems in the ten years since.

After the 2008 fires, the county had created a fifth route off the Ridge, paving an old gravel road that wound through mountains to the north. Paradise vigorously revamped and expanded the emergency plans it had in place. The town had been carved into fourteen evacuation zones; these were reorganized to better stagger the flow of cars. Paradise introduced the idea of "contraflow," whereby traffic could be sent in a single direction across all lanes of a given street if necessary. Maps and instructions were mailed to residents regularly. There were evacuation drills, annual wildfire-preparedness events, and other, more meticulous layers of internal planning, too. Paradise's Wildland Fire Traffic Control Plan identified, for example, twelve "priority intersections" where problems might arise for drivers leaving each evacuation zone, and stipulated how many orange cones or human flaggers would ideally be dispatched to each.

"The more you study the Camp Fire," said Thomas Cova, a University of Utah geographer who has analyzed wildfire evacuations for twenty-five years, "the more you think: This could have been way worse. *Way* worse." Cova called Paradise "one of the most prepared communities in the state." A *USA Today*–California Network investigation found that only six of California's twenty-seven communities at highest risk for fire had robust and publicly available evacuation plans.

One architect of Paradise's planning was Jim Broshears, who had spent the bulk of his forty-seven-year career as an emergency planner and firefighter struggling to mitigate his community's idiosyncratically high risk of disaster. After the Camp Fire, Broshears confessed that, in his mind, the upper limit of harrowing scenarios against which he'd been defending Paradise was the 1991 Tunnel Fire in the Oakland hills—a wildfire that consumed more than 2,900 structures and killed twenty-five people: "I'll be honest," he told me, "we simply didn't see it being much worse than that." Recently, Broshears showed me a copy of the Traffic Control Plan in a big, thick binder and said, with admirable directness, "It mostly didn't work." Then he clacked the binder shut and insisted, "That is still going to work 98 percent of the time, though."

The *Los Angeles Times* and other newspapers would later dig up many city planning mistakes and communication failures that appeared to compound the devastation on the morning of

November 8. But the core of the problem was that there just wasn't any time. The fire was moving so astonishingly fast that, only a few minutes after Paradise started evacuating its first zones, it was obvious the entire community would have to be cleared.

There was no plan for evacuating all 27,000 residents of Paradise at once. "I don't think it's physically possible," Paradise's mayor, Jody Jones, told me. And building enough additional lanes of roadway to *make* it possible, she added, would have seemed preposterous for a town of Paradise's size, and like a waste of taxpayer money had anyone thought to propose it. Our communities, as they currently exist, were planned and built primarily to be lived in, not escaped. Fully prioritizing evacuation could mean ripping them apart.

Paradise evolved without any genuine planning at all: Three adjacent communities just kept expanding until they merged. This produced a town of tangled side streets and poorly connected neighborhoods, often with a single outlet and many dead ends. "In towns all up and down the Sierra, we've got the same pattern," said Zeke Lunder of Deer Creek Resources, which often contracts with the state on wildfire-mapping projects. "I think it's inevitable that this will happen again."

That morning in Paradise, streets were blocked by fallen trees, disabled cars, or even fire blowing crosswise over them. Flaming roadside vegetation slowed or halted traffic on major evacuation routes like Skyway so that many of the cross streets that fed them, like Pearson, backed up, penning even more drivers defenselessly into the side streets that fed *them*.

Just ahead of Tamra and Larry, a woman named Lorena Rodriguez watched flames absorb the space around her car. She reached for her phone to tell her children goodbye, but then she reconsidered, worried the memory of her frightened voice would permit her kids to more vividly imagine her burning alive and keep imagining it for the rest of their lives. This enraged Rodriguez—that she had been put in a position to have such a thought. So she decided to run, sprinting in a pair of Danskos, threading the lanes of idling vehicles and moving faster on foot than all of them. She kept expecting to find some obstacle blocking the road, a reason for the traffic. All she saw was more cars.

Rodriguez ran for two and a half miles, all the way west on Pearson until she reached Skyway. She says the street was bumper-to-bumper most of the way, the vehicles alongside her perfectly still. It was as if time had stopped for everyone but her.

Tamra was thinking about her father, a former fire captain who was protective to the point of pitilessness. To teach his little girls not to play with matches, he showed them gruesome photographs of bodies extracted from houses that burned down.

Those pictures had been flashing through Tamra's mind all morning. Now, on Pearson Road, she sensed she was inside one. She knew there had to be people dying around her and Larry, good people who wanted to live just as much as she did—surely, who wanted it more.

Tamra inhaled deeply to rein in her crying and told Larry: "I gotta say something. I've tried to kill myself multiple times, and now, I'm scared." It was true. She felt guilty about it. She also knew, in that moment, that she wanted to live.

It had been all of ten minutes since Larry waved Tamra into his truck. While some people might have recoiled from a stranger making this kind of admission, Larry didn't pass judgment or see Tamra as a burden. As a kid, he went to parochial school, though the faith never took; he asked too many questions. Still, he liked the way his wife talked about spirituality, not God so much as a form of godliness that arises whenever two human beings connect. In that moment, he told me, his only thought was: *This person needs to talk, and I can certainly listen.*

After getting turned around on Pearson, Larry instantly felt deflated—and then a little foolish, too. He was starting to reprimand himself for driving into a fire. For what? A chair?

Tamra, meanwhile, was exhausted, having so far shouldered the responsibility for her survival alone all morning. "I just wanted to be with somebody," she explained.

For Larry, "Something clicked—now I had someone to be responsible for."

They were together now, but still trapped, and the windows of Larry's truck were getting hotter. Until then, the fires blooming erratically around Paradise were so-called spot fires, birthed from embers that the wildfire sprayed ahead of itself as it grew. Now an impregnable riot of heat and flame was cresting the hillside under Pearson Road. This was the fire itself.

There's a dismaying randomness to how a wildfire can start: The tire on a trailer goes flat and its rim scrapes against the pavement, producing sparks; the DIY wiring job on someone's hot tub melts. (These were the causes of the 2018 Carr and 2015 Valley fires, respectively. More than 300,000 acres burned, combined.) But by now, there is also a feeling of predictability: In 2017, for example, seventeen of twenty-one major fires in California were started accidentally by equipment owned by Pacific Gas and Electric (PG&E), which, as California's largest electrical utility, is in the precarious business of shooting electricity through 175,000 miles of live wire, stitched across an increasingly flammable state. Under state law, the company may be liable for damage from those fires, whether or not the initial spark resulted from its negligence. And so, PG&E found itself looking for ways to adapt.

Two days before the Camp Fire, as horrendously blustery and dry conditions began settling on the Ridge and the risk of fire turned severe, PG&E began warning 70,000 of its electricity customers in the area, including the entire town of Paradise, that it might shut off their power as a precaution. This was one of the new tactics that the company had adopted—a "last resort," PG&E called it: In periods of extreme fire danger, if weather conditions aligned to make any accidental spark potentially calamitous, PG&E was prepared to flip the switch, preventively cutting the electricity from its lines. Life would go dark, maybe for days—whatever it took. It was clear that the unforgiving environment in which PG&E had been operating for the last few years was, as the company put it, California's "new normal."

Wildfires have always remade California's landscape. Historically, they were sparked by lightning, switching on haphazardly to sweep forests of their dead and declining vegetation and prime them for new, healthier growth. Noticing this cycle—the natural "fire regimes" at work—Native Americans mimicked it, lighting targeted fires to engineer areas for better foraging and hunting. But white settlers were oblivious to nature's fire regimes; when blazes sprung up around their towns, they stamped them out.

Those towns grew into cities; the land around them, suburbs. More than a century of fire suppression left the ecosystems abutting them misshapen and dysfunctional. To set things right, the maintenance once performed naturally by fire would have to be conducted by state and federal bureaucracies, timber companies, private citizens, and all the other entities through whose jurisdictions that land splinters. The approach has been feeble and piecemeal, says William Stewart, a co-director of Berkeley Forests at the University of California, Berkeley: "Little pin-pricks of fuel reduction on the landscape." We effectively turned nature into another colossal infrastructure project and endlessly deferred its maintenance.

Then came climate change. Summers in Northern California are now 2.5 degrees hotter than they were in the early 1970s, speeding up evaporation and baking the forests dry. Nine of the ten largest fires in state history, since record-keeping started in 1932, have happened in the last sixteen years. Ten of the twenty most destructive fires occurred in the last four; eight in the last two. California's Department of Forestry and Fire Protection, known as Cal Fire, expects that these trends will only get worse. It's possible that we've entered an era of "megafires" and "mega-disturbances," the agency noted in its 2018 Strategic Fire Plan. And these fires are no longer restricted to the summer and early fall: "Climate change has rendered the term 'fire season' obso-lete."

Even deep into last fall, much of the landscape still seemed restless, eager to burn. A bout of heavy rains that spring pro-duced a record growth of grasses around the Ridge—the fastest-burning fuels in a landscape. But then the rain stopped. By the time of the Camp Fire, in November, there hadn't been any sig-nificant precipitation since late May, and July had been Califor-nia's hottest month on record: All that vegetation dried out. "Everything is here," explained a veteran wildland firefighter named Jon Paul. "All you need is ignition."

The Camp Fire glinted into existence around 6:15 that Thurs-day morning. A hook on a PG&E electrical tower near the com-munity of Pulga snapped, allowing a cable to spring free and slap against the skeletal metal tower. Electricity arced between them, melting the aluminum in the cable and the steel in the tower—

maybe only for a fraction of a second before the system's safety controls would have flipped. Still, it was enough: The flecks of molten metal dropped into the brush of the base of the tower. Those sparks started a fire; the fire spread.

In the end, PG&E had chosen not to de-energize its lines. Even with warm, dry air gushing through the canyon early that morning, blowing thirty miles per hour and gusting up to fifty-one, the company claimed that conditions never reached the thresholds it had determined would necessitate a shut-off. "That revealed a failure of imagination on PG&E's part," says Michael Wara, who directs the Climate and Energy Policy Program at the Stanford Woods Institute for the Environment. PG&E was largely forced into the position of having to shut off people's power in the first place, Wara argues, because it failed for decades to invest in the kind of maintenance and innovation that would allow its infrastructure to stand up to more hostile conditions, as climate change gradually exacerbated the overall risk. But the decision to keep operating that morning suggested that the company still wasn't prepared to be as resolute as this new reality demanded, Wara said. Three weeks earlier, PG&E had instituted its first, and ultimately only, shutdown of the 2018 fire season, cutting electricity during a windstorm to nearly 60,000 customers in seven counties. It took two days to restore everyone's power; citizens and local governments fumed. "One has to wonder," Wara says, "if the negative publicity and pushback PG&E received influenced decision-making on the day of the Camp Fire." ("We will not speculate on past events," a PG&E spokesman said in an email.)

An even starker truth: It probably wouldn't have mattered. The lines at that particular tower in Pulga wouldn't have been included in a shut-off that morning anyway; PG&E's protocols at the time appeared not to consider such high-voltage transmission lines a severe risk. A shutdown, however, would have de-energized other lower-voltage lines a few miles west of the tower—which, shortly after the first fire started, were struck by a blown down Ponderosa pine tree, triggering a second blaze.

In its report on the disaster, Cal Fire's investigators regarded this subsequent event as negligible, however. Within thirty minutes of igniting, this second fire had been consumed by the first, which was ripping through a fast-burning landscape, powered forward by its own metabolism and pushed by the wind. It had advanced four miles and was already swallowing the small town of Concow. The Camp Fire was moving too fast to be fought.

"It was pretty much complete chaos," Joe Kennedy said. Kennedy is a Cal Fire heavy-equipment operator based in Nevada City, southeast of Paradise. He was called to the Camp Fire at 7:16 that morning and hurtled toward the Ridge with his siren on, in an eighteen-wheeler flatbed with his bulldozer lashed to the back.

Kennedy is thirty-six, a fantastically giant man with a shaved head and a friendly face but the affect of a granite wall; he spoke quietly and, it seemed, never a syllable more than necessary. He had operated heavy equipment his entire adult life, working as a contractor in the same small mountain towns around the Sierra where he grew up, then joined Cal Fire in 2014, just before he and his wife had a child. He claimed his supremely taciturn nature was a by-product of fatherhood; until then, he explained, he was a more reckless adrenaline junkie. But Kennedy loved bulldozers, and he loved the rush of barreling toward a fire in one. "Dozer driver" seemed to be less his job description than his identity, his tribe. "In ten years," he joked, "they'll probably consider it a mental disorder."

Kennedy was dispatched to the Adventist Health Feather River hospital on Pentz Road. By the time he arrived, spot fires were igniting everywhere. The chatter on the radio was hard to penetrate. Now that he was in position, Kennedy couldn't get in touch with anyone to give him a specific assignment, so he fell back on his training and a precept known as "leader's intent": If someone were to give him an order, he asked himself, what would it be?

By then, the hospital staff had completed a swift evacuation of the facility. Nurses later described doing precisely what they practiced in their annual drills but at three or four times the speed: wheeling patients through the halls at a sprint, staging everyone in the ER lobby, then sorting all sixty-seven inpatients into a haphazard fleet of ambulances and civilians' cars arriving outside to carry them away. Many didn't make it far. One ambulance, carrying a woman who had just had a C-section and was still immobilized from the waist down, quickly caught fire in the traffic on Pentz. Paramedics hustled the woman into a nearby empty house. Others took shelter there as well. A Cal Fire officer, David Hawks, mobilized them into an ad hoc fire brigade to rake out the gutters and hose down the roof as structures on either side began to burn.

Kennedy caught snippets on his radio about this group and others hunkered in nearby houses. He'd found his assignment. He climbed into his bulldozer, a colossal Caterpillar D5H that traveled on towering treads like a tank and was outfitted with a huge steel shovel, or "blade." It also had a pretty killer sound system, and as Kennedy turned the ignition, the stereo automatically Bluetoothed to his phone and started playing Pantera. Kennedy's technical skill and experience as a heavy-machinery operator was formidable; so was his knowledge of wildland firefighting tactics. But, given the scale of disaster unfolding around him, all that expertise now concentrated into one urgent, almost blockheadedly simple directive in his mind: *Take the fire away from the houses.*

Of course, Kennedy had no idea which houses any of these people were sheltered in. All around the hospital lay a sprawl of mostly ranch homes, packed together on small, wooded lots. A great many were already burning, so Kennedy homed in on the others and started clearing anything flammable, or anything already in flames, away from them. Ornamental landscaping, woodpiles, trees—he ripped it all out of the ground, pushed it aside or plowed straight through it, clearing a buffer around each home. He worked quickly, brutally, unhindered by any remorse over the collateral damage he was causing; it's impossible, he explained, to maneuver an eighteen-ton bulldozer between two adjacent houses and not scrape up a few corners.

Before long, Kennedy lost track of exactly where he was; he hadn't even bothered to switch on the GPS in his dozer yet. "It seemed like forever, but it was probably a half hour," he said. "I think I got eight or nine houses. I made a pretty big mess."

Wildfires are typically attacked by strategically positioned columns of firefighters who advance on the fire's head, heel, or flanks like knights confronting a dragon. If a fire is spreading too rapidly for such an offensive, they instead work to contain it, drawing boundaries around the blaze—a "big box," it's called. Work crews or bulldozers clear vegetation and cut firebreaks to harden that perimeter. Aircraft drop retardants. Everything in the big box can be ceded to the fire; if you have to, you let it burn. But ideally, you hold those lines, and the flames don't spread any farther.

As wildfires get fiercer and more unruly, firefighters aren't just unable to mount direct attacks but are also forced to draw larger and larger boxes to keep from being overrun themselves. "The big box is a lot bigger now," one Cal Fire officer explained. (He asked not to be named, hesitant to publicly concede that "our tactics need to change.") But this strategy breaks down when the fire is racing toward a populated area. The extra space you would surrender to the fire might contain a neighborhood of several hundred homes.

Wildfires aren't solid objects, moving in a particular direction at a particular speed. They are erratic and fluid, ejecting embers in all directions, producing arrays of spot fires that then pull together and ingest any empty space between them. On November 8, the wind was so strong that gusts easily lofted embers from one rim of the Feather River Canyon to the other like a trebuchet, launching fire out of the wilderness into Tamra's neighborhood.

As this swirl of live embers descended, like the flecks in a snow globe, each had the potential to land in a receptive fuel bed: the dry leaves in someone's yard, the pine needles in a gutter. Those kinds of fuels were easy to find. It was November, after all, past the time of year that wildfires traditionally start, and Paradise's trees had carpeted the town with tinder. And every speck of flame that rose up in it had the potential to leap into an air vent and engulf a home. Now it's a spot fire—a beachhead in the built environment, spattering its own embers everywhere, onto other houses, rebooting the entire process.

Within two hours of the first spot fires being reported near Tamra's house, others had leapfrogged from one end of Paradise to the other. The progression was unintelligible from any one point on the ground. As one man who was at the hospital later told me, "I thought that the only part of Paradise that was on fire was the part of Paradise we were looking at." And, as happened with Tamra, this generated a horrifying kind of dissonance: scurrying away from the fire only to discover that the fire was suddenly ahead of you and alongside you, too.

"Take deep breaths," Larry said.

Tamra had just told him about trying to kill herself. They were barely moving. Embers darted by like schools of bioluminescent fish. Evergreen trees alongside them burned top to bottom. These were the town's famous pines, stressed from years of drought; the pitch inside was heating to its boiling point and, the moment it vaporized, the length of the trunk would flash into flame all at once. This became one of the more nightmarish and stupefying sights that morning on the Ridge: giant trees suddenly combusting.

The topography of that particular stretch of Pearson Road made it a distinctly horrible place to be stranded. Beyond the guardrail to Tamra and Larry's left, a densely wooded ravine yawned open, with a stream known as Dry Creek Drainage far below. Already, the spot fires and burning trees on either side of the road were casting heat inward. But as the mass of the wildfire moved in, the ravine appeared to create a chimney effect, funneling flames up and over the street—only to be overridden periodically by the prevailing winds, which pushed the flames right back down the same chimney. Everyone on Pearson was caught in the middle.

A Cal Fire branch director, Tony Brownell, told me that he was astonished to watch fire doubling back across Pearson, washing over the same land it had just scorched. It was only the second such immediate "reburn" he'd witnessed in his thirty-one-year career. This was about fifteen minutes before Tamra's car ignited. Brownell, it turns out, was the fireman in the white pickup truck whom she'd initially followed into that gridlock from back on Pentz Road. Brownell managed to escape quickly, but as he turned his vehicle around and drove away, he told me, he looked at the flames in his rearview mirror and thought, *I just killed that girl.*

"You'd think that people would just hurry up and go," Tamra said.

"There's no place to go," Larry told her. "They're trying. Cal Fire's here to help."

He could see a fire engine a few car-lengths ahead. After fighting to weave forward, it, too, had been more or less swallowed by the same intractable traffic. Larry silently made the calculation that if his own truck caught fire, he and Tamra would make a run for it and climb inside to safety.

This would have been a mistake. The Cal Fire captain driving the fire engine, John Jessen, later estimated that the outside temperature was more than two hundred degrees, the air swirling with lethally hot gases. Cars were catching fire everywhere; four drivers fled toward that fire truck and, one after another, crammed themselves into the cab alongside its three-man crew. When two more people came knocking, Jessen turned them away—no more room, he said. "That was probably the worst thing I've ever had to do," Jessen said later. "I don't know if those people made it to another car. I don't know what happened to them."

This was Jessen's twenty-fourth fire season in California. He'd fought five of the ten most destructive fires in state history and was beginning to feel beaten down. "When I started this career twenty-five years ago, a ten-thousand-acre fire was a big deal," he said. "And it was a big deal if we weren't able to do structure defense and the fire consumed five homes. We took that to heart. We felt like we lost a major battle." Just moments earlier, around the corner on Pentz, Jessen had watched fire consume dozens of homes within minutes. He'd been knocking on the door of another, to evacuate any stragglers, when he saw the actual fire front for the first time. It was already climbing the near side of the canyon, pounding toward town. The wall of flame was two hundred feet tall, he estimated, and stretched for more than two and a half miles. That was the moment Jessen scrambled back to his truck and told his crew it was time to move.

Now, marooned on Pearson, Jessen radioed for air support. Later, he would seem embarrassed by this request, chalking it up to "muscle memory": The smoke was clearly too thick for any aircraft to fly in. The paint on his hood started burbling from the heat. Inside, the plastic on his steering console was smoking; the stench of its off-gassing filled the cab. The barrel-shaped fuel tanks beneath the doors were splashing diesel around the truck; the brass plugs in their openings got so hot they liquefied.

Jessen, meanwhile, was making a desperate calculation of his own: If their truck caught fire, he decided, they would extinguish it quickly and take off, saving the civilians aboard by pushing other cars out of the way with the front of his fire engine.

Maybe this was the lowest point. The fire overwhelmed every system people put in place to fight or escape it; now it was scrambling their consciences, too. "That's something I never imagined I would be thinking about," Jessen confessed, "pushing people closer to the fire so that I could get out."

Jessen sat there, watching for signs that his truck was about to catch fire. Larry sat watching his own truck, ready to run for Jessen's. Then someone shouted, "Let's go, let's go, let's go!" Larry saw a bulldozer churn into view behind him, clobbering one burning car after another.

Joe Kennedy had been mashing through people's landscaping on Pentz when he heard Jessen's distress call. There was no time to use the standard, numeric identifiers over the radio. "John," Kennedy responded. "Where you at?"

He switched on the iPad in his dozer and found Jessen's position near the corner of Pearson and Stearns Road. It was more than a mile away. The dozer's maximum speed was 6.3 miles per hour. But Kennedy clipped that distance by disregarding the roads and right angles on his street map and barging his bulldozer through backyards at a diagonal, then eventually barreling down the steep, wooded incline overlooking Pearson and spilling, sloppily, into the middle of the street.

He produced a spectacular ruckus as he pushed the machine down the hill on its treads. From the road, it sounded like trees crashing—and some of it probably was. As Kennedy leveled off, he came upon a group of people, including four nurses from the hospital in scrubs. They were stranded in the middle of Pearson, battered by gusts of embers roaring up from the ravine. They were buckling over, struggling to breathe and keep walking. One nurse, Jeff Roach, was walking straight at Kennedy's bulldozer, with his arms in the air. Later, Roach explained that he had decided the bulldozer driver would either see him and rescue him and his three friends, or would not see him, keep advancing, and crush him under the vehicle's treads. The burning in Roach's lungs was so bad, he said, that he had made his peace with either outcome.

Kennedy stopped. Two of the nurses climbed aboard then scampered to rejoin the others, who had piled into a fire engine that appeared behind him. Kennedy began fighting his way up Pearson, toward Jessen, but found cars crammed into both lanes and the shoulder. Some people were idling right beside other vehicles that were expelling fountains of flame. Kennedy turned up the Pantera. He knew what he had to do: take the fire away from the people.

He approached the first burning car and pushed it off the embankment and into the ravine with his dozer blade, then backed up to discover a flaming rectangle of asphalt underneath it. He drove through that, pushed more cars. "I was basically on fire," Kennedy said. A photo later surfaced of an old Land Cruiser shoved so far up the adjacent hillside that it became snared in some sagging power lines. "That was me," Kennedy explained with a noticeable quantum of pride.

At least one of the vehicles Kennedy was shoving around had a body in it: Evva Holt, an eighty-five-year-old retired dietitian who lived at Feather Canyon Gracious Retirement Living, close to Tamra's house. Holt had phoned her daughter that morning to come get her—her daughter and son-in-law lived nearby and frequently came to perform for Holt and the other residents with their choral group—but there was no time. An independent caretaker named Lori LeBoa was readying to leave with a 103-year-old woman, and a police officer put Holt in her Chevy Silverado as well. Moments later, the three women wound up stuck on Pearson. As the fire curled over LeBoa's pickup, she'd jumped out and handed off the older woman to another driver. Turning back for Holt, she saw only fire and two arms reaching out.

Months later, over coffee, I asked Kennedy if he remembered moving that Silverado. He did. The memory seemed painful; he preferred not to talk about it on the record, except to stress that it had been clear that he arrived too late to help whoever was inside.

I asked if he knew any details about the woman, if he wanted me to tell him. He did not. "I like the story in my head," he said.

Kennedy opened enough space for the stranded drivers on Pearson to maneuver and slowly advance. Moments earlier, one nurse who'd leapt into his dozer accidentally knocked into his iPad, switching his GPS into satellite view. Eventually, when Kennedy looked down at the map again, his eyes locked on to a conspicuous bare rectangle, free of any vegetation or structures—any fuels to burn. It was a large gravel lot right near Jessen's fire engine; the firefighters just couldn't see it through the smoke. Once Kennedy arrived, the firefighters began herding the entire traffic jam—more than a hundred cars—into that clearing.

"Pull over there," a firefighter hollered at Larry and Tamra as they crept uphill.

"And then what?" Larry asked.

"Hunker down and keep your windows rolled up."

"Are you serious?" Tamra erupted. She was hoping for a more sophisticated plan.

"They wouldn't have put us here unless it was safer than where we were," Larry said.

He eased his truck into place, parallel with the others. Directly in front of them, through the windshield, the frame of a large house burned and burned. For a moment, it was quiet. Then Tamra broke down again, very softly this time. "I don't have anything," she said. "I don't have anything."

Fires are unique among natural disasters: Unlike earthquakes or hurricanes, they can be fought, slowed down, or thwarted. And virtually every summer in Paradise, until that Thursday morning, they had been. There was always trepidation as fire season approached but also skepticism that evacuation would ever truly be necessary and worth the hassle. "I confess my sense of denial," said Jacky Hoiland, who had lived in Paradise most of her life and worked for the school district for twenty years. Initially, after hearing about the Camp Fire, she took a look at the sky and then made herself a smoothie.

Still, even before the Camp Fire, many people in Paradise and around California had started to look at the recent succession of devastating fires—the Tubbs Fire, the Thomas Fire; blazes that ate through suburban-seeming neighborhoods and took lives—and intuit that our dominion over fire might be slipping. Something was different now: Fire was winning, finding ways to overpower our fight response, to rear up recklessly and break us down. That morning, in Paradise, there hadn't even been time for that fight response to kick in. And the flight response was failing, too. Those who study wildfire have long argued that we need to reshuffle our relationship to it—move from reflexively trying to conquer fire to designing ways for communities to outfox and withstand it. And in a sense, that's what was happening with Larry and Tamra, though only in a hasty and desperate way: Hunkered in that gravel lot, everyone was playing dead.

After the fire, stories surfaced of people retreating into similar so-called temporary refuge areas all over the Ridge: clearings that offered some minimal protection or structures that could be easily defended. One large group sheltered in the Paradise Alliance Church, which had been scouted and fortified in advance as part of the town's emergency planning. Another group sheltered outside a bar on Skyway and, when it caught fire, scampered, en masse, to an adjacent building and sheltered there. The Kmart parking lot became an impromptu refuge. So did an antique shop called Needful Things. In Concow, one firefighter instructed at least a dozen people to jump into a reservoir as the fire approached.

The group on Pearson wasn't in the gravel clearing long, less than ten minutes, it seems, from videos on Tamra's phone. Eventually, there was a knock on Larry's window. "We're going to get out of here," a firefighter said, though he didn't specify where they would go. Moments later, another firefighter on a bullhorn shouted, "We're going to go toward the hospital."

"Oh, shit," Larry blurted.

"We're going back?" Tamra said. She sounded both terrified and incensed. The hospital was on Pentz Road, near where she'd started. The trauma of the last two hours appeared to be flooding back.

Joe Kennedy led the way in his bulldozer, crawling through the thick smoke on Pearson to batter any obstacles out of their way. The core of the fire had passed, though it had left a kind of living residue everywhere: All the wooden posts of a roadside metal barricade were still burning, and shoals of flames dotted the road where Kennedy had removed burning cars.

The cars were still burning, too, wherever he had deposited them, belching solid black smoke as the caravan of survivors slowly passed.

"There's my car," Tamra said, and turned to film it. Fire spouted from its roof like the plume of a Roman helmet. "It has my Raggedy Ann in it!" she said. The doll was one of the few things she grabbed before evacuating. She had had it since she was six and had expected to be buried with it one day. "Oh, my God," she said. "I'm crying over something so stupid!"

At the hospital, a fire alarm quacked robotically as a small outbuilding, not far from where Larry and Tamra parked, expelled smoke from behind a fence. A group of nurses had scavenged supplies from the evacuated emergency room and erected a makeshift triage center under the awning to treat any wounded trickling in. Larry got out of his truck to see how he could help.

The hospital campus was ringed and speckled with fire. Some of the men were peeing on the little spot fires that danced in the parking lot's landscaped medians. Still, the influx of firefighters that morning had largely succeeded in defending the main building when the fire front moved through. Eventually, a call went out on the radio that the hospital campus was "actually the safest place to be."

Tamra and Larry's group waited in the parking lot for close to three hours. Then those lingering fires nearby began to swell and expand, threatening the hospital again. The firefighters were losing pressure in their hoses. The nurses were told to pack everything up. The road out was clear; they had a window in which it was safe to move. Everyone would finally be driving off the Ridge.

As they pulled out of the parking lot, back onto Pentz Road, Larry noticed his eye-doctor's office burning top to bottom, directly in front of them.

"It's gone," Tamra said.

"It's gone," Larry said.

"It's gone," Tamra repeated. "That house is gone! And that house is gone!"

They went on gesturing at everything as they drove—or rather, at its absence: all the homes still burning and others that had already settled into static masses of scrap and ash. As with any small town, every part of Paradise had been overlaid with memories and meanings; each resident had his or her own idiosyncratic map of associations. As Tamra and Larry coasted down Pentz, they tried to reconcile those maps with the disfigured reality in front of them, speaking the names of each flattened side street, noting who lived there or the last time they'd been down there themselves. The iconic home at the corner of Pearson, with the ornate metal fence and sculptures of lions, had been devoured: "It used to be on the garden tour," Larry said.

"Right here, that was my dog groomer's house."

"My sister is just right up here."

"Are these the people that used to have the Halloween stuff up?"

It was 1:45 p.m. Thirty-nine minutes later, and 460 miles to the south, a small brush fire would be reported near a Southern California Edison substation north of Malibu. Firefighters wouldn't contain the Woolsey Fire until it had swallowed nearly 100,000 acres and 1,600 structures and charged all the way to the Pacific, where it ran out of earth to consume. This time, as photos surfaced, all of America could find reference points on the map the fire had clawed apart: Lady Gaga evacuated. Miley Cyrus's home was a ruin. The mansion from *The Bachelor* was encircled and singed.

"Oh, God, it's all gone," Tamra said again. She gaped at the east side of Pentz Road, facing the canyon, where there didn't appear to be a single home left: just chimneys, wreckage, the slumping carcasses of cars, everything dun-colored and dead.

Five months after the Camp Fire, at the end of March, the wreckage in Paradise was still overpowering: parcel after parcel of incinerated storefronts, cars, outbuildings, fast-food restaurants, and homes. Patches of rutted pavement, like erratic rumble strips, still scarred Paradise's roadways wherever vehicles had burned. On Pearson Road, I knelt beside one and found a circular shred of yellow plastic, fused into a ring of tar: a piece of

Tamra's car. It was startling how similar Paradise looked to when I first came, ten days after the fire. Except that it was spring now: Clusters of daffodils were blooming, carefully arranged, bordering what had been fences or front steps.

That week, the city had issued its first rebuilding permit, though roughly a thousand residents were already back, somehow making a go of it, either in trailers or inside the scant number of houses that survived, even as public-health officials discovered that the municipal water system was contaminated with high levels of benzene, a carcinogen released by the burning homes and household appliances, then sucked through the pipes as firefighters drew water into their hoses. Driving around at dusk one evening, letting acre after acre of obliterated houses wash over me, I spotted a lone little boy in what appeared to be the head of a cul-de-sac—it was hard to tell—with heaps of houses all around him. He was standing with his arms raised, like a victor or a king, then he hopped back on his scooter and zipped away.

Jim Broshears, Paradise's emergency-operations coordinator, pointed out that many of the homes still standing tended to be in clusters: "a shadow effect," he called it, where one property broke the chain of ignitions—maybe because its owners employed certain fire-wise landscaping or design features, or maybe just by chance. It showed that, while the destructiveness of any fire is largely random, there are ways a community can collectively lower the odds. "It's really a cultural shift that requires people to look at their home in a different way," Broshears said: to see the unkempt azalea bush or split rail fence touching your home as a hazard that will carry the next fire forward like a fuse, and not just to your house but also to the others around it—to recognize that everyone is joined in one massive pool of incalculable and unconquerable risk.

The free market, meanwhile, has continued adjusting to that risk according to its own unsparing logic. Insurance companies have steadily raised premiums or even ceased to renew policies in many fire-prone areas of California, as payouts for wildfire claims will now exceed $10 billion for the second year in a row. Two months after the Camp Fire, PG&E filed for bankruptcy protection. Then it announced, along with two of California's other major utilities, that it would be expanding its Public Safety Power Shutoff program this year. The company is now prepared to preventively cut electricity to a larger share of its infrastructure—high-voltage wires, as well as lower-voltage ones—and across its entire range. Nearly five and a half million customers could be subject to shutdowns at one time or another this summer, "which is all of our customer base," a PG&E vice president, Aaron Johnson, told me: every single one. "With the increasing fire risk that we're seeing in the state," he added, "and the increasing extreme weather, this program is going to be with us for some time to come."

In California, the prospect of life without electricity from time to time—a signature convenience of the twentieth century—has become an unavoidable, even sensible, feature of the twenty-first.

How did it end? With smoke—with colossal shapes of smoke gurgling out of Paradise behind Larry and Tamra as they glided downhill, and with a stoic figure somewhere inside the smoke, single-mindedly grinding through neighborhoods in his bulldozer, music blaring, chasing after flames as they stampeded uphill, but mostly failing to get ahead of them, as he and every other firefighter labored to keep fire away from structures that seemed, in the end, determined to burn.

The houses had revealed themselves: They were just another crop of tightly clustered, dried-out dead trees, a forest that had grown, been felled and milled, then rearranged sideways and hammered together by clever human beings who, over time, came to forget the volatile ecosystem that spawned that material and still surrounded it now. Some of that wood most likely lived a hundred years or more and had been lumber for almost as long: a storehouse of energy that was now bursting open, joining with the burning forests around the Ridge into a single, furious outpouring of smoke—ominous because it was dark and high enough to challenge the sun, but also because it was largely composed of carbon: an estimated 3.6 million metric tons of greenhouse gases that, as seems to happen at least once every fire season lately, was more than enough to obliterate the progress made by all of California's climate-change policies in a typical year.

How did it end? With smoke—with smoke that signaled the world Tamra had known at the beginning of the day was gone, and that surely signaled something just as grave for the rest of us. Within hours, and for nearly two weeks after that, smoke would swamp the lucid blue sky over the valley where Tamra was now heading; where, for weeks, she would be afraid to be left alone and, for months, refuse to drive, terrified by the sensation of slowing down in traffic, even momentarily; where she found herself repeatedly checking the sky to make sure it wasn't black; where she kept showering but swore she still smelled the smoke on her skin. And before long, the smoke had floated all the way to the coast, where it forced the city of San Francisco to close its schools.

How did it end? It hasn't. It won't.

This Story About Charlie Kaufman
Has Changed

| 2020 |

"So they required rewrites?" Charlie Kaufman asked.

Yes, I explained. It was late spring, the year 2020, and I'd just received some discouraging feedback from the editors of *The New York Times Magazine* about a draft of a story I'd turned in two weeks earlier. The story was a profile of him: Charlie Kaufman, the sixty-one-year-old Oscar-winning screenwriter, known for films so rich with surreality and self-referential lunacy that they feel as if they might be spun apart by the force of their strangeness, yet miraculously cohere. (He first made his name in 1999 with *Being John Malkovich,* about a morose, avant-garde puppeteer who takes a temp job on the seventh-and-a-half floor of a Manhattan office building and discovers a dumbwaiter-shaped portal into the actor John Malkovich's brain.) The occasion for the profile was the publication, on July 7, of Kaufman's first novel, *Antkind,* a book that's a half-foot thick and absolutely synopsis-resistant.

Our initial plan had been for me to fly to New York to interview him one Wednesday that March, but that plan evaporated when the nation's first COVID-19 outbreak started flaring near my home in Washington State. Instead, as I explained in my first draft of the story:

Kaufman and I quickly settled into a routine of talking on the phone every Wednesday, usually for an hour and a half or longer at a time. At least once, to be polite, I offered to give him a break, but Kaufman didn't seem to want one. "The more we talk, the more I have a chance of saying something that's not idiotic," he said. Those phone calls were often the only entries on either of our calendars. It felt good to have them fixed there, dependably marking time.

Relatively quickly, the curve in my corner of the country started to flatten while the one in New York spiked, and Kaufman found himself somewhat dislocated at the epicenter of a pandemic. He only recently moved to Manhattan from Pasadena and was living alone in a temporary rental, still figuring things out. "How are you?" I would ask each week when he picked up the phone, and Kaufman would say, "I think I'm the same, but I'm always anticipating the next thing" or "I still seem to be avoiding getting sick, but who knows" or "Everything is threatening." One week he told me that he'd dropped his glasses on the floor in Whole Foods and couldn't bring himself to put them back on, even after washing them five times. ("What happens when your glasses break?" he asked. "What do you do?") And one week, when I asked how he was doing, he could only burst out laughing. And then I burst out laughing. Then Kaufman said, "How are you?" Then, after more laughing, the laughing died down and, very quietly, he told me, "I'm in a panic."

Eight weeks, this went on. It was a bizarre way to get to know a stranger, at a time when there was scant opportunity to discover anything new in life at all. A bond formed: not friendship, not therapy, but a kind of reciprocal Stockholm syndrome with qualities of both. "I wonder if you and I are ever going to meet after this intimate thing we've had," Kaufman asked during our final call on April 29.

"I've had that thought, too," I said. "It's strange the degree to which you've been the only real relationship in my life during this time, beyond my wife and kids." I had tried setting up weekly calls with family or friends, I told him, but nothing else stuck.

"Mine, too, really," Kaufman said. Friends reached out, wanting to talk, but he usually felt too gloomy or anxious to engage. One guy, the previous week, had been uncommonly persistent, "and I finally had to text him back and say: 'I can't. I just can't.' But I couldn't do that with you," Kaufman told me. "That's been good for me. I've had to do it."

The whole first draft read like that, more or less. It was slow-moving and a little weird. But given the disordered circumstances, I'd decided that the most honest approach was simply to write a portrait of one specific human being talking to another specific human being (me), to present a record of conversations that seemed to have been made more intimate by the dismaying stretch of time in which they took place. It was preposterous, but it almost felt as though Kaufman and I had somehow lived through that first phase of the pandemic together.

The problem was, in the two weeks since I'd turned in the story, hundreds of thousands of Black Lives Matter protesters had taken to the streets; things had taken an unmistakable, turbulent turn. What I heard my editors saying, and what I tried to explain to Kaufman now on the phone, was something I had sensed myself: The world was furious and roiling, and the profound introspection and "baroque interiority" of the piece I'd written (my editors' words) felt out of sync. Didn't that dissonance need to be resolved, or at least acknowledged, in the story somehow if it were going to run in a weekly magazine right now? After receiving some slightly murky instructions about how that might be accomplished, I agreed to start by calling Kaufman back, to at least bring the chronology of our conversations up to date.

"They're saying it seems quaint at this point," Kaufman ventured. "But that's a bizarre thing in and of itself," he pointed out: how swiftly reality seemed to be shifting, the awkwardness of people's attempts to instantly react. "They want you to come back to talk to me because the piece doesn't have anything to do with the time we live in. If it *did* ever have anything to do with the time we live in"—and Kaufman was skeptical—"I think it's important to point out that that was two weeks ago!"

"I don't think that's exactly what they're saying," I said. "They're not saying it's irrelevant. . . ." But I'm not sure this was totally honest. Everything except a small number of things did feel pretty irrelevant to me just then.

"It may be irrelevant!" Kaufman gladly interrupted. "I accept that it's irrelevant." It's why he had felt wary of doing the profile in the first place, he said. No part of him believed that he, as a person—not just his work—warranted this kind of attention. He'd written a book, and this profile was proposed, and it clearly seemed worth doing even if it made him uncomfortable. "At the time, it was fine, because I liked you, and it's been nice talking to you," he said. "But now, just because I wrote a book, are you going to have to keep coming back to me until July 5, or whenever this thing is published, for updates on the world? It's embarrassing," he said. "It's embarrassing to me."

I suddenly felt embarrassed, too. I was also angry at myself;

my job required me to grapple with a problem with no obvious solution and, out of weakness, I had foisted my confusion on him. Months earlier, when I set out to interview some of Kaufman's collaborators for this article, he declined to give me their contact information. The virus was tearing through New York and Los Angeles at the time, disrupting people's lives, ending people's lives, and Kaufman didn't feel comfortable helping me bother his friends and colleagues in the middle of all that, just so they could say nice things about him in *The New York Times*. It felt both wrong and shameful. Reminding him of that, I now told him, "So I'm not surprised that you find it embarrassing to have a big story written about you right now."

"Ever!" Kaufman said. "Ever! Like, ever!" But yes, that included right now. Moreover, the profile still wouldn't be published for another three weeks, and he and I both had been reading that morning about states blindly reopening and the explosion of new COVID-19 cases in Arizona, the hospitals overloading. It seemed the future would be different from the present. It always is.

"You know what this is like?" Kaufman went on. "You know the British documentary series that started with *Seven Up*?" (Beginning in 1964, the filmmaker Michael Apted followed fourteen children, revisiting them to document their lives every seven years; in the most recent installment, the subjects are all sixty-three.) "That's what this is like, except it's seven weeks instead of years," Kaufman said. "And it's not even seven weeks, it's two weeks." And each time I called, the world, and his small, insignificant life within it, would have swerved unthinkably from last time. "I'm living in a trailer in the Scottish Highlands now," Kaufman said, laughing.

He was right. Time did seem to be compacting, I said. It felt like, at some point in the last few months, a truck backed up and started pumping years' worth of reality into every single week. The lever kept cranking, increasing the rate of flow.

On the other end of the phone: silence.

"Jon, you're breaking up," Kaufman said.

In my first draft of the story, there was a section dated Wednesday, April 15, that began like this:

> "I didn't even know it was Wednesday when I got your email this morning," Kaufman said. "I was planning to go out, to go to the store." The grocery deliveries on which he'd been relying had stopped being reliable. Was the system caving in? The website said orders would now take a month to complete. I apologized, offered to call back later. But Kaufman didn't mean that he was too busy to talk. His point was: "I had no idea what day it was."

This was how most of those weeks felt: languorous and flat. Also, bewildering and fraught. Periodically, Kaufman would wind his way from some other subject into expressions of empathy, terror, or indignation at the pain and governmental ineptitude unfolding in the world beyond his apartment. That sense of distance, he observed, gave a strange, new cast to those feelings. "It's all very weird," he pointed out. For those of us who weren't essential workers or touched personally by the virus, "this thing is largely virtual. It's disembodied." Every day he absorbed new information, but his mind struggled to settle on any confident interpretation of it. When New Yorkers started cheering for frontline health-care workers every evening, for example, Kaufman found it well intentioned, but he struggled to go along with it and feel uplifted. "There's a sentimentality to it that doesn't take into account the gross negligence of the government in making sure that these people are protected at their jobs," he said. "It's the equivalent of tweeting. When you're tweeting your support for people who work in grocery stores or are delivering the products you buy, what is that getting them?" It wasn't a rhetorical question. Was it getting them something? He earnestly wanted to know.

In April, he busied himself a little, taking a job adapting a short story for Ryan Gosling's production company. Early on, Kaufman's college-age daughter came to stay with him, and they got in the habit of taking nine-mile walks around Manhattan and felting together, as they did when she was young. (At one point, Kaufman sent me a photo of one of his creations: a felt bust of Federico García Lorca.) But mostly, he explained, "I feel like I've been spinning my wheels and wasting my time and looking at stuff online that I shouldn't be. It's making me very anxious. I feel like I've got some kind of obligation that I'm not meeting right now, an obligation to do something, to not waste time—to find the world and not have it delivered to me."

Antkind had been finished for several months, as had a new film Kaufman wrote and directed, *I'm Thinking of Ending Things,* which would be out in a few months. Kaufman was proud of the film, but called it "odd, small, and a little complicated" and felt certain it would not produce any significant upswing for his career. "I honestly approached it as my last directing job."

Kaufman is in the curious position of being admired in Hollywood but also constantly thwarted by its business model. Somewhere along the line, his actual stature and the perception of it had slipped awkwardly out of alignment. (When an interviewer from *The Hollywood Reporter* asked Kaufman in 2016, "Would Charlie Kaufman ever consider doing television?"

Kaufman replied, "Charlie Kaufman has tried.") After a trio of his earliest films, *Being John Malkovich, Adaptation,* and *Eternal Sunshine of the Spotless Mind* earned him three Oscar nominations and one win, he accumulated enough clout to direct one of his own scripts for the first time: *Synecdoche, New York,* starring Philip Seymour Hoffman as a theater director whose warped ambition leads him to build (somehow) a full-scale replica of Manhattan inside a warehouse in Manhattan, which includes (somehow) a replica of the warehouse, which contains (somehow) another Manhattan inside it. *Synecdoche* came out in the fall of 2008, when the economy was in free fall. Roger Ebert called it "the best film of the decade," but commercially, it was not a success. Then the film industry rapidly contracted and turned risk-averse. The big studios Kaufman had worked with, like Sony, no longer seemed interested in greenlighting the kind of mid-budget, idiosyncratic films he wanted to write and direct.

"I have a lot of things that could spark, but won't," he told me one of the first times we spoke. He spent nearly a decade seeking financing for a script he wrote called *Frank or Francis,* a musical about an Internet troll's deranged feud with a film director that included fifty original songs. The only way a studio would let Kaufman direct it, he was told, was if he loaded it with movie stars. So he got Steve Carell and Jack Black attached. Also Cate Blanchett, Nicolas Cage, Emma Thompson, Kevin Kline, Elizabeth Banks, and Catherine Keener. But still, it wasn't enough. He developed ideas for television, then watched them founder. He took jobs to pay his mortgage, including an uncredited rewrite on *Kung Fu Panda 2.* In 2015, he co-directed, with Duke Johnson, the critically exalted stop-animation film *Anomalisa,* based on a script Kaufman wrote for a live radio play—but only after Johnson's company raised the initial chunk of the project's budget on Kickstarter. And in all that time, Kaufman made a point of being disarmingly transparent with the press about the obstacles he met with, which the press at times overemphasized, much to his embarrassment. (*New York* magazine, 2016: "Charlie Kaufman Is Having a Pretty Depressing Existential Crisis: 'I Wonder If It's Not Cool or Sexy to Be in Business With Me.'")

When a book editor first approached Kaufman, in 2011, asking if he'd ever thought about writing a novel, he recognized how liberating that might be. Whatever he chose to write wouldn't have to be filmed or budgeted, or screened for a test audience, or tweaked to get a particular rating. If he wanted to write about an army of animatronic Donald Trumps, known as "Trunks," or place a new mountain range in the middle of North America, he could. And if he wanted his protagonist to have sexual intercourse with that mountain range, he could do that, too. And more than that: He *had* to do it. Though he hadn't seriously written prose in forty years, and kept imagining critics punishing him for his ineptitude, or just his audacity for trying something new, he took the same approach that he does with his screenplays. Ideas that came up that felt like "Oh, you absolutely can't do that"—those were the ideas that Kaufman forced himself toward. "I have to put myself in a position to fail ridiculously," he said.

This was never clearer to me than when he talked about writing *Adaptation.* In short: Kaufman signed on to adapt *The Orchid Thief,* by Susan Orlean—a delicate, wide-ranging, meditative book about orchids, loosely centered on the story of an oddball Floridian plant poacher but without any hint of conventional plot—precisely because he had no idea how it could be done. After spending months in an "overwhelming depression" over the project, as he put it, he finally stepped back from the source material to consider what was preoccupying him at that moment in his own life, hoping to find something that felt alive, or sufficiently kinetic, to push him forward. And what was preoccupying him was obvious: "This idea occurred to me," he says, "and it opened things up."

In the end, *Adaptation* centered on the screenwriter Charlie Kaufman, struggling to adapt *The Orchid Thief*. In one of the first scenes, we see Nicolas Cage, as Kaufman, flop-sweating at lunch with a befuddled Hollywood executive, waving a copy of Orlean's book in the air and ranting about how he doesn't want to "cram in sex or guns or car chases, or characters learning profound life lessons . . . or overcoming obstacles to succeed in the end. The book isn't like that," he insists, and "life isn't like that. It just isn't." It was precisely what the real Kaufman explained to a real Hollywood executive before taking the job.

Discussing Kaufman's creative process in my first draft, I described him as essentially constructing tortuous escape rooms for himself, then writing his way out. This approach seemed to cause him so much suffering that I eventually asked him:

"Is there any part of you that feels afflicted by your convictions?" Did he ever just wish he could write an action film or something? "There's no part of you that wishes it were easier?"

"I would like to have money that I don't have," he replied, "and I tell myself that I could write a commercial blockbuster." But he also understood that he might be flattering himself; he'd never actually tried. He was proud of his commitment to do original, meaningful work. "There's lots and lots of garbage out there that isn't honest and isn't trying to help clarify or explore the human condition in any way," he told me, "and it sends people down the wrong road"—skews our perceptions of our own lives, and each other—"and it's mind-numbing and it's toxic, and I don't want to have that on my résumé. I don't even mean my professional résumé, but my résumé as a human being."

Spike Jonze, who directed both *Adaptation* and *Being John Malkovich*, compared Kaufman to Kanye West—albeit haltingly and with a number of disclaimers. "This is a weird comparison," Jonze told me, "and I hesitate to bring him up because everyone has an opinion about this person, but . . ." Jonze and West have been friends and collaborators for fifteen years, he said, almost as long as Jonze has been a friend and collaborator of Kaufman's. "And the thing about Kanye is," Jonze said, "it's not that Kanye doesn't care what people think about him. It hurts his feelings if he's misunderstood, like anybody. But he can't not be himself. He has no choice in the matter. And I think Charlie's the same way."

Jonze stuttered a bit, then added: "Again, I hesitate to make the comparison. They're so different in every other way." Then he was quiet for a moment, a long moment, searching for another way to capture it.

To be fair, almost everyone I interviewed appeared to struggle to express what it was they admired about Kaufman. The actress Jessie Buckley told me, "I guess the thing with Charlie is that he's the most human kind of otherworldly kind of Greek god I've ever met." And what did that mean? She tried again: "He's so beautifully and strongly vulnerable as a human, but he's also not. Oh, God," she said, "now I feel like a twat because I just hate myself for even trying to describe the man." The actress Catherine Keener, a close friend of Kaufman's who has appeared in three of his films and been attached to a few of his stalled projects over the years, actually took the proactive step of signaling to me in advance, via text, how lousy she would be at talking about Kaufman and started crumpling under that difficulty within a few seconds of my getting her on the phone: "If you could see my face, you would know how I feel when I talk about

Charlie," she insisted, though it was, in fact, completely apparent to me—not only from the warmth of Keener's tone but in the vigorous determination with which she kept trying to describe Kaufman, how sincerely she wanted me to know what she knew. "Charlie is, you know, out of this world and kind of normal at the same time," she said. "I feel like he can have a conversation with anybody and also . . . he can not." Finally, having again failed to put some other elemental quality of Kaufman's into words, Keener just told me, with defeat and delight, "Charlie knows what he is!"

I don't mean to be flip about this; I empathized with the problem because I was experiencing it myself. I worried that the conversations Kaufman and I were having wouldn't translate well in print either; that people would skim through the article I was writing impatiently, feeling exhausted by Kaufman and his tendency to process every minuscule facet of existence through a vast, clattering, Rube Goldberg machine of introspection. But in real life, it was actually pretty moving to listen to. His vulnerability didn't make you want to turn away from him; it made you want to be vulnerable, too.

Jonze remembered Kaufman's telling him about the novel he was working on a few years ago at a diner. He could still picture the diner perfectly, he said, down to where in the diner he and Kaufman were seated, and he remembered how excited he was by everything Kaufman was communicating about the story. But the specifics had gone weirdly fuzzy for Jonze since then. "It almost feels like trying to remember a dream," he told me. "The ideas, they were so—I don't know what the right word is: They occupy the same part of my brain that dreams do."

"Was there something about a film archive?" Jonze asked me. "Is that still in there?"

I started telling Jonze about the book. A fifty-eight-year-old, excruciatingly self-important academic film critic named B. Rosenberger Rosenberg, who teaches "a cinema studies elective at the Howie Sherman Zoo Worker Institute in Upper Manhattan," travels to Florida to research his next monograph, on an obscure silent film. But Rosenberg abandons that project when he has a chance encounter—or is it chance?—with a centenarian shut-in named Ingo Cutbirth, who has spent his life shooting a stop-motion animation movie in his apartment. Rosenberg seizes on it as a potential work of outsider art. And because Kaufman has written his narrator as a satire of white-savior arrogance, Rosenberg considers it a tantalizing bonus that the reclusive artist behind this presumed masterpiece is African American. Rosenberg smells glory and prestige—for himself, the discoverer of the film.

He watches the movie. It has to do with the creation of the universe, time travel, and a future civil war, plus an old-timey comedy duo known as Mudd and Molloy and their escalating, murderous feuds with other, competing comedy duos. There's a donkey and a giant and a hyperintelligent ant named Calcium. The film is three months long. That's how long it takes to view it, straight through. (It is structured with set bathroom and sleep breaks.) And at some point, while Rosenberg is watching it, Cutbirth drops dead.

Consumed with despicable ambition masquerading as a calling, Rosenberg packs everything into a U-Haul and heads back to New York, intent on carrying Cutbirth's genius into the culture, posthumously. But the truck catches fire, everything is destroyed, and when Rosenberg resurfaces from a coma, he has forgotten the entire film, of which only a single, meaningless frame survived.

That covers about the first eighty pages, I explained to Jonze. *Antkind* was seven hundred pages long.

"Oh, my God, it's seven hundred pages?" Jonze blurted out. He was elated.

Something about the book knocked me off balance: the relentlessness of its language, the increasing claustrophobia of Rosenberg's interior monologue, and the mushrooming absurdity of his suffering as, struggling to reconstruct Cutbirth's film over the course of the novel, he loses his job and apartment and his life grinds into a kind of nonsensical dust. The humiliation and indignities fly at him from all directions. He's plagued by improbable accidents. He falls into an open manhole. Then he falls into another open manhole. Then another. Each time, he happens to be bad-mouthing the filmmaker Charlie Kaufman, deriding him as "a pathetic narcissist on the scale of Adolf Hitler or, quite frankly, beyond, who the world is fortunate does not have any real power," or recounting a lecture he delivered to the San Antonio chapter of the League of Women Voters, titled "I Vote with My Feet When It Comes to Kaufman."

As a critic, Rosenberg has an antagonistic relationship with comedy. He disapproves of it, considers it violent and abusive: A coyote must always be bonked by an anvil so a roadrunner can laugh. But now, he's being debased the same way, the three-dimensionality of his pain flattened into a punch line.

"I have come to the conclusion that I am ridiculous," he eventually announces. "The mishaps. The open manholes. Even the fire that ruined Ingo's film and my life. But perhaps more horrific are my thoughts. My thinking is silly. My memories are preposterous. My ideas are laughable. I am a pompous clown. I can, on occasion, become aware of this. There are moments of clarity that I find all the more humiliating because I can see myself as others likely do, but I cannot control any of it."

"A lot of fiction or screenplays are written from a distance," Kaufman had told me one Wednesday, early in our succession of Wednesdays together. "There's a perspective of knowing"— a retrospective awareness of what happened. Consider a tooth-ache, he said. A truly searing, excruciating toothache can over-come you entirely: your mouth, your body, your mind. "It can be a very primal moment in your life," he said. "But compare that to a year later, telling the story of having a toothache to a friend at dinner. You no longer have a toothache, presumably. You've got a story about having a toothache, with a beginning, middle, and end. You can tell it as an anecdote. But when you're in the middle of the toothache, you don't have that perspective. It's a very chaotic moment."

Kaufman's point was that he strove as much as possible to write with an imperfect sense of where a story is going, to keep its meaning a secret from himself. "I don't have any lessons to impart," he said, "and I want to make sure I can't." This accounts for the many dreamlike elements of his work, like the suburban house in *Synecdoche, New York* that is perpetually on fire, even as a character lives in it for decades. These images sweep in from the fringes of his intellect, just like dreams. But, for Kaufman, this approach is fundamentally a matter of realism. "It allows me to tell the story not as a story that is untrue or dishonest," he said.

"It goes back to that feeling of not understanding the world," he went on, "not understanding what we're doing here and why the things that happen to us happen to us—not having a clue! We're all very vulnerable, and everything is uncertain moment to moment. That's always the case, in every moment of our life. But our face is being rubbed in it right now." The virus, he meant; it was still, at that point, the thing that people seemed to be referring to when they said "right now."

"I've always worried about all possible outcomes for anything

I ever embarked on," he said. Even growing up, on Long Island and in Connecticut, Kaufman doesn't remember feeling invincible, the way kids often do. Writing and directing appeared to be "a way for me to take chances without the same fear," he went on. "I feel like I'm a lot more open to making mistakes and failing, of doing the wrong thing, in work. I often think about that and wish I could be more like that in my real life."

Kaufman thought a lot about embarrassment: He came to the conclusion recently that it's at the root of most of his characters' struggles—the hazard that impedes them, the sting in their wounds—and central to his own experience, too. As a child, Kaufman loved acting in plays and musicals, but when he went to study acting at Boston University, he suddenly found it very embarrassing and, swamped by that embarrassment, transferred to film school at New York University, intending to become a screenwriter and director, which also felt embarrassing, but bearably so.

He remembered, once in high school, cracking a joke while driving with a friend, sending the kid into a fit of laughter. But then the friend stopped laughing, abruptly, signaling that he hadn't found the joke funny at all. He was messing with Kaufman. This wasn't some horrendous trauma, Kaufman said; growing up, he was teased a lot and bullied physically and made to feel small and powerless in any number of ways. Still, when he mentioned embarrassment, this was the memory that burbled up: "I had made myself vulnerable," he said. "I trusted it. And I felt so humiliated and mortified and just—embarrassed: not only that he was faking the laugh and that I had believed it, but that I'd let myself laugh, too. That distrust," he went on, "became a kind of fabric in my psyche."

We'd been on the phone for an hour and a half by then, far past the point of me asking Kaufman actual questions. The conversation had roamed somewhere formless but important, and I registered for the first time how accustomed we had grown, here in our fourth week, to sitting on the phone together like this, collaborating on this strange, joint project of revealing and deciphering who Charlie Kaufman is, like two men showing up every morning to paint a house.

After another four weeks, our conversations essentially collapsed in on themselves: I confessed to Kaufman how freaked out I was about having to sit down and actually write this piece, and we started spitballing ideas for how I might construct it.

The problem, I explained, was that "I have to do exactly what you said you don't like to do!" Instead of writing from within the confusion of the present, it was my job to look back on this time we'd spent together on the phone and compress it into the form of a magazine article, driving the details toward some simplified understanding of who he was. It felt dishonest. Also, inadequate: like a waste of such an unusual experience.

"Well, maybe don't do that," he said. "Maybe don't feel constrained by that. Maybe surprise yourself."

So, surmounting some discomfort, I tried, and turned the rest of that conversation into the opening of my first draft:

"I would never, and I am not, presuming to tell you how to write this," Kaufman began. "But just as a thought experiment: If I were writing this article about me from your perspective—and I was still me—I would start to think about that tension I'm feeling in writing the article. And I would include that in the article. Not even 'include' it. I might even hinge the entire thing on that tension. Because that's the truth."

This was one simplified understanding of who Charlie Kaufman was: He was someone who valued truth. When he detected the absence of it, it pained him. He would prefer, for example, if film critics prefaced their negative reviews by disclosing that they'd just had a fight with their spouse, or: "I don't like this guy because I don't like the way he looks." Because those things are true, he said. Our thoughts and feelings are true. They are facets of the world at whichever moment we attempt to describe it.

"You'd be called self-indulgent, which I am all the time," Kaufman said. "But if it's done in a way that's expansive, to me it's very interesting. Because that is what's going on. Because it's true."

I was terrified of being called self-indulgent. But we agreed that whatever I turned in would have to face head-on the weirdness of the circumstances that produced it. It would be too hard, and probably ultimately more embarrassing, to try and contort myself around that reality and write a conventional profile, acting as though the entire process had been unremarkable. At a minimum, I told him, "I'll have to explain why it doesn't read like, you know, 'I sat across from him at lunch and he ordered a salad.'"

Right, Kaufman said. "Because what would we have done if there was no quarantine—or no social distancing." He paused, unable to come up with the right phrase. "What is this called? We're 'something in place.' Shelter in place!" Kaufman said. "How much would we have talked? Just one day?"

"Maybe two?" I said. It was still being negotiated when the pandemic swept in. I'd been in frequent contact with his publisher for months, operating under the assumption that Kaufman, being a famous filmmaker, was a Beyoncé-like figure whose time must be haggled for through official channels. When I'd asked a publicist, however, what Kaufman would be doing this spring, in the hopes of tagging along, I was forwarded this reply from Kaufman: "On March 11, I am going to the D.M.V. to get my New York driver's license. He can come with me for that."

And so, that was the plan for the story: Charlie Kaufman Goes to the DMV—an odd premise for a celebrity profile, but the celebrity being profiled was odd, so it struck everyone as reasonable, even like a stroke of luck. ("I think the reason the DMV sounds like a good idea is because it sounds like a scene from one of his films," my editor told me.) But then circumstances changed, and I had to improvise and account for the new restrictions and constraints. Then those circumstances changed, and I had to improvise again.

But the thing needed to be honest. What else could a person do?

Another Wednesday. Kaufman was talking again about his desire to write from within the tumult and unpredictability of the present tense, striving to give his writing something similar to the feeling of spontaneity that makes a good actor's performance seem real.

Think about it, he said: "Everything we do in life is an improvisation. We're improvising right now"—me and him. Neither of us knew what the other person was about to say nor could we understand the secret slop of motives, judgments, or insecurities from which it would emerge. "We often have scripts that we abide by," Kaufman said. "But at any moment, we can break out of that script and find something new. We can all do that in real life."

To be clear, Kaufman hardly ever does this. He often walks around with a presumption that individual strangers hate him, or attuned to currents of potential conflict or humiliation humming between him and every other human being. And now, the virus had literalized that psychic vulnerability, made it lethal. In New York, he said, everybody's mindset seemed to be: "'You're the enemy. You're the virus'—which, in essence, you are. You could really be the thing that's going to make me sick and possibly die."

Still, he explained, on one of their long walks around the West Side of Manhattan recently, he and his daughter encountered a man standing outside his home on a desolate-feeling street. "We were getting very close to him," Kaufman said—"not within the prescribed distance or anything, but we're pretty close." The man wasn't wearing a mask. As they approached, the man smiled.

"It was really moving to me," Kaufman said. "I actually got a little emotional. It was a very genuine smile." Telling me this, Kaufman went silent. The feeling had caught hold of him again.

"It just felt kind," he went on. "And you know when someone's kind to you—it can be very small; it doesn't have to be anything in particular, just a moment you have with somebody, and they're kind. You know how that can change you? It can soften you. It can open you up to something—for hours. If you can keep that feeling and use it, it can spread.

"I don't know," Kaufman said. "But that's improvisation. That man's smile was not canned. I know that. I could *feel* it. It was just a genuine smile."

As they walked by, Kaufman smiled back. He forced himself to—a pretty big smile, at that. But Kaufman was wearing a mask and worried the man wouldn't be able to tell. So then he had to screw up his courage. He raised his arm a little. He waved. "I hoped he understood on some level that I was appreciative of it."

Swing State

| 2012 |

The monkey appeared behind a Bennigan's. The Bennigan's was one in a row of freestanding, fast-casual joints in Clearwater, Florida, just outside Tampa, that also includes a Panda Express and a Chipotle. At one end of the complex, a Perkins Family Restaurant flies a preposterously large Stars and Stripes in its front yard, as if it were a federal building or an aircraft carrier.

Someone had spotted the monkey poking through a Dumpster around lunchtime. When a freelance animal trapper named Vernon Yates arrived, all he could make out was an oblong ball of light brown fur, asleep in the crown of an oak. It was a male rhesus macaque—a pink-faced, two-foot-tall species native to Asia. It weighed about twenty-five pounds.

No pet macaques had been reported missing around Tampa Bay; there wasn't even anyone licensed to own one in the immediate area. Yates, who is called by the state wildlife agency to trap two or three monkeys a year, was struck by how "streetwise" this particular animal seemed. Escaped pet monkeys tend to cower and stumble once they're out in the unfamiliar urban environment, racing into traffic or frying themselves in power lines. But as Yates loaded a tranquilizer dart into his rifle, this monkey jolted awake, swung out of the canopy, and hit the ground running. It made for the neighboring office park, where it catapulted across a roof and reappeared, sitting smugly in another tree, only to vanish again. Yates was left dumbstruck, balancing at the top of a ladder. (By then, a fire truck had been called in to assist him.) "There's no way to describe how intelligent this thing is," he said.

The Florida Fish and Wildlife Conservation Commission, a state agency known as the FWC, was quickly convinced that the macaque wasn't a pet either; it believed the animal had wandered out of a small population of free-roaming wild macaques that live in a forest along the Silver River, a hundred miles away. Soon, the FWC was warning the public that wild macaques can carry the herpes B virus, which, though not easily transmitted to humans, can be fatal. A spokesman also explained to the press, "They're infamous for throwing feces at things they don't like."

Sightings stacked up in the following days. The macaque appeared to have been crossing the highway again and again, threading traffic like a running back. One afternoon, Yates and an FWC investigator named James Manson managed to dart the animal in a church parking lot but lost track of the macaque before the drug could take effect. At one point, the two men were side by side, staring blankly into a tangle of brush, completely stumped, when Manson slowly tilted his head and saw the monkey perched with ninja-like stillness above him, close enough to touch. The two primates locked eyes. Then the monkey turned and was gone. "And that's really when the story began," Manson told me.

That was the middle of January 2009. More than three and a half years later, as the Republican National Convention was about to get underway in Tampa, the macaque was still on the loose. After outmaneuvering the cops in Clearwater, the animal had eventually showed up on the opposite side of Old Tampa Bay, somehow crossing the West Courtney Campbell Causeway, a low-lying bridge nearly ten miles long. (The FWC posits that it hid in the back of a covered truck.) It materialized in a low-income neighborhood in East Tampa, crouching in a tree. Guessing it was a raccoon, an FWC lieutenant scaled a ladder and barked at it. The monkey urinated on him and disappeared.

Eventually, a long string of sightings showed the macaque doubling back around the bay, overland, then boogying down the Gulf Coast and into St. Petersburg, where it scrambled over the roof of a Baptist church during evening service. ("He came to worship," one witness told the *Tampa Bay Times*.) A woman watched it swing off a tree limb and flop into her swimming pool. On Coquina Key, homeowners would climb ladders to prune their trees before hurricane season and find spent citrus peels littering their roofs.

And on it went, with the monkey zigging and zagging around Tampa Bay, dodging the government agencies bent on capturing it. The state considers the animal a potential danger to humans and, like all invasive species, an illegitimate and maybe destructive part of Florida's ecology. But the public felt differently; people came to see the monkey as an outlaw, a rebel—a nimble mascot for "good, old-fashioned American freedom," as one local reporter put it.

I flew to Tampa late in the summer of 2012, with thousands of pumped-up and deeply aggrieved Republicans about to pour into the city. It was Mitt Romney's moment, but also the Tea Party's; Obamacare was law and anti-Obamacarism was gospel;

and a real estate developer named Donald J. Trump wouldn't let Birtherism die.

Everywhere in America, the beginnings of some prodigious, national fuss had been kicked up, and there promised to be a big bout of belligerent hand-wringing and self-scrutiny at the convention center downtown. And yet, the most fundamental questions—What exactly is government for? Where are the lines between liberty, tyranny, and lawlessness?—had been shaking the trees around Tampa for years.

Vernon Yates is fifty-nine, with a broad, serious face and mussed-up, dusty-brown hair. He lives on the west side of Tampa Bay, in the suburb of Seminole, and came to open his front gate for me wearing camouflage Crocs and khaki shorts. He threw on a Jack Hanna–style khaki shirt as he walked, but never went so far as to button it.

Yates had been hosing down his bear cage when I rang. He has about two hundred exotic animals at his home. Most had been confiscated by the FWC from pet owners who failed to comply with state regulations, then entrusted to Yates's one-man nonprofit, Wildlife Rescue and Rehabilitation. There were seventeen tigers, some leopards, cougars, a pile of alligators in a concrete pool, and a dusty battalion of large African spurred tortoises. Yates has a special affection for tortoises—he also keeps a single Galápagos tortoise as a pet. "I've been married five times," he told me. "In one of my divorces, I lost a hundred thousand dollars' worth of tortoises."

At his desk, Yates unfolded a map of Tampa Bay. But he found he had to flip the map over, then consult other maps, at different scales, to trace the macaque's entire odyssey. "It's an amazing feat, when you think about his travels," he said. Since 2009, Yates estimates, he has gone after the animal on roughly a hundred different occasions; the monkey was his white whale. He claimed to have darted it at least a dozen times, steadily upping the tranquilizer dosage, to no avail. The animal is too wily; it retreats into the woods and sleeps off the drug. A few times, the monkey stared Yates right in the eye while it pulled the dart out of its body.

For the last two years, the macaque seemed to have been lingering in the same area of South St. Petersburg, ranging between a bulbous peninsula and the small island of Coquina Key, about two miles away. Yates still received calls about the animal—one came in the previous week. But the trail had gone cold a long time ago. Sightings were seldom reported now. As a woman on Coquina Key named Rosalie Broten told me: "Nobody wants the monkey to be captured. Everybody wants it to be free."

The citizenry of Tampa Bay was emphatically pro-monkey. People had long been abetting the animal, leaving fruit plates on their patios. One FWC officer told me that a few people called the agency's monkey hotline to report that they'd seen the macaque several hours or even a couple of days earlier, offering totally useless intelligence, in other words, presumably just to stick their thumbs in the government's eye. The Mystery Monkey of Tampa Bay, as people called it, had very quickly become a celebrity. There were at least two styles of Mystery Monkey T-shirts on offer, a Facebook page, and a catchphrase: "Go, Monkey, Go." As the macaque passed through the town of Oldsmar, a self-storage facility threw the monkey's picture on a digital billboard with the message: STAY FREE MYSTERY MONKEY. "The taxpaying citizens of Tampa have been driven bananas by the out-of-touch political establishment," a blog, purportedly written by the monkey, declared at the end of 2010. The monkey was using this post to announce its run for mayor.

At no point had the macaque threatened or hurt anyone. So it was easy for the public to see the authorities—who, on at least a couple of occasions, surrounded the macaque with rifles and Tasers drawn, or hovered overhead in helicopters, beaming video surveillance to troops on the ground—as bullying or wasteful. ("In this economy," one television reporter quipped, "you have to wonder if it's time to stop monkeying around.") Lieutenant Steve De Lacure told me, "The general public perceives that we're the Gestapo." He was adamant that his agency was not "chasing" the animal, and had deployed officers only a handful of times, when they felt they had a reasonable shot at capturing the macaque. He didn't even like it when I used the word "pursue."

I sympathized with the FWC. What they had to do was unpopular, but their sense of duty was unshakable. They were even prepared to shoot the animal dead if a situation arose in which tranquilization wasn't an option. And they knew they'd be vilified if it came to that. Still, they took a somewhat traditional view: that the American people have a right to be protected by their government from wild monkeys. It was disorienting to watch the people of Tampa Bay champion the monkey's rights instead.

Vernon Yates came in for a special kind of ridicule. He seemed to have been caricatured as a small-town sheriff determined to kill the monkey or lock it up. (He'd also received death threats from pro-monkey radicals.) The vitriolic assumptions people were making about him offended Yates. "I don't hate the monkey!" he told me. "I don't hate the monkey at all!"

I took him at his word. He's not paid by the FWC for the trapping work he does, but instead volunteers because, he explained, he doesn't trust law enforcement to handle exotic animals with the level of expertise and caliber of equipment he can offer.

Yates seemed to think very little of government in general. "I love my country, but I hate my government," he told me at one point. Among his many complaints was the attitude of the USDA bureaucrats who inspect his menagerie. He filled me in on a protest he was planning: During the Republican convention, he'd take one of his tigers—three of the seventeen at his home are personal pets—load it on his boat, and just sit on the river in front of the convention center: just a man with a live tiger and a big sign condemning the USDA.

When it came to the Mystery Monkey, Yates insisted that his only interest was the welfare of the macaque. Once he captured the Mystery Monkey, he planned to surrender it to a pet owner who already kept a female macaque. The monkey would be put into captivity, but with its own kind. Both he and the FWC believed that this was the only compassionate resolution, arguing that a monkey this habituated to humans couldn't simply be put back in the wild. It was also the safest outcome for the macaque. Out there, in the subdivided wilds of Tampa Bay, the monkey was in danger. It could eat rat poison. Or it could be accidentally provoked by someone feeding it and lash out, all but forcing the government to shoot it. Besides, macaques, like humans, are social creatures. They live in groups—like the troop of macaques this one had come from, along the river in Central Florida. Researchers believe that the animals' mental and physical well-being can suffer if they're shorn from that community.

In other words, the Mystery Monkey's lone-wolf, fugitive lifestyle, which was so inspiring to liberty-loving Floridians, might actually have been, from the monkey's point of view, a kind of traumatic exile. This idea had gained traction briefly around

Labor Day 2010, when a retired newspaperman named Don McBride photographed the macaque among some crags of modern art in his neighbor's yard. The animal was staring into a metallic, mirrored cube, pressing its cheek against its own reflection.

"Everyone's shouting, 'It's gotta be free, it's gotta be free,'" Yates told me. "Well, go find the guy who's living on the street with his family and ask him how it feels to be free." Yates seemed to be arguing that sometimes we need a hand to reach down and nudge us, however forcefully, back into place. "Sometimes, freedom isn't necessarily a good idea."

This is not the first time that monkeys have incited a minor populist uprising in Florida.

The population of wild rhesus macaques in the middle of the state—the tribe from which, the theory goes, the Mystery Monkey strayed—was established in the late 1930s by a New Yorker named Colonel Tooey. (Colonel was his first name.) Tooey ran boat tours on the picturesque Silver River, a premier tourist destination. A brazen showman, he wanted to ratchet up the scenery another notch. So he bought a half dozen macaques and plopped them on a small island. Macaques are strong swimmers; Tooey had no idea. According to local lore, the animals were off the island within minutes.

By the mid-1970s, that population had expanded to about eighty macaques, living in two separate troops on either side of the river. They were fed constantly by tourists but were also encountered as many as twenty-five miles away. ("Reports of monkeys riding on the backs of wild pigs have not yet been confirmed," one university researcher wrote.) The troops continued to grow until, in 1984, a forerunner to the Florida Fish and Wildlife Conservation Commission started trapping the animals, citing herpes among other risks. Residents of the town of Silver Springs and neighboring Ocala were outraged. For years, a grassroots opposition made all the noise it could. When the state compiled a report of alleged monkey attacks and property damage—one macaque was said to have bitten a three-year-old in the neck—activists hired a private investigator to debunk it.

In 1993, a state legislative committee held a hearing about exterminating the monkeys once and for all. Tish Hennessey, an Ocala schoolteacher and leader of the resistance, was hospitalized for a respiratory condition at the time, but nevertheless made it to the state capitol in Tallahassee, entering the hearing room attended by a nurse and oxygen tank. "Hear the sound of our voices," Hennessey cried. Then, with a *thwunk,* she dropped a petition to save the macaques on the chamber floor, signed by twenty-five thousand citizens. The committee recommended that the killing be called off. "I think the will of the people was heard," Hennessey told me.

In truth, though, the controversy was never resolved. The State of Florida still holds that the monkeys don't belong on the land around the river, but officials are no longer racing to clear them out. I decided to trace the mystery of the Mystery Monkey to its roots—to see, at the very least, how large the population of macaques on the river had become, and how far its range had expanded. But all I'd find was more mystery. A retiree named Bob Gottschalk, who has a background in biology and, as a hobby, has been studying the monkeys from a kayak over the last three years, told me he believes there are no more than a hundred monkeys on the Silver River today. But state officials also pointed me to an independent count done in 2010 that estimates there may be as many as five more troops living along twenty miles of the neighboring Ocklawaha River to the east. "We don't really have good answers," an FWC spokeswoman said.

"I think there's probably *way* more monkeys than anybody imagines," Captain Tom O'Lenick told me one afternoon, as we drifted down the Silver River in his pontoon boat. Captain Tom is sixty-three, a spindly, aging Popeye of a man with a bristly white beard, white captain's hat, and jagged grin. He has led tours of the river two hundred days a year for twenty-nine years, hollering, "Monkey! Monkey! Monkey!" into the cypresses, to coax out the marquee attraction.

We couldn't find any macaques that afternoon. But Captain Tom filled the time with stories of his young adulthood as an antiwar activist, his stint as a roadie on tour with the Doors, and his high hopes for, and subsequent disillusionment with, President Obama. ("It doesn't matter which clown you vote for," he said, "you always get the same bozo.") Mostly, we talked monkeys. He warned me against underestimating the macaques or overestimating the authorities' grasp on the macaques' whereabouts and behavior. The monkeys are opportunistic and adaptable animals, he said. It seemed inevitable that they would have steadily expanded their territory since the 1930s. He has personally spotted macaques as far as forty miles away, on waterways that don't connect directly with the Silver River. Sometimes they turn up at his girlfriend's mobile-home park, "just grazing and eating, minding their business," he said.

"They just kind of mill around?" I asked.

"It's not like they got an agenda," he said.

When I asked about the Tampa macaque, Captain Tom reiterated what both the FWC and an anthropologist at Notre Dame who studies macaques, Agustín Fuentes, told me: In the wild, young macaques that challenge their troop leaders and lose are often forced out, left to wander in search of a new troop. The

Mystery Monkey is presumed to be one of these disenfranchised males; it just kept wandering until it hit a city full of human primates instead.

It sounds like a freak thing. It may not be. As Gary Morse, a thirty-four-year veteran of the FWC, told me, "We're starting to see macaques show up in places we haven't seen them before." In May, another lone male macaque was spotted near a Sunoco station northeast of Orlando, sixty-five miles from Silver Springs. And last September, one appeared in St. Cloud, eighty miles away. It's possible that all three spilled out of these woods—that they are the far-flung refugees of a population that might itself be more far-flung than anyone realizes.

Linda Wolfe, an East Carolina University anthropologist who studied the Silver River macaques in the 1980s, disagrees. "There's no such thing as rogue monkeys," she told me. "The state wants to play it up so that they can say they're overrun with monkeys" and start killing them again. But I had trouble gauging how much Wolfe's position was colored by old political resentments. Wolfe was part of the original pro-monkey protest movement and, twenty-five years later, was still angry about the government's tactics. She described the law-enforcement division of the FWC as "essentially a paramilitary organization. They answer to no one."

Captain Tom, however, seemed to have the whole thing mapped out in his head: the network of greenways that a single macaque could travel undetected between here and Tampa. I asked if this scenario didn't sound a little improbable: a lone rambler ups and walks a hundred miles to Tampa. Sure does, Captain Tom said. "But I don't think it's one, lone monkey." Just maybe, he said, the Mystery Monkey that everyone is spotting is actually several different monkeys—or one particularly audacious monkey acting as a sentinel for a group. That is,

Florida wasn't dealing with a monkey migration, but a monkey diaspora—or else, something even worse.

"I hate to say *invasion*," Captain Tom confessed, "because it sounds so alarming. But I would say it's a natural expansion of the troops."

That night, I stayed up late at a La Quinta inn in Ocala reading *Planet of the Apes.* I never knew the movies were based on a novel. (The author, the Frenchman Pierre Boulle, was a prisoner of war during World War II and also wrote *The Bridge over the River Kwai.*) In the book, a journalist accompanies an interstellar expedition to the planet Soror, where, their party is horrified to discover, apes wear tailored suits and hold scientific symposia, while human beings—naked, mewling, incapable of language— scurry through the forests like terrified deer.

Eventually, a kind of oral history is unlocked, explaining how the planet's animals came to power and how its humans devolved into animals. Originally, people had trained the apes to be their slaves. But gradually, the stress-free lifestyle this servant class enabled sapped human society of its willpower and curiosity. "A cerebral laziness has taken hold of us," one man narrates; folks couldn't even be bothered to read cheap detective novels anymore.

The apes, meanwhile, never stopped learning. And slowly, individual animals began to stand up for themselves. One night, a gorilla butler decided to sleep in its master's bed. Soon circus orangutans were forcing their *tamers* to do the tricks. In every case, it was just easier for the humans to go along with it—to surrender their bed to their ape and sleep on an armchair in the living room; to turn a few somersaults when the orangutans told them to. "Most of us are adapting to this regime," one woman says. "To give them their due, the apes treat us well and give us plenty to eat. . . . I'm not unhappy. I have no more worries or responsibilities." It hardly seemed alarming when the first chimpanzees used language. Eventually, humans withdrew to camps—and from there, the wilderness.

Maybe it was because I'd listened to so much conservative talk radio while driving around Tampa—because I'd absorbed all those biting, riled voices urging me to buy gold before the federal government started limiting ATM withdrawals, and so forth. But there at the La Quinta I experienced what can only be described as a waking nightmare. Reality and science fiction sloshed together. Some of us in America seemed to be sliding into the same disillusioned lethargy that undid humanity in the novel, while others of us were doing the exact opposite: vigilantly looking for the worst in our government, and in one another, to keep from being conned out of even the thinnest sliver of our freedom. And it seemed to me that the two mindsets—apathy and paranoia—probably yield the same result: You wind up off to the side of real democracy, disengaged from the strenuous project of brokering a better society.

"What is happening could have been foreseen," one witness to history on the planet Soror claims. But the thing is, no one saw it.

I saw the Mystery Monkey of Tampa Bay my last morning in town.

Earlier that year, a retired man in South St. Petersburg had emailed Emily Nipps, a reporter at the *Tampa Bay Times*. The macaque had been out of the news for a while, and the man wanted the public to know that the animal was alive and well. For more than six months, the monkey had been hanging out on his patio and swinging through the surrounding woods. He and his wife were feeding the monkey; they'd become close.

The couple asked Nipps to write a story, on the condition that she wouldn't print their names or the location of their house. What Nipps described in the article was essentially the scenario that the FWC and Vernon Yates had feared: the wild animal losing its wariness of people, endangered by human kindness. Yates, with a heavy heart, had described these people's actions to me as "signing the monkey's death warrant." I managed to get a message to the couple. The husband asked me to call him "Clas," a fragment of his email address. Eventually, he invited me to visit.

Clas came ambling out of the house in socks and sandals to prep me when I pulled in the driveway. "Monk" was out on the patio right now, he whispered. The animal usually flees from strangers, so Clas advised me not to look directly at it—that's a threat—and to just sort of check it out in my peripheral vision while he and I pretended to have a conversation.

We walked onto the screened-in porch. All at once, I spotted the monkey squatting over something on the patio outside. It paused to size me up, then scooped a pile of peanuts off the ground and hopped out of sight as quickly as it could. I'd totally blown the peripheral-vision thing. Clas gave a shrug. Then he introduced me to his wife—I'll call her Mrs. Clas—and we sat down to talk.

They'd heard about the monkey on the news, they said, but were still shocked one morning when they suddenly saw a macaque skitter up a post and vanish onto their roof. Mrs. Clas set out a banana and rushed inside to watch. The monkey hesitantly descended, sat on their woodpile, and ate the banana. That was a year ago. "He's been here ever since," Clas said.

The morning banana-feeding had become a routine. Sometimes grapes. Once in a while, Mrs. Clas left the monkey Oreos that he would twist apart and lick the frosting out of, just like a child. After a while, the monkey seemed to have packed on ten pounds. He looked husky; Clas took to calling him Banana Butt. So they dialed back the feeding, mostly leaving the monkey to forage for itself in the woods. "And he toned down!" Clas said, with amazement and pride. "I think he looks great."

Clas spread snapshots of the monkey across the table for me to see—scenes from their life together. The macaque watched them play gin rummy from the patio and thundered over the roof to the kitchen window to watch Mrs. Clas make dinner. It tracked their movements inside the house; it followed them, Clas explained. "It's pretty incredible. You're sitting on the crapper, and a monkey swings by."

Eventually, Clas's mother—I'll call her Mama Clas—joined us on the porch. She was 106 years old, a wobbly but astoundingly together woman for her age, and had recently moved in. "Is Monk here?" she asked casually, having lowered herself into a chair without first turning to check the patio. She and the monkey had their own relationship. Every morning, Mama Clas would walk down the long driveway with her walker to collect the newspaper and the monkey would escort her, staying twenty feet ahead or behind, keeping watch. "Like a guard," Clas said, showing me a photo of the two of them and laughing. "Honest to God, like a guard."

Otherwise, though, the family made an effort to keep their distance from the animal. They were principled enough not to turn it into a pet. "We really don't want to be friends with him too much," Clas said. "We like our critters wild out here." Living alongside a monkey clearly had its inconveniences. The macaque throws the wire screens off their rain barrels when it needs a drink. It eats the honeybell oranges off their favorite tree. And though they wouldn't elaborate, I suspected they'd glimpsed a temperamental side of the animal from time to time, too.

"Everybody has good days and bad days" was all Clas kept saying. "But it doesn't carry over. It's just forgotten."

I'd been listening to more conservative talk radio on the way to their house. Florida's governor, Rick Scott, had denied the mayor of Tampa's request to temporarily ban firearms around the Convention Center during the Republican convention for the sake of public safety; "We have the Second Amendment for a reason, and that's to make sure that we can always defend our freedom," Scott said. Meanwhile, in New Mexico, a Christian photographer had refused to take a job photographing a lesbian couple's commitment ceremony; a court ruled this violated the couple's civil rights, while the photographer insisted that shooting the ceremony would have gone against her religious convictions. Everywhere, it seemed, everyone's inalienable rights were grinding against everyone else's, and even more abrasively against the government, with all those opposing ideals refusing to settle into a sloppier, if relatively equitable, society. Against that backdrop, what was playing out at the Clas household was so radical that it took me a moment to recognize it: It was a compromise.

Granted, it was a tense, untidy, and maybe untenable compromise—more of a détente. The displaced monkey hadn't actually found a new troop, and for all I knew, it would freak out the next morning and shove Mama Clas to the pavement as she reached for her *Tampa Bay Times*. But for the time being, strange neighbors were making a go of it, being reasonable, getting along.

Maybe there's some muddled metaphor for America in that. Or maybe it's only tempting to look for one because there's such hunger for a hint of any way forward. Maybe it's not a metaphor. Maybe we're on our own. Maybe it's just a macaque.

Birdman

| 2015 |

1. Heavy Is the Head That Wears the Crown

The Pigeon King delivered his closing statement to the jury dressed in his only suit. His name was Arlan Galbraith, and he was representing himself. He had abruptly fired his lawyer nearly two years earlier, during the long lead-up to the trial, and then ignored the judges who kept advising him to hire another. He seemed adrift but also supremely confident. One of his former employees, who testified for the prosecution, speculated that he must have watched too much *Law & Order:* "I think he sat down one day and said, 'Yeah, I can do this.'"

It was December 2013, and Galbraith was being tried in Ontario Superior Court in the city of Kitchener for engineering what the Canadian government described as "one of the biggest frauds in our history." He was sixty-six and heavyset with graying hair, narrow eyes, and a listless, nasal voice. "A very nice-looking, trusting face," is how one woman, who invested $80,000 in his company, described him.

The suit Galbraith wore was dark, and we know it was his only suit because one of the many outlandish and haphazard questions he put to witnesses during the monthlong trial was this: "Do you believe that this suit is the only suit I own and that I bought it in 1997? Do you believe that?" He worked into the same rambling cross-examination the fact that he was now "homeless," staying in a friend's sixteen-square-foot cabin in the "remote bush of far northern Ontario"—a detail that, like his only suit, he felt undermined the idea that he'd allegedly stolen money from hundreds of people. Two days later, he mentioned to another witness that the cabin had no indoor toilet.

Galbraith's reign as Pigeon King lasted seven years, from 2001 to June 2008, when his empire imploded. The prosecution likened his company, Pigeon King International, to a Ponzi scheme—much like Bernie Madoff's operation, which happened to crumble just months after Galbraith's, except that where Madoff's scheme centered on stocks and securities, Galbraith's used live birds.

Pigeon King International sold breeding pairs of pigeons to farmers with a guarantee to buy back their offspring at fixed prices for ten years. Initially, Galbraith told farmers that the birds were high-end racing pigeons, and that he planned to sell the offspring to the lucrative markets that support the sport overseas. Later, Galbraith changed his story, telling farmers that the birds were part of his trailblazing plan to elevate pigeon meat, known as squab, from a fringe delicacy in North America into the next ubiquitous chicken. But in the end, "they were neither," the prosecutor said; Galbraith never sold a single pigeon for sport or meat. He seemed to have merely taken the young birds he bought from Pigeon King International farmers and resold them, as breeding pairs, to other Pigeon King International farmers, shuttling pigeons from one barn to another. And this meant continually recruiting new investors so he would have the cash to buy the pigeons his existing investors produced every month. When Galbraith's scheme finally fell apart, Pigeon King International had almost a thousand breeders under contract in five Canadian provinces and twenty U.S. states. He'd taken nearly $42 million from farmers and walked away from obligations to buy back $356 million worth of their baby birds, ruining many of those investors. A forensic accountant determined that signing up enough new pigeon breeders to pay off those contracts would have dug him into an even deeper, $1.5 billion hole.*

As more details came to light, Pigeon King didn't look like a reasonable business. But it didn't make much sense as a scam, either. For seven years, until the day Galbraith shut down the company, he picked up his people's young pigeons on time and never broke a contract or missed a payment. In one three-year period, he paid out $30 million to these farmers and other creditors. Many of his early investors walked away with six-figure returns. "I was doing the opposite to what a criminal would do," Galbraith argued at the end of the trial. He paid the business's major expenses in full, sometimes months in advance, and didn't flee and vanish when it was clear his company was coming apart. Instead, he stuck it out and wound up with virtually nothing. (Some years, Galbraith paid himself about $400,000, but he used much of that money to bail out the company.) Even his paranoid-sounding claims that he was taken down by a "fearmonger's smear campaign" turned out to be basically true. He'd had no trouble signing up new investors until his credibility was attacked by a prominent Amish intellectual, an eccentric with a bullhorn and a small, muckraking farming magazine.

* All figures are in Canadian dollars.

"I am not a lawyer," Galbraith told the jury, summing up his case. "I am just a farmer and an entrepreneur, trying to defend myself against charges, which, I believe, should have never been brought against me in the first place." He compared himself to Steve Jobs, a "risk taker and visionary," and explained that all he ever wanted was to put "joy on people's faces, by providing them with a better life through pigeon farming." Even a few of his victims weren't sure whether he intended to con them. During the trial, Galbraith asked a farmer named Ken Hoffman, "In spite of losing approximately $125,000, if Arlan Galbraith invited you to join him for dinner, to talk about the past, the present, and the future, would you have dinner with him?" Without hesitation, Hoffman responded, "I certainly would."

The story Galbraith was telling was simple: He started a business and failed. Then again, the prosecution's story was even simpler: Galbraith was a liar. "Use your everyday common sense," the prosecutor told the jury. "This isn't a mistake." The legal case against Galbraith seemed irrefutable: He misled many people, destroying lives. But to understand who the Pigeon King actually was—skilled con man, hapless businessman, hapless con man, or all three—it may help to put common sense aside.

2. Everlasting Trust

Pigeon racing is a centuries-old sport, a test of the birds' speed and navigational skills, which is to say a test of humans' ability to breed exceptional birds. Typically, pigeon racers compete by transporting their flocks long distances, then timing the birds' flights home. Pigeons have been known to travel seven hundred miles in a day, at average speeds of ninety miles an hour.

The pigeon-racing world is small, but it has become much more professionalized over the last twenty years. While the members of a local club in the Bronx might get together on weekends to compete for a couple of hundred dollars, international promoters stage bigger races with astronomically larger purses. In January, the nineteenth annual Million Dollar Pigeon Race in South Africa paid its first-place finisher $150,000. As the stakes have risen, the atmosphere around races has intensified—testing pigeons for doping is now standard practice—and the value of the pigeons has soared. Birds from top-performing breeders are auctioned off to racers wanting to inject their own flocks with quality genes. In 2013, a gifted Belgian pigeon named Bolt, after the Olympic sprinter Usain Bolt, sold for $400,000 to a Chinese businessman.

Galbraith, who declined to be interviewed for this article, told a court official that he started raising pigeons when he was six, during a much simpler era for the sport. He was apparently introduced to the hobby in the 1950s by aging neighbors in Stouffville, Ontario, northeast of Toronto. Both his parents came from farming families, and Galbraith knew from an early age that he wanted to be a farmer, too. He dropped out of school after eleventh grade—he was disappointed in the teachers and bored, he recalled—and bought a farm with his parents and older brother, Norman. They raised and slaughtered pigs and cattle. But the business faltered, and they declared bankruptcy in 1980, when Galbraith was in his early thirties. With his own family to support, he moved around, picking up farm work. On the side, he bred high-end rabbits and exotic birds for show. For a time, he had a tame cockatiel who had the run of the house.

In February 1989, Galbraith's wife, Elizabeth, was en route to a nursing seminar in Toronto when a snowstorm hit, whiting out the highway, and another vehicle slammed into her car. The wreck left Elizabeth a quadriplegic, and Galbraith spent several years caring for her and their two small children until the couple separated. This was difficult for Galbraith, a family member explained: He "has a strong sense of duty," and the divorce was "largely" Elizabeth's decision.

Through all this strain and upheaval, pigeons appear to have been a constant in Galbraith's life. For decades, he was active in Ontario's pigeon-racing and pigeon-fancying circles. At his trial, he proudly noted membership in several organizations: the Canadian Racing Pigeon Union, the Canadian National Tippler Union, the National Birmingham Roller Club. He was charter president of the Saugeen Valley Fur and Feathers Fanciers Association.

By 2001, when Galbraith started running ads in small farming magazines, recruiting investors for Pigeon King International, he'd been breeding pigeons for about fifty years. He referred to himself as the Pigeon King and claimed to have developed his own genetic line, which he called Strathclyde Genetics, after his ancestral region of Scotland. He also showed many farmers a photograph of Mike Tyson, the world's most famous pigeon racer, to whom he claimed to have sold birds. Galbraith always insisted he had a clear business plan—he'd mention the big money paid for racing pigeons in the Middle East or allude to contacts he had in Saudi Arabia—but offered few specifics. Many farmers respected that reticence. If Galbraith had found a niche market, it was smart to keep it to himself.

Investors describe Galbraith as talkative but low-pressure. "He could care less whether you invested or not," one said. In a promotional mailing, he recommended that prospective investors visit families already breeding birds for Pigeon King and wait until they were "absolutely satisfied" before buying in— even if it took years. A large share of his investors, especially at first, were Amish and Mennonite families, people for whom trusting others is central to living a meaningful life. Prosecutors would argue that Galbraith deliberately targeted these groups, that he exploited their credulousness and knew that Mennonites, especially, are committed to absolute forgiveness, typically unwilling to participate in the legal process and unlikely to bear witness against him. (An employee would testify that he overheard Galbraith mocking the Amish as "aliens.") Often, Galbraith threaded his rhetoric with biblical-sounding aphorisms. He signed an early flyer: "He who does not trust is not to be trusted. My business is built on everlasting trust."

When Pigeon King International grew enough to move out of Galbraith's basement into a proper office, he taped a sign with that credo on the front door.

In late 2004, Galbraith visited the hog farm of Christine and Ron Bults. The Bultses had recently bought the property, which was not far from the Pigeon King office in Waterloo, Ontario. They had five kids and were looking for extra income. Christine told me that Galbraith arrived in pin-striped overalls like an "everyday hick farmer," which put her at ease. She invited him in for coffee.

Christine Bults is fifty but looks much younger; when we met last fall, she wore muted gold eye shadow and a denim jacket. She remembered that Galbraith talked about his family, recounting his wife's accident, and explained that the work of raising pigeons, unlike with larger livestock, was oriented around family. Christine and the kids could do the work together safely, while Ron worked his job off-farm. The Bultses talked with Galbraith for more than three hours that day. Rather than attempt to close the deal, Galbraith insisted they do some research and think it over.

Several months later, the Bultses borrowed $125,000 against their farm and bought 360 pairs of pigeons at $165 a pair. There were only a few dozen Pigeon King breeders at the time, but Christine had learned what she could and didn't feel especially suspicious. Still, she's strong-minded and vigilant by nature; she has her father's temper, she told me, adding, "My husband's a little afraid of me when I get pissed." At one point, she glared at Galbraith across the kitchen table and heard herself telling him, "If this goes bad, I will come and find you." Ron, shocked, kicked her under the table. They were trying to do business with the guy, after all.

There's a temptation to dismiss farmers who were taken by Galbraith as ignorant or blinded by greed. But typically, their motivations were nuanced, their ambitions modest. Families dreamed of giving each child his or her own bedroom or keeping both spouses from having to take second jobs away from the family and the farm. "We didn't see dollar signs," one man told me. "We saw more time together." And many, like the Bultses, did their due diligence only to find that watchdogs and regulators were unconcerned about Galbraith, even after a former Pigeon King employee says he warned Ontario's Ministry of Agriculture, Food and Rural Affairs about the company in 2006. An Ohio couple who lost a quarter of a million U.S. dollars described in an affidavit how they'd called half a dozen agricultural and law-enforcement agencies before investing, as well as Better Business Bureaus in the United States and Canada, and turned up no red flags.

Feeling compassion for Galbraith's victims—and possibly, understanding this story at all—may mean getting past some disparaging stereotypes of pigeons, as well. To a New Yorker, a pigeon is flying trash; but to a small poultry farmer, accustomed to stretching and diversifying, the bird could reasonably be seen as one more animal with potential value. At the time, commodity prices were low. Even the market for pregnant-mare urine had tanked. (Mare urine, which is used in hormone-replacement therapy, was a long-standing sideline in farming communities.) Many investors were simply looking for a way to ease the strain of running a small family farm. They saw Galbraith as one of them, and he offered a means to preserve a way of life they believed in. He called the values and work ethic they shared "Pigeon Religion."

As Galbraith hired salesmen and pushed across Ontario and into Pennsylvania and the American Midwest, the monthly newsletter he started, *The Pigeon Post*, became a sort of small-town newspaper for the community he was building. Among the pigeon nutrition tips, pigeon trivia, and mazes for kids were testimonials from Pigeon King investors. One chronicled the escalating misfortunes of a family with eight children—one with a brain tumor, another in a wheelchair with spina bifida—who lived in a falling-down old house, but ended: "And then came the pigeons. WHAT A BLESSING."

3. "We at the Office Have Sure Had Lots of Good Laughs About These Rumors"

As the business grew, Pigeon King became more precarious. But it also appeared more credible. By late 2007, hundreds of breeders were making thousands of dollars a year selling pigeons back to Galbraith. It became easier for prospective investors to quiet their skepticism. When a man appeared outside a company open house in Ontario, warning that Pigeon King was a scam on the verge of collapse, people thought he was crazy. Then again, he *looked* crazy: he was standing on a log in the cold, shouting through a megaphone.

The man on the log was David J. Thornton. He is seventy-three, and runs a website called CrimeBustersNow, a one-man vigilante regulatory force bent on taking down pyramid and Ponzi schemes. In conversation, Thornton comes off as erratic, abrasive, and unnervingly fixated on the sins of the con men he calls "dream stealers"; when we spoke, he had difficulty relaying information chronologically, or in any sort of linear fashion, and broke down crying more than once. He told me he'd been arrested many times—for harassment, disturbing the peace, and assault. In 2010, for example, he got into an altercation with an elementary-school girl while handing out CrimeBustersNow literature outside a school near Toronto. According to court documents, Thornton grabbed at the girl's wrist to get her to pay attention. The school's vice principal had to intervene. (Thornton was convicted of assault and breach of probation but later won an appeal on procedural grounds.) Thornton told me that he was living off a pension, rent-free in the basement of a friend in Quebec, and he seemed almost debilitated by the impassioned tunnel vision with which he goes after his enemies. "I've lost everything," he said. And yet, he was one of the first people to see through Galbraith's operation.

Thornton began investigating Pigeon King in the summer of 2007 after being tipped off by a Mennonite nut grower. "It was just like Madoff," he told me. "I saw this thing could destroy all the farming communities in North America." He knew the only way to stop a scheme like Galbraith's was to choke off new investment. So he posted screeds about the company online, then started phoning bankers and feed companies in agricultural communities around North America, urging them to spread the word. (To reach Amish farmers, he telephoned blacksmiths.) He contacted television stations and law enforcement and visited the federal prosecutor's office near Pigeon King's headquarters, where he was escorted out by the police. He then stood outside that office with a bullhorn as well, shouting about Pigeon King.

By the fall of 2007, almost in spite of himself, Thornton was starting to hamstring Pigeon King. Bankers referred farmers to the CrimeBustersNow website when they came in for pigeon loans. Many farmers called Thornton, and Thornton began collecting numbers and cold-calling others preemptively. He apparently talked many people out of investing. But because he often phoned these people late at night, and also asked them for money to fund various CrimeBustersNow campaigns, it was hard for many of those farmers to take him seriously. "He sounded like he was on a tirade against anyone and everyone," one American investor told the police. A farmer in Ontario named Dale Leifso told me, "He sounded slightly unhinged." Leifso was already skeptical of Pigeon King when Thornton called him late one night, but Thornton sounded so unbalanced that Leifso thinks he may have even wound up defending Galbraith on that call. Leifso eventually cut a check to Pigeon King for $125,000. The company folded before he could sell back any birds.

In early December 2007, Pigeon King was attacked again. *Better Farming*, a magazine with a full-time editorial staff of three, working out of an office on the editor's own farm in eastern Ontario, published a sixteen-page "special investigation" of Pigeon King International, by far the longest piece of reporting the magazine had ever tackled. Its editor, Robert Irwin, told me that *Better Farming* was stonewalled by provincial and federal authorities. ("The police had no interest in what was going on," he said.) Even so, Irwin's team assembled an exhaustive and devastating exposé, a heroic piece of public-interest journalism that pulled together all kinds of agricultural data and quotes from pigeon fanciers and squab processors to undermine Galbraith's claim that there could ever be a market for so many birds.

This bad press crippled Pigeon King. Farmers began showing

the *Better Farming* article to Galbraith's salesmen, asking for explanations. One salesman, Mark DeWitt, drove out to *Better Farming*'s office—Irwin's farmhouse—to photograph it; he seemed to think that showing Pigeon King's investors the magazine's unimpressive headquarters would undercut its credibility. There was an altercation. In a letter Galbraith sent to breeders, DeWitt said that Irwin "went absolutely ballistic," jabbing a shovel in his face. (Irwin told me he put the shovel up to block DeWitt's camera, and DeWitt grabbed it through the driver's-side window of his truck and wouldn't let go.) DeWitt explained that he then drove off with one end of the shovel still in his truck. Irwin says he was dragged for several yards; DeWitt denies this. Eventually, *Better Farming* published an investigative profile of DeWitt, reporting that he was a disbarred lawyer who'd swindled clients out of at least $100,000 in the 1980s. Moreover, he still owed *Better Farming* for some classified ads he took out years earlier. DeWitt denies these allegations, insisting he's not that Mark DeWitt. But documents provided by *Better Farming* show that the disbarred lawyer, Mark DeWitt, and the pigeon salesman, Mark DeWitt, happen to have the same middle initial and date of birth.

Until then, Galbraith had dealt with his critics calmly. Earlier that year, an influential Amish figure, David Wagler, warned farmers about Pigeon King in a prominent Amish newspaper, *Plain Interests*. Galbraith's responses in *The Pigeon Post* had been breezy: "Judge not lest ye be judged yourself," he wrote, adding, "We at the office have sure had lots of good laughs about these rumors." But now, as David Thornton, and then *Better Farming,* piled on, Galbraith hit back harder. He railed in *The Pigeon Post* against the "destructive purveyors of fear" out to destroy innocent farmers. And though he resisted divulging all the details of his business plan—"Toyota did not become the world's largest carmaker by publicizing all their plans in advance"—he announced his intention to build a pigeon meat processing plant at Sacred Dove Ranch, a property he had purchased in far northern Ontario, so he could start delivering squab to the masses. In the past, Galbraith insisted his birds were racing pigeons and dismissed squab as unprofitable, but now he described the birds that Pigeon King farmers were raising as part of a long-term breeding program to create a superior meat bird. At this stage, Galbraith claimed, he was merely building up his flocks, working to achieve the quality and scale he would need to capture a chunk of the chicken market—that is, if the "fear mongers and envious critics" didn't destroy him first. He would call his brand Hinterland Squabs.

"The global demand for quality squab at reasonable prices is unlimited," Galbraith insisted, and he was resolute, even cocky, as the assaults kept coming. Soon, the attorney general of Iowa issued a civil investigative demand, asking Galbraith for proof that his company was not "a Ponzi-type of investment scheme" if it wanted to keep doing business in the state. Maryland and Washington followed with similar actions. "I feel like an old oak tree with a very strong wind trying to blow me down," Galbraith wrote in *The Pigeon Post* in the spring of 2008. "I have been battered and wounded, but I am still standing."

Inside the company, though, Galbraith was scrambling. A year earlier, Pigeon King didn't have enough pigeons to supply all its new breeders with birds. Now there was a backlog. The so-called holding barns—facilities that Pigeon King rented across the United States and Canada to house pigeons it purchased from farmers, before shipping them off to new investors—were filling up. Desperate to lure in new business, Galbraith offered referral fees and progressively more lucrative contracts. He pushed salesmen into the untapped territory of western Canada. "You could tell he was just log-jammed with pigeons," the owner of one holding barn in Ontario told me. "There was clearly no way to get rid of them."

In a typical Ponzi scheme, like Bernie Madoff's, the scammer moves money between investors to pay what he claims are dividends on an investment that doesn't actually exist. But Galbraith didn't have a fake investment as a front. He had birds—lots of birds. *Living* birds. And those birds created more birds, which he, in turn, was obligated to buy, house, feed, and medicate at considerable cost until he could sell them off to someone else. He appeared to miss the whole point of a Ponzi: He'd taken the fungible fictions that give the scam its power and turned them into tangible liabilities.

There were fourteen holding barns in Ontario alone. The largest ones held upward of forty thousand pigeons. The fact that Galbraith maintained those flocks instead of killing or releasing them—that he kept behaving as if the pigeons weren't disposable props but products with genuine value—suggests either that he didn't believe he was running a Ponzi or that he was just exceptionally bad at it. During the trial, one former employee remembered Galbraith unlocking his desk drawer one day, pulling out a ledger, and telling him, "You realize we're going to have to sell $125 million worth of contracts in 2008 and 2009 to use up all the birds."

4. Reduced to Ashes

"My heart is breaking as I write this letter," Galbraith began. It was June 17, 2008. In a mailing to all of Pigeon King International's breeders and barn operators, Galbraith explained that his company was now "dead in the water." It had been "reduced to ashes by FEAR" and by the "slanderous, underhanded smear campaign brought upon me by a handful of jealous protesters bent on destroying me. Some of you may feel better if you have someone to blame for what is happening," Galbraith went on. "In that case, blame the FEAR MONGERS AND ESPE-CIALLY THEIR RING LEADER," by whom he appeared to mean David Thornton.

When Christine Bults got the news, she sat on her kitchen floor and cried. For the last three years, Galbraith had picked up her young pigeons himself every month, buying them back at twenty-five dollars a head. He and Bults would chat while load-ing the crates onto his pickup together, or over a cup of coffee. Galbraith would write her a check for the pigeons on the spot, for four thousand dollars or more, often without double-checking her count. Soon, Bults had enough money to give her oldest daughter a proper wedding; the family was living comfortably for the first time in fifteen years.

Still, as she'd watched Galbraith drive so many pigeons off her property every month, she wondered where they could possibly be going. Initially, Galbraith told her he wanted a hundred in-vestors, but she saw him expand relentlessly beyond that target. The contracts and referral fees advertised in *The Pigeon Post* suggested he was desperate for cash. Months before the *Better Farming* story broke, Bults had become convinced that Pigeon King International was unsustainable, if not an outright scam. She just had a feeling that "something stupid is going to hap-pen," she told me, and no longer felt comfortable offering tours of her barn to prospective investors. Still, she didn't want to make too much noise. Her attitude, she would confess regretfully at the trial, became "survival of the fittest." She wanted to sell enough pigeons back to Galbraith to pay down her loan and get out.

When Pigeon King crashed, the Bultses still owed about $86,000. It took Christine a day, maybe two, to decide what to do next. Her first thought was to crate up her pigeons and have a truck-driver friend leave them on Galbraith's lawn. Ron, her husband, nixed that idea. So instead, Christine began her own investigation, half hoping to prove to herself that the company hadn't been a scam. She phoned breeders, who connected her with other breeders, and she listened patiently to dozens of victims vent or weep. Galbraith was incommunicado, but Bults pieced together where he lived, in part by tracking down a woman who cleaned his house, and drove to the address. And while Ron hollered, "Chris, get back in the vehicle," she circled the property on foot, going window to window, until she was satisfied that Galbraith wasn't there.

Four days after the collapse of Pigeon King International, Bults went to a meeting for investors in Stratford, Ontario, that had been called by Ken Wagler, one of the company's salesmen. Wagler, no relation to the Amish writer David Wagler, is seventy-one and travels to Zambia regularly to do missionary work digging wells. He not only worked for Pigeon King but also bought birds from Galbraith with a partner and lost $125,000.

When Wagler got word the company was finished, he was on his way to promote Pigeon King at an agricultural expo in Saskatchewan. He considered Galbraith a friend and felt hurt that he hadn't called him after the collapse. "Have you ever heard the saying 'There's none so blind as he who will not see'?" Wagler asked me last fall. "Maybe I was guilty of that."

Several hundred farmers attended that first meeting in Stratford. The group eventually broke off into committees, and Wagler joined one tasked with finding another market for everyone's pigeons. Soon, they connected with a processed-food entrepreneur and began meeting monthly at Wagler's church. The sessions became makeshift dinner parties, with the entrepreneur working up gourmet recipes for the committee to taste: smoked pigeon breast, pigeon soup. ("He'd bring dessert and everything," Wagler remembered.) The dishes were delicious, but it turned out the pigeons yielded so little meat that even if the collective were to charge thirty dollars for what Wagler called these "glorified TV dinners for two," they'd still have little hope of turning a profit.

Around North America, it was dawning on Pigeon King breeders that their birds were worthless—too small for squab, not refined enough to be taken seriously by any racer. ("I saw these birds, and they made no sense to me," a longtime supplier to pigeon racers told me. "What he had was a bunch of junk—crossbreeds and just nothing.") In his letter, Galbraith had told investors they were free to do what they pleased with the pigeons, even to open their barn doors and set them free. Officials in Ontario realized they had a potential avian refugee crisis on their hands. Farmers in the province had been left holding an estimated 400,000 pigeons—birds they suddenly had no incentive to keep. There was concern the pigeons could swarm into downtown Toronto like a plague.

The province's agricultural ministry was inundated with calls. It gave out advice about euthanasia and resources for proper disposal. Then in July, the agency began clearing out some of the largest barns itself. Crews gassed 175,000 pigeons in five weeks, working sixteen-hour days, six days a week. An internal assessment noted that, in retrospect, it would have been wise to have grief counselors on hand, as many of the breeders had grown attached to their birds.

Christine Bults served on the same committee with Wagler and hung on to her birds as long as she could. "Finally," she told me, "one day, I came home and said, 'Today's the day.'" Like many investors, the Bultses kept their pigeons in an old barn that couldn't be sealed off for gassing, so when the sun went down and the pigeons became docile, Christine, Ron, and their five children trapped them one by one in feedbags and drowned them in a trough. (Other farmers I spoke to wrung their pigeons' necks by hand—even the day-old babies, one woman confessed.) Bults told me, "I cried the whole time." There were about three thousand birds in her barn. The work took two and a half hours.

Galbraith, meanwhile, had retreated to Sacred Dove Ranch, the planned site of his future processing plant. Years earlier, he'd built a home and guest cottage on the property and hired two caretakers, Debbie Zabek and Del Mountain. Now, Zabek told me, Galbraith "kind of went into seclusion." He was living in the basement of the main house; all the lights upstairs were off, the shades drawn. "He might have been falling apart," she said. In an interview with a Canadian news show that November, Galbraith was unrepentant. When asked what his ruined investors were supposed to do now, he blared: "Same thing as me! Try to put their life back together!"

Pigeon King International declared bankruptcy with less than $50,000 in assets. Eventually, Galbraith would declare personal bankruptcy, too. In the end, the Pigeon King was left to clean up the same mess as his subjects. Zabek recalled looking out the window one day and watching Galbraith remove bulging garbage bags from Sacred Dove's pigeon barn, load them onto the back of a four-wheeler, and drive off. Zabek figured he was snapping the birds' necks and dumping them in the bush.

It was hard to watch. Lies and misdirection aside, Galbraith always seemed to sincerely love the birds. In the past, Zabek had sometimes seen him release a group of pigeons, then stand in the cold with his head up, just watching them circle. "To each his own, I guess," she said.

5. Catharsis

The Crown attorney, or prosecutor, in the Pigeon King International case was Lynn Robinson, a frenetic and charmingly pugnacious woman known for her ruthless cross-examinations of defense witnesses. ("She breaks them," a colleague told me. "Puts them over her knee and breaks them.") Robinson had spent her twenty-two-year career prosecuting sexual-assault and child-abuse cases. But she suffered from rheumatoid arthritis and had just been laid low for almost a year by a severe flare-up. In the spring of 2009, as a way to ease Robinson back into work, her supervisors handed her boxes of documents about Pigeon King International and asked her to determine whether the government could bring a case. "They said, 'What do you know about fraud?'" Robinson remembered. "I said, 'Nothing.' They said, 'Here you go.'"

Robinson and her investigators started tracing the whole maze of sensational subplots. They discovered a couple of chilling instances when Galbraith's affable farmer persona fell away and a more sinister Pigeon King could be glimpsed beneath it. One centered on a company bookkeeper, Darryl Diefenbacher, who despite being a chartered accountant, didn't piece together that Pigeon King was a Ponzi scheme until he'd been working in the office for four months. Diefenbacher would later testify that when he confronted Galbraith with his suspicions, in the summer of 2007, Galbraith told him coldly, "This is a very awkward discussion we're having." Diefenbacher responded: "No, Arlan. This is nothing like the one you're going to have with the FBI."

William Top, Pigeon King's first U.S. salesman, forced his own cinematic confrontation with Galbraith in early 2006. Top explained to me how his doubts about the company were cemented through a series of coincidences, including a chance encounter with a crowd of fanatical pigeon fanciers in a Pennsylvania Waffle House. (Top compared the old men to Shriners: "Buttons and vests and funny hats.") The men had never heard of Galbraith, which seemed impossible to Top, given how small the pigeon-breeding world is. Eventually, Top went to Galbraith's office demanding answers. When the Pigeon King explained that he was, as Top later relayed it, "strictly in the business of selling breeders," with no outside customers for his birds, Top admonished him for running a scam. Galbraith bowed his head. "And then when he raised his head," Top would tell the jury, there was "a different look on his face. It was a different Arlan." Galbraith threatened to ruin Top's reputation, and that of his family, if he exposed Pigeon King. Top quit on the spot. He told me he subsequently called many farmers and other employees to warn them, but everyone was making good money; many didn't want to upset the arrangement. "People loathed me," Top said. "I've had my life threatened."

The story Lynn Robinson saw unspooling was elaborate and unwieldy. And because there was no money to recover for the victims, her job was simply to find an efficient way to send Galbraith to jail, without paying to fly in dozens of witnesses or getting bogged down in a twenty-month trial. Her office decided to let all of the company's employees off the hook. She would narrow the scope of the case to the 917 farmers who had signed with Galbraith since 2005 and prosecute the Pigeon King for fraud.

Galbraith was charged in December 2010, two and a half

years after he sold his last pigeon. Then came three years of postponed court appearances and other delays, with Galbraith periodically slowing the procedural machinery by firing his lawyer or filing odd motions.

The long lag disillusioned many farmers. It felt as if the peculiarities of the fraud—and the fact that, as Christine Bults put it, Galbraith was a farmer moving pigeons between barns in rural areas, not a banker moving numbers around a spreadsheet on Wall Street—gave authorities permission not to take his victims seriously. It had taken the police seven months from the time Pigeon King imploded to open an investigation and another year to complete it. By comparison, seven months after Bernie Madoff's scam fell apart, Madoff was already in prison, serving 150 years.

Once the trial began, in November 2013, the case against Galbraith coalesced quickly, as Robinson and her co-counsel piled up his inconsistent statements about the ultimate market for his birds. But they had to prove only that he took investors' money through "deceit, falsehood, or other fraudulent means." The more intriguing question—what Galbraith actually thought he'd been doing—was legally irrelevant and, as a consequence, never became any less mystifying.

Witnesses portrayed the Pigeon King as a commandeering and eccentric businessman—he didn't let employees sign checks or open the mail—but often in ways that didn't seem crooked or even calculating, just weird. Each month, for example, Galbraith would pay off his salesmen's credit cards in full (upward of $40,000 in gas and travel expenses), then cut up the cards and issue new ones. And though there were reasons why constructing a squab-processing plant at a remote site like Sacred Dove Ranch seemed idiotic, from a business perspective, Galbraith made a plausible case, during his cross-examination of the engineer he hired to draw up the plans, that he was serious about constructing it anyway.

Maybe Pigeon King had been a scam from the start, or maybe it had devolved into one at some unknown point, as sales to farmers swelled and Galbraith lost control. It was tempting to reread his *Pigeon Post* columns for some veiled confession. The essence of Pigeon Religion, he wrote in January 2007, was this: "United people are builders of the positive. Negative people divide and knock down a good thing." Really, he was describing the psychological architecture of a Ponzi scheme, a community fused precariously by optimism and trust.

Robinson expected Galbraith to stitch together a convoluted counternarrative that she'd have the pleasure of shredding. ("Be careful," a veteran lawyer warned her. "The only defense to a big fraud is a bigger fraud.") But it never happened. Galbraith declined to take the stand and called only one witness. He didn't even make an opening statement. His side of the story emerged piecemeal from random assertions that he slipped into the proceedings. They expanded on his earlier rebuttals to Thornton and *Better Farming:* The pigeons that farmers were left holding when Pigeon King collapsed, he explained, were only "breeding stock"—an intermediary step on the path to Hinterland Squabs. Galbraith even brought a visual aid to illustrate his sophisticated "up-breeding" program, but never figured out how to introduce it as evidence. He tried to unveil it repeatedly during one cross-examination, but the judge, Justice G. E. Taylor, kept disallowing it, because the witness had not seen the document before. "Your Honor, I'm not allowed to show him this genetic formula?" Galbraith finally asked the judge glumly. Then he gave up.

In general, his clumsiness as an attorney so disrupted the flow of the trial that Justice Taylor, and even Robinson, repeatedly stepped in to assist him. The jury was occasionally excused so Galbraith could be given longer tutorials as well. Still, Galbraith kept floating bizarre hypotheticals while cross-examining witnesses and lacing his questions with insults and accusations. Because there were often no legitimate questions to answer, witnesses frequently took the opportunity to tell Galbraith off. At one point, Dale Leifso, the Ontario farmer, erupted at him: "I've got places I gotta be, I've got a thousand things to do at home, and I'm sitting here in a courtroom answering these stupid questions!" The defense Galbraith was mounting, in other words, seemed just as rudderless as his company. And that, however unwittingly, may have been the best evidence he offered in his favor.

Christine Bults was the first breeder called by the prosecution, and she seized every opportunity to dress Galbraith down. But as Galbraith's cross-examination wore on, something extraordinary happened: The Pigeon King's own wounded feelings became just as conspicuous as hers. The catharsis was happening on both sides. Galbraith asked Bults if, knowing him as well as she did, she didn't understand that he was too "paralyzed with depression" to call farmers once his company fell apart?

"I was depressed, too!" Bults said shakily. "Was I not?"

He told her—again, ostensibly in the form of a question—how shocked and disappointed he was that, after years of what he considered friendship, she would turn against him.

"Seriously?" Bults shot back. "What a dumb question, Arlan! I didn't turn against you. You walked away from us!"

It wasn't a cross-examination anymore; it was an unrestrained showdown between two estranged friends. Soon, Galbraith was lashing out. "Do you realize," he asked, "you're a prime example of a two-faced, fair-weather friend, ready to stab me in the back when things don't go your way?" But Bults interrupted him, which meant that after some refereeing from the judge, Galbraith was required to repeat the question. He did, verbatim.

"Are you done?" Bults asked this time, goading him.

"Yes," he said.

It was her moment, and she tried to rise to it, pushing the final words out slow and hard. "And *you* didn't stab me in the back," she said, "my fair-weather friend?"

6. A Lack of Insight

It took the jury two days to find Arlan Galbraith guilty. He appeared for sentencing in March 2014 looking deadened and unshaven. His leg was shackled to the floor, and his suit—the only suit he owned—was now several sizes too big; he'd lost about forty pounds in custody since the trial.

Galbraith had finally hired a lawyer, but there wasn't much the man could do at this point. He merely noted that his client was a senior citizen with no criminal history, whose life had taken a tragic turn after his wife's accident. The prosecution was asking for nine to twelve years, which Galbraith's lawyer called a "crushing sentence" for a man who, as these last months showed, clearly wouldn't fare well in prison. "He's certainly a diminished man," he said.

The judge was not sympathetic. Galbraith, he said, appeared to have a "lack of insight into his serious criminal conduct" and absolutely no sympathy for his victims. The judge had read through statements that farmers filed with the police, outlining their stories. They were devastating. Farmers with too much pride to file for bankruptcy wrote vulnerably about their deep feelings of shame and regret. "Every day I feel that I have let my children down," one said. Another explained, "All the hours that my husband spent away from our babies when they were little— all for nothing."

Marriages suffered. "We are still together," one man wrote, "but we do not talk about the pigeon deal at all." Victims' children were ridiculed at school. There were anxiety attacks, depression, suicidal thoughts, heart attacks, teeth falling out from stress. "Cancer has come back into my life after a 30-plus-year absence," one woman wrote. Worst of all, the experience broke some fundamental decency in many people. "We have learned not to trust," one couple confessed. "This is against our very nature."

The judge sentenced Galbraith to seven years and three and a half months. The Pigeon King said nothing at the hearing. Last year, from a prison in northern Ontario, he quietly dropped his appeal. Christine Bults told me she was grateful to prosecutors for putting Galbraith away, but it was hard to appreciate his sentence as justice when she was still paying a thousand dollars a month on her loan. Then she thought about it and added that, as a taxpayer, "It's costing me money again to have him sit in jail."

Bults attended the entire four-week trial and told me that, during a lunch recess one day, she came back from having a cigarette and found Galbraith sitting on a bench in an empty hallway of the courthouse with his head down. Bults sat on the bench right across from him. She stared at him, hard. "I never moved," she told me. "I just stayed there."

She was trying to force Galbraith to look at her, to acknowledge her. At one point, the Pigeon King finally lifted up his head. For a split second, Bults caught his eye. Then he looked away.

A Cloud Society

| 2016 |

Gavin Pretor-Pinney decided to take a sabbatical. It was the summer of 2003, and for the previous ten years, as a sideline to his graphic-design business in London, he and a friend had been running a magazine called *The Idler*. *The Idler* was devoted to the "literature for loafers." It argued against busyness and careerism and for the ineffable value of aimlessness, of letting the imagination quietly coast. Pretor-Pinney anticipated all the jokes: that he'd burned out running a magazine devoted to doing nothing, and so on. But it was true. Getting the magazine out was taxing, and after a decade, it seemed appropriate to stop for a while and live without a plan—to be an idler himself and shake free space for fresh ideas. So he swapped his flat in London for one in Rome, where everything would be new and anything could happen.

Pretor-Pinney is forty-seven, towering and warm. His face is often totally lit up, as if he's being told a story and can feel some terrific surprise coming. He stayed in Rome for seven months and loved it, especially all the religious art. One thing he noticed:

The paintings and frescoes he encountered were crowded with clouds. They were everywhere, he told me recently, "these voluptuous clouds, like the sofas of the saints." But outside, when Pretor-Pinney looked up, the real Roman sky was usually devoid of clouds. He wasn't accustomed to such endless, blue emptiness. He was an Englishman; he was accustomed to clouds. He remembered, as a child, being enchanted by them and deciding that people must climb long ladders to harvest cotton from up there. Now, in Rome, he couldn't stop thinking about clouds. "I found myself missing them," he told me.

Clouds. It was a bizarre preoccupation, even a frivolous one, but he didn't resist it. He went with it, as he often does, despite not having a specific goal or even a general direction in mind; he likes to see where things go. When Pretor-Pinney returned to London, he talked about clouds constantly. He walked around admiring them, learned their scientific names and the meteorological conditions that shape them, and argued with friends who complained they were oppressive or drab. He was realizing, as he later put it, that "clouds are not something to moan about. They are, in fact, the most dynamic, evocative, and poetic aspect of nature."

Slowing down to appreciate clouds enriched his life and sharpened his ability to appreciate other pockets of beauty hiding in plain sight. Pretor-Pinney couldn't help noting that we were entering an era in which "miraculousness" was losing its meaning. Novel, purportedly amazing things ricocheted around the Internet so quickly that, as he put it, we can now all walk around with an attitude like, "Well, I've just seen a panda doing something unusual online, what's going to amaze me *now*?" His fascination with clouds was teaching him that "it's much better for our souls to realize we can be amazed and delighted by what's around us."

At the end of 2004, a friend invited Pretor-Pinney to give a talk about clouds at a small literary festival in Cornwall. The previous year, there were more speakers than attendees, so Pretor-Pinney wanted an alluring title for his talk, to draw a crowd. "Wouldn't it be funny," he thought, "to have a society that defends clouds against the bad rap they get—that stands up for clouds?" So he called his talk "The Inaugural Lecture of the Cloud Appreciation Society." And it worked. Standing room only! Afterward, people came up to him and asked for more information about the Cloud Appreciation Society. They wanted to *join* the society. "And I had to tell them, well, I haven't really got a society," Pretor-Pinney said.

He set up a website. It was simple. There was a gallery for posting photographs of clouds, a membership form, and a florid manifesto. ("We believe that clouds are unjustly maligned and that life would be immeasurably poorer without them," it began.) Pretor-Pinney wasn't offering members of his new Cloud Appreciation Society any perks or activities, but, to keep it all from feeling ephemeral or imaginary, as many things on the Internet do, he eventually decided that membership should cost fifteen dollars and that members would receive a badge and certificate in the mail. He recognized that joining an online Cloud Appreciation Society that only nominally existed might appear ridiculous, but it was important to him that it not feel meaningless.

Within a couple of months, the society had two thousand paying members. Pretor-Pinney was surprised and ecstatic. Then Yahoo placed the Cloud Appreciation Society first on its 2005 list of Britain's "Weird and Wonderful Websites." People kept clicking on that clickbait, which wasn't necessarily surprising, but thousands of them also clicked through to Pretor-Pinney's own website, then paid for memberships. Other news sites noticed. They did their own articles about the Cloud Appreciation Society, and people followed the links in those articles, too. Previously, Pretor-Pinney had proposed writing a book about clouds and was rejected by twenty-eight editors. Now he was a viral sensation with a vibrant online constituency. He got a deal to write a book about clouds.

The writing process was agonizing. On top of not actually being a writer, he was a brutal perfectionist. But *The Cloudspotter's Guide*, published in 2006, was full of glee and wonder. Pretor-Pinney relays, for example, the story of the United States Marine pilot who, in 1959, ejected from his fighter jet over Virginia and during the forty minutes it took him to reach the ground, was blown up and down through a cumulonimbus cloud about as high as Mount Everest. He surveys clouds in art history and Romantic poetry and compares one exceptionally majestic formation in Australia to "Cher in the brass armor bikini and gold Viking helmet outfit she wore on the sleeve of her 1979 album 'Take Me Home.'" In the middle of the book, there's a cloud quiz. Question No. 5 asks of a particular photograph, "What is it that's so pleasing about this layer of stratocumulus?" The answer Pretor-Pinney supplies is "It is pleasing for whatever reason you find it to be."

The book became a bestseller. There were more write-ups, more clicks, more Cloud Appreciation Society members. And that cycle would keep repeating, sporadically, for years, whenever an editor or blogger happened to discover the society and set it off again. (There are now more than forty thousand paid members.) The media tended to present it as one more amusing curiosity, worth delighting over and sharing before moving on. That is, Pretor-Pinney's organization was being tossed like a pebble, again and again, into the same bottomless pool of interchangeable content that he was trying to coax people away from, by lifting their gaze skyward. But that was OK with him; he understood that it's just how the Internet works. He wasn't cynical about it, and he didn't feel his message was being cheapened either. It felt as if he were very small, peering up, observing the whole thing from afar, and he tried to appreciate it.

Then Pretor-Pinney noticed something odd.

"The way I felt when I first saw it was: Armageddon," Jane Wiggins said. Wiggins was a paralegal, working in downtown Cedar Rapids, Iowa, in June 2006, when she looked out her office window and saw an impenetrable shroud of dark clouds looming over town. Everyone in the office stood up, Wiggins told me, and some drifted to the window. The formation was so enormous, so terrible and strange, that it would make the evening news. Wiggins, who had recently taken up photography, reached for her camera.

Soon after that, Wiggins discovered the Cloud Appreciation Society website and posted one of her pictures in its gallery. But the anomaly Wiggins thought she had captured wasn't actually anomalous. Similar photos turned up in the Cloud Appreciation Society's gallery from Texas, Norway, Ontario, Scotland, France, and Massachusetts. Pretor-Pinney assumed that this phenomenon was so rare that, until now, no one had recognized it as a repeating form and given it a name. "As the hub of this network, a network of people who are sky-aware," he said, "it's easier to spot patterns that, perhaps, weren't so easy to spot in the past."

In fact, many aspects of meteorology already rely on a global network of individual weather observers to identify cloud types with the naked eye, filing them into a long-established scientific framework: not just as cumulus, cirrus, stratus, or cumulonimbus clouds, as schoolchildren learn, but within a recondite system for describing variations of those basic shapes. Atypical clouds are either fitted into that existing map of the sky or set aside as irrelevant. Pretor-Pinney liked classifying clouds using these names; he was thankful to have that structure in place. And yet, it seemed a shame to repress the glaring, deviant beauty recorded in Wiggins's photograph by assigning it a name that didn't sufficiently describe it. He supposed, if you had to, you could call this thing an *undulatus*—the standard classification for a broad, wavy cloud. But that seemed to be selling the cloud tragically short, stubbornly ignoring what made it so sublime. This was *"undulatus* turned up to eleven," he said. So he came up with his own name for the cloud: *asperatus*. (The word "asperatus" came from a passage in Virgil describing a roughened sea; Pretor-Pinney had asked his cousin, a high-school Latin teacher, for help.) He wondered how to go about making such a name official.

In 2008, while shooting a documentary for the BBC about clouds, Pretor-Pinney pitched his new cloud to a panel of four meteorologists at the Royal Meteorological Society. The scientists sat in a line behind a table; Pretor-Pinney stood, holding blown-up photos of asperatus for them to consider. "It was a lot like *The X Factor*," he said, referring to the TV talent show. The scientists were encouraging but diplomatic. A new cloud name, they explained, could be designated only by the World Meteorological Organization, an agency within the United Nations, based in Geneva, which has published scientific names and descriptions of all known cloud types in its *International Cloud Atlas* since 1896. The WMO is exceptionally discerning; for starters, Pretor-Pinney was told, he would need more carefully cataloged incidences of these clouds, as well as a scientific understanding of their surrounding "synoptic situation." The process would take years. And even then, the chances of inclusion in the atlas were slim. The WMO hadn't added a new cloud type to the *In-*

ternational Cloud Atlas since 1953. "We don't expect to see new cloud types popping up every week," a WMO official named Roger Atkinson told me. When I asked why, Atkinson said, "Because fifty or sixty years ago, we got it right."

A cloud is only water, but arranged like no other water on earth. Billions of minuscule droplets are packed into every cubic foot of cloud, throwing reflected light off their disordered surfaces in all directions, collectively making the cloud opaque. In a way, each cloud is an illusion, a conspiracy of liquid masquerading as a floating, solid object.

But for most of human history, what a cloud was, physically, hardly mattered; instead, we understood clouds as psychic refuges from the mundane, grist for our imaginations, feelings fodder. Clouds both influenced our emotions and hung above us like washed-out mirrors, reflecting them. The English painter John Constable called the sky the "chief organ of sentiment" in his landscapes. And our instinct, as children, to recognize shapes in the clouds is arguably one early spark of all the higher forms of creative thinking that make us human and make us fun. Frankly, a person too dull to look up at the sky and see a parade of tortoises or a huge pair of mittens or a ghost holding a samurai sword is not a person worth lying in a meadow with. In *Hamlet*, Polonius's despicable spinelessness is never clearer than when Hamlet gets him to enthusiastically agree that a particular cloud looks like a camel, then not a camel at all, but a weasel. Then not a weasel, but a whale. That is, Polonius will see whatever Hamlet wants him to; he is a man completely without his own vision.

We also look for meaning—portents—in the clouds, the more grown-up version of picking out puffy animals. "There's a long history of people finding signs in the sky," Pretor-Pinney told me, from Constantine seeing the cross over the Milvian Bridge to the often-belligerent protesters outside Pretor-Pinney's talks, who are convinced that the contrails behind commercial airplanes are evidence of a toxic, secret government scheme and are outraged that Pretor-Pinney—the righteous Lorax of clouds—refuses to expose it. In short, clouds exist in a realm where the physical and metaphysical touch. "We look up for answers," Pretor-Pinney says. And yet, we often don't want *empirical* answers. There has always been a romantic impulse to protect clouds from our own stubbornly rational intellects, to keep knowledge from trampling their magic. Thoreau preferred to understand clouds as something that "stirs my blood, makes my thought flow" and not as a mass of water. "What sort of science," he wrote, "is that which enriches the understanding but robs the imagination?"

The scientific study of clouds grew out of a collection of madly appreciating amateurs who struggled with this same tension. The field's foundational treatise was first presented to a small scientific debating society in London one evening in 1802 by a shy Quaker pharmacist named Luke Howard. Howard, then thirty, was not a professional meteorologist but a devoted cloud-spotter with a perceptive, if wandering, mind. His interest in clouds started early. His biographer, Richard Hamblyn, explains that as a young student in Oxfordshire, Howard seems to have found school magnificently boring. He couldn't bring himself to pay attention, except to his Latin teacher, who punished daydreaming with beatings. Today Howard might covertly pull out his phone and read a link a friend shared about, say, an eccentric society in England that appreciates clouds. But poor Howard's boredom was analog: All he could do was look out the classroom window at the actual clouds rolling by.

Howard's intention that night in London was to bring clouds

down to earth without depleting their loftiness. After years of closely observing clouds, his appreciation of them had hardened into analysis. He now insisted that, though clouds may appear to be blown around in random, ever-changing shapes, they actually take consistent forms, forms that can be distinguished from one another and whose changes correspond to changes in the atmosphere.

Clouds could be used to read what Howard called "the countenance of the sky"; they are an expression of its moods, not just in a poetic way, as Constable meant, but meteorologically.

Howard's lecture was eventually published as "On the Modifications of Clouds, and on the Principles of Their Production, Suspension and Destruction." It stands as the ur-text of nephology, the branch of meteorology devoted to clouds. Howard divided clouds into three major types and many intermittent varieties of each, all similarly affixed with Latin names or compounds. (He had learned his Latin well.) Like Linnaeus, who used Latin to sort the fluidity of life into genera and species, Howard used his new cloud taxonomy to wrest our understanding of the world's diversity from superstition and religion. His signature assertion that "the sky, too, belongs to the Landscape" can be read as a call for empiricism—a conviction that science can, in fact, measure out the mystical.

Nearly a century later, Howard's work would be picked up by another energetic amateur, the Honorable Ralph Abercromby. Abercromby was the bookish great-grandson of a celebrated English war hero. He was apparently so meek and frail ("never robust, even as a boy," one tribute read after his death) that he was forced to drop out of school and was rarely able to hold a job. He served briefly in the military but seemed completely un-

suited to soldiering; deployed to Newfoundland in 1864, Abercromby began theorizing about how the fog there was produced.
Later, stationed in Montreal, he scrutinized the wind. It would
have been tempting for his superiors to label him "absent-
minded" or "unfocused" but, in retrospect, it was just another
case of a young man intensely focused on something few people
considered worthy of attention—another case of a young man in
love with clouds.

In 1885, Abercromby took his first round-the-world voyage.
He was a civilian again, and his private physician hoped the sea
air would restore his pitiable health. But he worked slavishly the
whole time, keeping a meticulous weather diary, photographing
the clouds at sea. He published many scientific papers and a
book about the clouds and weather that he encountered. And he
kept traveling: Scandinavia and Russia, Asia and the United
States, compelled, as he wrote, to "continue the observation and
photography of cloud forms in different countries." Looking up,
Abercromby came to realize that clouds looked essentially the
same everywhere. Colonialism was sending goods, resources,
and culture around the planet; suddenly, it must have seemed
obvious that we also shared the same sky.

Abercromby's primary interest was in refining the science of
weather-tracking and forecasting, and he knew that meteorologists everywhere would need a standard way to discuss and share
their observations. Eventually, collaborating with a Swedish
cloud scientist named Hugo Hildebrand Hildebrandsson, he
convened a Cloud Committee to hammer out a "Nomenclature
of Clouds." They declared 1896 "the International Year of the
Cloud." By year's end, the committee produced the first *International Cloud Atlas*.

The atlas is now in its seventh edition, and its meticulous taxonomy provides for ten genera of clouds, fourteen species, nine

varieties, and dozens of "accessory clouds" and "supplementary features." The atlas also establishes a grammar with which these terms can be combined to allow for the instability of clouds—the way they morph from one form into another—or to note their altitude. A cumulus, for example, might just be a cumulus; or it might be a cumulus fractus, if its edges are tattered; or a cumulus pileus, if a smaller cloud appears over it like a hood. An altocumulus lenticularis, meanwhile, is a vast, tightly bunched flock of clouds stretching across the sky at altitudes from 6,500 to 23,000 feet.

Of course, not everything in the sky needs to be precisely described. As a reference book for meteorologists, the atlas has been concerned only with clouds that have "operational significance"—that reliably reveal something about atmospheric conditions. As far as other clouds go, says Roger Atkinson of the WMO, one person might look at a cloud and say: "It's wonderful. It looks like an elephant," and someone else might think, "It's a camel." But the WMO doesn't care. It does not see its mission as settling disagreements about elephants and camels.

Soon after Pretor-Pinney appeared on the BBC, championing his asperatus cloud, the media seized on the possibility, however remote, that the WMO would add asperatus to its atlas. Suddenly, there were stories about the Cloud Appreciation Society all over the place, all over again. This time, Pretor-Pinney— previously cast as a charming English eccentric with a funny website—was presented as the crusading figurehead of a populist meteorological revolt. Pretor-Pinney had initially turned defeatist after shooting the documentary and never bothered reaching out to the WMO; the bureaucracy seemed too formidable. Now he didn't quite know what to say. When reporters called, he suggested they contact the WMO themselves, impishly channeling them as de facto lobbyists.

Then, in 2014, the WMO announced it was preparing the first new edition of the cloud atlas in nearly forty years; the agency felt pressure to finally digitize the book, to reassert its authority over the many reckless cloud-reference materials proliferating online. One of the WMO's first steps was to convene an international Task Team to consider additions to the atlas. "Most public interest," a news release noted, "has focused on a proposal by the Cloud Appreciation Society" to recognize the so-called asperatus. The Task Team would report to a so-called Commission for Instruments and Methods of Observation. Last summer, the commission recommended to the World Meteorological Organization's 17th World Meteorological Congress in Geneva that the cloud be included. Everyone seemed confident that the recommendation would soon be ratified by the WMO's executive council. Except, the new cloud wasn't asperatus anymore; it was now *asperitas*. The Task Team had demoted it from a cloud "variety," as Pretor-Pinney had proposed, to a "supplementary feature," and the elaborate naming convention for clouds required supplementary features to be named with Latin nouns, not adjectives. "One of those things that's so close, but different," Pretor-Pinney told me, with a tinge of both amusement and spite.

When I spoke to Roger Atkinson, he stressed that the WMO was codifying asperatus as merely "a fourth-order classification, not a primary genus, not one of the primary cloud types, not one of the Big Nine." Neither was it the only new classification the Task Team recommended adding; it was just the most famous one. The prominence of the cloud seems to have forced the scientists' hand. Asperitas didn't appear to have any operational significance, but the public enthusiasm Pretor-Pinney had gathered around the cloud ultimately made asperitas too prominent to ignore. One Task Team member, George Anderson, told me that not giving such a well-known cloud a definitive name would only create more confusion.

Pretor-Pinney conceded all this, happily. "My argument is not that this is some hugely significant thing," he told me. By now, he was mostly using the cloud to make a point—to needle the "human vanity" inherent in "the Victorian urge to classify things, to put them into pigeonholes and give them scientific names." Clouds, he added, "are ephemeral, ever-changing, phenomenal. Here you have a discrete, scientific, analytic urge laid onto the embodiment of chaos, onto these formations within these unbounded pockets of our atmosphere where there's no beginning and no edge." All he wanted was to encourage people to look at the sky, to elevate our perception of clouds as beautiful "for their own sake."

Slowly, over the last two hundred years, the impulse of cloud lovers like Howard and Abercromby to make the mystical empirical had ossified into something stringent and reductive. Pretor-Pinney wanted to clear a little more space in our collective cloudscape for less distinct feelings of delight and wonder. His championing of asperatus was, in reality, somewhat arbitrary. There were a few other unnamed cloud forms he saw repeating in the society's photo gallery. He just happened to pick this one.

The cultural history of clouds seemed to be shaped by a procession of amateurs, each of whom projected the ethos of his particular era onto those billowing blank slates in the troposphere. Pretor-Pinney was our era's, I realized—the Internet era's. He wasn't just challenging the cloud authorities with his crowdsourced cloud; he was trolling them.

I was one of the many reporters who contacted Pretor-Pinney when the first photos of asperitas made the rounds in 2009. I had seen an Associated Press article, with Jane Wiggins's photo of the cloud in Iowa and a reference to Pretor-Pinney and his Cloud Appreciation Society, and felt a kind of instant and exhilarated envy: Apparently, some people cultivated a meaningful connection to what I'd only ever regarded as vaporous arrangements of nothingness. I wanted in. I was even more impressed that these enthusiasts seemed to be rattling the self-serious strictures of the scientific establishment. And so it was disappointing to realize, in those early days and as I checked back with him periodically, that nothing was really happening yet and that no one seemed particularly rattled. Pretor-Pinney even sounded slightly exhausted by asperitas. "It's the zombie news story that will never die!" he said.

He was, by then, closing in on his tenth year as head of the Cloud Appreciation Society and, as he'd done after ten years with *The Idler* magazine, he was questioning his commitment to it. Somehow, being a cloud impresario had swallowed an enormous amount of time. He was lecturing about clouds around the world, sharing stages at corporate conferences and ideas festivals with Snoop Dogg and Bill Clinton, and appearing monthly on the Weather Channel. Then there was the Cloud Appreciation Society's online store, a curated collection of society-branded merchandise and cloud-themed home goods, which turned out to be surprisingly demanding to run, particularly in the frenzied weeks before Christmas. The Cloud Appreciation Society was basically just Pretor-Pinney and his wife, Liz, plus a friend who oversaw the shop part-time and a retired steelworker he brought on to moderate the photo gallery. It was all very arduous now, which Pretor-Pinney seemed to find a little embarrassing. "My argument about why cloud-spotting is a worthwhile activity is that it's an aimless activity," he said. "And I've turned it into something that is very purposeful, that is work."

At the same time, he realized that he'd conjured a genuine community of amateur cloud lovers from all over the world but regretted never doing anything to truly nourish it; it felt so "fluffy," he said, "with no center to it, like a cloud." Soon, that spectral online society—that cloud of people—would be celebrating its tenth anniversary. "I'm thinking that it might be a nice reason to get everyone together," he said.

One morning last September, Pretor-Pinney was fidgeting and fretting in the auditorium of the Royal Geographical Society building, at the edge of Kensington Gardens in London. Escape to the Clouds, a one-day conference to celebrate the Cloud Appreciation Society's tenth anniversary, would be underway in ninety minutes, and Pretor-Pinney was impatiently supervising the small team of balloon-installation artists he had commissioned to rig inflatable cloud formations around the stage. This was the first big event that he organized for the Cloud Appreciation Society. The evening before the conference, he was expecting 315 attendees. But there had been a late surge of ticket-buying, and now he was panicking about running out of artisanal cloud marshmallows for the gift bags. Outside, Pretor-Pinney kept pointing out, the London sky was impeccably blue. Not a single cloud. It was terrible.

Bounding onstage to kick off the conference, Pretor-Pinney seemed overwhelmed but cheerful. He reminded the muddle of cloud appreciators from all over the world, now crammed into the theater, that "to tune in to the clouds is to slow down.

It's a moment of meteorological meditation." And he celebrated the transcendence of cloud-spotting: how it connects us to the weather, the atmosphere, to one another. "We are part of the air," he told everyone. "We don't live beneath the sky. We live *within* the sky."

Who were they all? Why were they there? They were a collection of ordinary people with an interest in clouds. Behind all those user names on the Cloud Society website were schoolteachers, skydivers, meteorologists, retired astronomy teachers, office workers, and artists. Many people had come alone, but conversations sparked easily. ("I've just seen the best cloud dress I've seen in my life," one woman said to another on the stairway. The second woman turned and said, "Well, yours is quite lovely, too.") The atmosphere was comfortable and convivial and amplified by a kind of feedback loop of escalating relief, whereby people who arrived at a cloud conference not knowing what to expect recognized how normal and friendly everyone was and enjoyed themselves even more.

The program Pretor-Pinney had pulled together was a little highbrow but fun. A British author recounted the misadventures of the first meteorologist to make a high-altitude balloon ascent. An energetic literary historian surveyed "English Literary Views of the Sky." Pretor-Pinney and a professor of physics tried to demonstrate a complicated atmospheric freezing process in a plastic bottle, but failed. And between the talks, a musician named Lisa Knapp performed folk songs about wind and weather. She had saved the obvious crowd-pleaser for her final turn onstage: the melancholy Joni Mitchell classic "Both Sides Now."

There would be one more talk after Knapp finished, but it didn't matter. This—the Joni Mitchell moment—was the conference's transformative conclusion. Knapp had an extraordinary voice, Bjork-like, but gentler, and performed the song alone, accompanying herself with only a delicate, monotonal Indian classical instrument resting in her lap, a kind of bellows called a shruti box. It let out a mournful, otherworldly drone. After hours of lectures and uncertain socializing with strangers, something about this spare arrangement and the sorrowful lyrics felt so vulnerable that, by the time Knapp had finished the first lines— "Rows and flows of angel hair, and ice cream castles in the air, and feather canyons everywhere. I've looked at clouds that way"—she was singing into an exquisite silence.

The performance moved me. But it was more than that, and weirder. Maybe, somewhere in this story about clouds and cloud lovers, I'd found a compelling argument for staying open to varieties of beauty that can't quite be categorized and, by extension, for respecting the human capacity to feel, as much as our ability to scrutinize the sources of those feelings. Whatever the case, as Knapp sang, I started to feel an inexplicable rush of empathy for the people I met that day, the people sitting around me—all these others, living within the same sky. And I let my mind wander, wondering about their lives. What I felt, really, was awe: the awe that comes when you fully internalize that every stranger's interior life is just as complicated as yours. It seemed very unlikely that a meeting of an online cloud society in a dark, windowless room could produce such a moment of genuine emotion, but there I was, in the middle of it. Just thinking about clouds, I guess, had turned a little transcendent, at least for me.

Then I heard the sniffle. It was very loud. With the room so transfixed, it easily cut through Knapp's voice from a few rows behind me, and when I turned to look, I saw Pretor-Pinney's wife, Liz, fully in tears. Then the woman right next to me—she was crying, too. And I heard others inhaling loudly, oddly, and got the impression there were more. Immediately afterward, out in the hall, the first person I walked past was bashfully apologizing to two others. It was so strange, she kept saying. She just didn't know why she'd been crying.

A couple of days later, I tried to describe it in an email to a friend: "Many people spontaneously cried, just releasing their tears like rain, and I realized that we are all human beings—that's the truth . . . in all our different forms and sizes, we are expressions of the same basic currents, just like the clouds." And when I read the email back, I was mortified by how fluffy and stoned it sounded, but still—even now—I can't pretend it's not true.

Neanderthals Were People, Too

| 2017 |

Joachim Neander was a seventeenth-century Calvinist theologian who often hiked through a valley outside Düsseldorf, Germany, writing hymns. Neander understood everything around him as a manifestation of the Lord's will and work. There was no room in his worldview for randomness, only purpose and praise. "See how God this rolling globe / swathes with beauty as a robe," one of his verses goes. "Forests, fields, and living things / each its Master's glory sings." He wrote dozens of hymns like this— awestruck and simplistic. Then he caught tuberculosis and died at age thirty.

Almost two centuries later, in the summer of 1856, workers quarrying limestone in that valley dug up an unusual skull. It was elongated and almost chinless, and the fossilized bones found alongside it were extra thick and fit together oddly. This was three years before Darwin published *The Origin of Species*. The science of human origins was not a science; the assumption was that our ancestors had always looked like us, all the way back to Adam. (Even distinguishing fossils from ordinary rock was beyond the grasp of many scientists. One popular method involved licking them; if the material had animal matter in it, it was supposed to stick to your tongue.) And so, as anomalous as these German bones seemed, most scholars had no trouble finding satisfying explanations. A leading theory held that this was the skeleton of a lost, bowlegged Cossack with rickets. The peculiar bony ridge over the man's eyes was a result of the poor Cossack perpetually furrowing his brow in pain—because of the rickets.

But one British geologist, William King, suspected something more radical. Instead of being the remains of an atypical human, they might have belonged to a typical member of an alternate humanity. In 1864, he published a paper introducing it as such—an extinct human species, the first ever discovered. King named this species after the valley where it was found, which itself had been named for the ecstatic poet who'd once wandered it. He called it *Homo neanderthalensis:* Neanderthal Man.

Who was Neanderthal Man? King felt obligated to describe him. But with no established techniques for interpreting archaeological material like the skull, he fell back on racism and phrenology. He focused on the peculiarities of the Neanderthal's skull, including the "enormously projecting brow." No living humans had skeletal features remotely like these, but King was under the impression that the skulls of contemporary African and Australian aboriginals resembled the Neanderthals' more than "ordinary" white-people skulls. So, extrapolating from his low opinion of what he called these "savage" races, he explained that the Neanderthal's skull alone was proof of the creature's moral "darkness" and stupidity. "The thoughts and desires which once dwelt within it never soared beyond those of a brute," he wrote. Other scientists piled on. So did the popular press. We knew almost nothing about Neanderthals, but already we assumed they were ogres and losers.

The genesis of this idea, the historian Paige Madison notes, largely comes down to flukes of "timing and luck." Because, while King was working, another British scientist, George Busk, had the same suspicions about the Neander skull. He had received a comparable one, too, from the tiny British territory of Gibraltar. The Gibraltar skull was dug up long before the Neander Valley specimen surfaced, but local hobbyists simply labeled it "human skull" and forgot about it for the next sixteen years. Its brow ridge wasn't as prominent as the Neander skull's, and its features were less imposing; it was a woman's skull, it turns out. Busk dashed off a quick report but stopped short of naming the new creature. He hoped to study additional fossils and learn more. Privately, he considered calling it *Homo calpicus,* or Gibraltar Man.

So, what if Busk—"a conscientious naturalist too cautious to make premature claims," as Madison describes him—had beaten King to publication? Consider how different our first impressions of a Gibraltar Woman might have been from those of Neanderthal Man: what feelings of sympathy, or even kinship, this other skull might have stirred.

There is a worldview, the opposite of Joachim Neander's, that sees our planet as a product of only tumult and indifference. In such a world, it's possible for an entire species to be ground into extinction by forces beyond its control and then, 40,000 years later, be dug up and made to endure an additional century and a half of bad luck and abuse.

That's what happened to the Neanderthals. It's what we did to them. But recently, after we'd snickered over their skulls for so long, it stopped being clear who the boneheads were.

I'll start with a confession, an embarrassing but relevant one, because I would come to see our history with Neanderthals as continually distorted by an unfortunate tendency to believe in ideas that are, in reality, incorrect—and then to leverage that conviction into a feeling of superiority over other people. And in retrospect, I realize I demonstrated that same tendency myself at the beginning of this project. Because I don't want to come off as self-righteous, or as pointing fingers, here goes:

Before traveling to Gibraltar last summer, I had no idea what Gibraltar was. Or rather, I was *sure* I knew what Gibraltar was, but I was wrong. I thought it was just that famous Rock—an unpopulated hunk of free-floating geology, which, if I'm being honest, I recognized mostly from the Prudential logo: that limestone protuberance at the mouth of the Mediterranean, that elephantine white molar jutting into the sky. True, I was traveling to Gibraltar on short notice; when I cold-called the director of the Gibraltar Museum, Clive Finlayson, he told me the museum happened to be starting its annual excavation of a Neanderthal cave there the following week and invited me to join. Still, even a couple of days before I left, when a friend told me she faintly remembered spending an afternoon in Gibraltar once as a teenager, I gently mansplained to her that I was pretty sure she was mistaken: Gibraltar, I told her, wasn't somewhere you could just *go*. In my mind, I had privileged access. I pictured myself and Finlayson taking a special little boat.

In fact, Gibraltar is a peninsula connected to Spain. It's a lively British overseas territory, with thirty thousand citizens living in a city on its western side—a city with bakeries and clothing stores and tourists buying all the usual kitsch. Some unusual kitsch, too—like the laminated child's place mat I spotted that, in a typical tourist destination, might say something unexceptional like SOMEONE WHO LOVES ME WENT TO GIBRALTAR, but here read WE SHALL NEVER SURRENDER! BRITISH FOREVER!

The history of Gibraltar, given its strategic location, is a grinding saga of military sieges and ruthlessly contested changes in ownership. The residue of that strife, today, is a pronounced British patriotism and a never-ending exchange of slights with Spain, which still disputes Britain's claim to the territory. After Queen Elizabeth II's Diamond Jubilee, in 2012, when Gibraltar projected towering images of Her Majesty on a Spain-facing side of the Rock—"a clear act of provocation," one reporter called it—Spain began inspecting vehicle after vehicle at the border, backing up the line for hours, stranding the bulk of Gibraltar's workforce, who commute in every day. The afternoon I showed up, activists from a far-right Spanish political party had crossed into Gibraltar and hung an enormous Spanish flag high up on the Rock. This wasn't just mischief. It was regarded as an act of symbolic terrorism. When one of the men appeared in court two days later, a woman screamed at him, "Gibraltar will never be Spanish!" She sounded like that defiant place mat come to life.

I happened to arrive in Gibraltar the week of the Brexit vote. Up in England, people were thundering about the working class versus elites, sovereignty, and immigration, warning that British identity was being fouled by the European project. But in Gibraltar—a far-flung, fully detached nib of Britain, flanked by water on two sides and Spain on the third—the question was less philosophical: If the United Kingdom left the European Union, Spain might seize the opportunity to isolate Gibraltar, leaving the territory to shrivel up, like a flap of dead skin. The Gibraltarian government had already called on the House of Commons for help. There was concern that Spain would jam up the border again, that it might happen right away.

Around town, REMAIN signs hung everywhere. The atmosphere was edgy, as though everyone was holding hands, waiting to see whether a meteor would hit. It was as though the hairline cracks between so many self-designated Us-es and Thems seemed to be widening, and some corrosive, molten goop was seeping out: mutual dependence curdled with contempt. Clearly it was happening back home in America, too.

All in all, it was a good week to spend in a cave.

Gorham's Cave is on Gibraltar's rough-hewed eastern coast: a tremendous opening at the bottom of the sheer face of the Rock, shadowy and hallowed-seeming, like a cathedral. Its mouth is 200 feet across at the base and 120 feet tall. It tapers asymmetrically like a crumpled wizard's hat.

Neanderthals inhabited Gorham's Cave on and off for 100,000 years, as well as a second cave next to it, called Vanguard Cave. The artifacts they left behind were buried as wind pushed sand into the cave. This created a high sloping dune, composed of hundreds of distinct layers of sand, each of which was once the surface of the dune, the floor of the cave. The dune is by now enormous. It reaches about two-thirds of the way up Gorham's walls, spilling out of the cave's mouth and onto the rocky beach, like a colossal cat's tongue lapping at the Mediterranean. Every summer since 1989, a team of archaeologists has returned to meticulously clear that sand away and recover the material inside. "I realized a long time ago, I won't live to see the end of this project," Finlayson, who leads the excavation, told me. "But I think we're in a great moment. We're beginning to understand these people after a century of putting them down as apelike brutes."

Neanderthals are people, too—a separate, shorn-off branch of our family tree. We last shared an ancestor at some point between 500,000 and 750,000 years ago. Then our evolutionary trajectory split. We evolved in Africa, while the Neanderthals would live in Europe and Asia for 300,000 years. Or as little as

60,000 years. It depends whom you ask. It always does: The study of human origins, I found, is riddled with vehement disagreements and scientists who systematically dismantle the premises of even the most straightforward-seeming questions. (In this case, the uncertainty rests, in part, on when, in this long evolutionary process, Neanderthals officially became "Neanderthals.") What is clearer is that roughly 40,000 years ago, just as our own lineage expanded from Africa into Eurasia, the Neanderthals disappeared. Scientists have always assumed that the timing wasn't coincidental. Maybe we used our superior intellects to outcompete the Neanderthals for resources; maybe we clubbed them all to death. Whatever the mechanism of this so-called replacement, it seemed to imply that our kind was somehow better than their kind. We're still here, after all, and their path ended as soon as we crossed paths.

But Neanderthals weren't the slow-witted louts we've imagined them to be—not just a bunch of Neanderthals. As a review of findings published last year put it, they were actually "very similar" to their contemporary *Homo sapiens* in Africa, in terms of "standard markers of modern cognitive and behavioral capacities." We've always classified Neanderthals, technically, as human—part of the genus *Homo*. But it turns out they also did the stuff that, you know, makes us human.

Neanderthals buried their dead. They made jewelry and specialized tools. They made ocher and other pigments, perhaps to paint their faces or bodies—evidence of a "symbolically mediated worldview," as archaeologists call it. Their tracheal anatomy suggests that they were capable of language and probably had high-pitched, raspy voices, like Julia Child. They manufactured glue from birch bark, which required heating the bark to at least 644 degrees Fahrenheit—a feat scientists find difficult to duplicate without a ceramic container. In Gibraltar, there's evidence that Neanderthals extracted the feathers of certain birds—only dark feathers—possibly for aesthetic or ceremonial purposes. And while Neanderthals were once presumed to be crude scavengers, we now know they exploited the different terrains on which they lived. They took down dangerous game, including an extinct species of rhinoceros. Some ate seals and other marine mammals. Some ate shellfish. Some ate chamomile. (They had regional cuisines.) They used toothpicks.

Wearing feathers, eating seals—maybe none of this sounds particularly impressive. But it's what our human ancestors were capable of back then, too, and scientists have always considered such behavioral flexibility and complexity as signs of our specialness. When it came to Neanderthals, though, many researchers literally couldn't see the evidence sitting in front of them. A lot of the new thinking about Neanderthals comes from revisiting material in museum collections, excavated decades ago, and reexamining it with new technology or simply with open minds. The real surprise of these discoveries may not be the competence of Neanderthals but how obnoxiously low our expectations for them have been—the bias with which too many scientists approached that other Us. One archaeologist called these researchers "modern human supremacists."

Inside Gorham's Cave, archaeologists were excavating what they called a hearth—not a physical fireplace but a spot in the sand where, around 50,000 years ago, Neanderthals lit a fire. Each summer, the Gibraltar Museum employs students from universities in England and Spain to work the dig, and now two young women—one from each country—sat cross-legged under work lights, clearing sand away with the edge of a trowel and a brush to leave a freestanding cube. A black band of charcoal ran through it.

The students worked scrupulously, watching for small animal bones or artifacts. They'd pulled out a butchered ibex mandible, a number of mollusk shells, and pine-nut husks. They'd also found six chunks of fossilized hyena dung, as well as "*débitage*," distinctive shards of flint left over when Neanderthals shattered larger pieces to make axes.

The cube of sand would eventually be wrapped in plaster and sent for analysis. The sand the two women were sweeping into their dustpans was transferred into plastic bags and marched out of the cave, down to the beach, where other students sieved it. Smaller bones caught in the sieve were bagged and labeled. Even the sand that passed through the sieve was saved and driven back to a lab at the museum, where I would later find three other students picking through it with magnifying glasses and tweezers, searching for even tinier stuff—rodent teeth, sea-urchin spines—while listening to "Call Me Maybe."

To an outsider, it looked preposterous. The archaeologists were cataloging and storing absolutely everything, treating this physical material as though it were digital information—JPEGs of itself. And yet they couldn't afford not to: Everything a Neanderthal came into contact with was a valuable clue. (In twenty-eight years of excavations here, archaeologists have yet to find a fossil of an actual Neanderthal.) "This is like putting together a five-thousand-piece jigsaw puzzle where you only have five pieces," Finlayson said. He somehow made this analogy sound exciting instead of hopeless.

By that point, the enormousness of what they didn't know—what they could never know—had become a big distraction for me. One of the dig's lead archaeologists, Richard Jennings of

Liverpool John Moores University, listed the many items they had found around that hearth. "And this is literally just from two squares!" he said. (A "square," in archaeology, is one meter by one meter; sites are divided into grids of squares.) Then Jennings waved wordlessly at the rest of the sand-filled cave. *Look at the big picture*, he was saying; *imagine what else we'll find!* There was also Vanguard Cave next door, an even more promising site, because while Gorham's had been partly excavated by less meticulous scientists in the 1940s and '50s, Finlayson's team was the first to touch Vanguard. Already they had uncovered a layer of perfectly preserved mud there. ("We suspect, if there's a place where you're going to find the first Neanderthal footprint, it will be here," Finlayson said.) The "resolution" of the caves was incredible; the wind blew sand in so fast that it preserved short periods, faithfully, like entries in a diary. Finlayson has described it as "the longest and most detailed record of [Neanderthals'] way of life that is currently available."

This was the good news. And yet there were more than twenty other nearby caves that the Gibraltar Neanderthals might have used, and they all were now underwater, behind us. When sea levels rose around 20,000 years ago, the Mediterranean drowned them. It also drowned the wooded savanna between Gorham's and the former coastline—where, presumably, the Neanderthals had spent an even larger share of their time and left even more artifacts.

So yes, Jennings was right: There was a lot of cave left to dig through. But it was like looking for needles in a haystack, and the entire haystack was merely the one needle they had managed to find in an astronomically larger haystack. And most of the rest of *that* haystack was now inaccessible forever. I could tell it wasn't productive to dwell on the problem at this scale, while picking pine-nut husks from the hearth, but there it was.

"Look, you can almost see what's happening," Finlayson eventually said. "The fire and the charcoal, the embers scattering." It was true. If you followed that stratum of sand away from the hearth, you could see, embedded in the wall behind us, black flecks where the smoke and cinders from this fire had blown. Suddenly, it struck me—though it should have earlier—that what we were looking at were the remnants of a single event: a specific fire, on a specific night, made by specific Neanderthals. Maybe this won't sound that profound, but it snapped that prehistoric abstraction into focus. This wasn't just a "hearth," I realized; it was a campfire.

Finlayson began narrating the scene for me. One evening, a few Neanderthals cooked the ibex they had hunted and the mussels and nuts they had foraged and then, after dinner, made some tools around the fire. After they went to sleep and the fire died out, a hyena slinked in to scavenge scraps from the ashes and took a poop. Then—perhaps that same night—the wind picked up and covered everything with the fine layer of sand that these students were now brushing away.

While we stood talking, one of the women uncovered a small flint ax, called a Levallois flake. After 50,000 years, the edge was still sharp. They let me touch it.

One of the earliest authorities on Neanderthals was a Frenchman named Marcellin Boule. A lot of what he said was wrong.

In 1911, Boule began publishing his analysis of the first nearly complete Neanderthal skeleton ever discovered, which he named Old Man of La Chapelle, after the limestone cave where it was found. Laboring to reconstruct the Old Man's anatomy, he deduced that its head must have been slouched forward, its spine hunched, and its toes spread like an ape's. Then, having reassembled the Neanderthal this way, Boule insulted it. This "brutish" and "clumsy" posture, he wrote, clearly indicated a lack of morals and a lifestyle dominated by "functions of a purely vegetative or bestial kind." A colleague of Boule's went further, claiming that Neanderthals usually walked on all fours and never laughed: "Man-ape had no smile." Boule was part of a movement trying to reconcile natural selection with religion; by portraying Neanderthals as closer to animals than to us, he could protect the ideal of a separate, immaculate human lineage. When he consulted with an artist to make a rendering of the Neanderthal, it came out looking like a furry, mean gorilla.

Neanderthal fossils kept surfacing in Europe, and scholars like Boule were scrambling to make sense of them, improvising what would later grow into a new interdisciplinary field, now known as paleoanthropology. The evolution of that science was haphazard and often comically unscientific. An exhaustive history by Erik Trinkaus and Pat Shipman describes how Neanderthals became "mirrors that reflected, in all their awfulness and awesomeness, the nature and humanity of those who touched them." That included a lot of human blundering. It became clear only in 1957, for example—forty-six years after Boule, and after several re-examinations of the Old Man's skeleton—that Boule's particular Neanderthal, which led him to imagine all Neanderthals as stooped-over oafs, merely happened to have several deforming injuries and severe osteoarthritis.

Still, Boule's influence was long-lasting. Over the years, his ideologically tainted image of Neanderthals was often refracted through the lens of other ideologies, frequently racist ones. In 1930, the prominent British anthropologist Sir Arthur Keith, writing in *The New York Times*, channeled Boule's work to justify colonialism. For Keith, the replacement of an ancient, inferior species like Neanderthals by newer, hardier *Homo sapiens*

proved that Britain's actions in Australia—"The white man . . .
replacing the most ancient type of brown man known to us"—
was part of a natural order that had been operating for millennia.

It's easy to get snooty about all this unenlightened paleoanthropology of the past. But all sciences operate by trying to fit
new data into existing theories. And this particular science, for
which the "data" has always consisted of scant and somewhat
inscrutable bits of rock and fossil, often has to lean on those
meta-narratives even more heavily. "Assumptions, theories, expectations," the University of Barcelona archaeologist João Zilhão says, "all must come into play a lot, because you are
interpreting data that do not speak for themselves."

Imagine, for example, working in a cave without any skulls or
other easily distinguishable fossils and trying to figure out if you're
looking at a Neanderthal settlement or a more recent, modern
human one. In the past, scientists might turn to the surrounding
artifacts, interpreting more primitive-looking tools as evidence
of Neanderthals and more advanced-looking tools as evidence
of early modern humans. But working that way, it's easy to miss
evidence of Neanderthals' similarities and intellectual equiva-
lence with us—because, as soon as you see that evidence, you assume they *were* us instead of them. So many techniques similarly
hinge on interpretation and judgment, even perfectly empirical-
sounding ones, like "morphometric analysis"—identifying fossils
as belonging to one species rather than another by comparing particular parts of their anatomy—and radiocarbon dating.
How the material to be dated is sampled and how results are
calibrated are susceptible to drastic revision and bitter disagree-
ment. (What's more, because of an infuriating quirk of physics,
the effectiveness of radiocarbon dating happens to break down
around 40,000 years ago—right around the time of the Neanderthal extinction. One of our best tools for looking into the past

becomes unreliable at exactly the moment we're most interested in examining.)

Ultimately, a bottomless relativism can creep in: tenuous interpretations held up by webs of other interpretations, each strung from still more interpretations. Almost every archaeologist I interviewed complained that the field has become "overinterpreted"—that the ratio of physical evidence to speculation about that evidence is out of whack. Good stories can generate their own momentum.

Starting in the 1920s, older and more exciting hominid fossils, like *Homo erectus,* began surfacing in Africa and Asia, and the field soon shifted its focus there. The Washington University anthropologist Erik Trinkaus, who began his career in the early 1970s, told me, "When I started working on Neanderthals, nobody really cared about them." The liveliest question about Neanderthals was still the first one: Were they our direct ancestors or the endpoint of a separate evolutionary track? Scientists called this question "the Neanderthal Problem." Some of the theories worked up to answer it encouraged different visions of Neanderthal intelligence and behavior. The "Multiregional Model," for example, which had us descending from Neanderthals, was more inclined to see them as capable, sympathetic, and fundamentally human; the opposing "Out of Africa" hypothesis, which held that we moved in and replaced them, cast them as comparatively inferior.

For decades, when evidence of a more advanced Neanderthal way of life turned up, it was often explained away, or mobbed by enough contrary or undermining interpretations that, over time, it never found real purchase. Some findings broke through more than others, however, like the discovery of what was essentially a small Neanderthal cemetery, in Shanidar Cave, in what is now Iraqi Kurdistan. There had been many compelling instances of Neanderthals' burying their dead, but Shanidar was harder to ignore, especially after soil samples revealed the presence of huge amounts of pollen. This was interpreted as the remains of a funerary floral arrangement. An archaeologist at the center of this work, Ralph Solecki, published a book called *Shanidar: The First Flower People*. It was 1971—the Age of Aquarius. Those flowers, he'd go on to write, proved that Neanderthals "had 'soul.'"

Then again, Solecki's idea was eventually discredited. In 1999, a more thorough analysis of the Shanidar grave site found that Neanderthals almost certainly did not leave flowers there. The pollen had been tracked in, thousands of years later, by burrowing, gerbil-like rodents. (That said, there are still paleoanthropologists at work on this question even a half century later. It might not have been gerbils; it may have been bees.)

But as more supposed anomalies surfaced, they became harder to brush off. In 1996, the paleoanthropologist Jean-Jacques Hublin and others used CT scanning technology to re-examine a bone fragment found in a French cave decades earlier, alongside a raft of advanced tools and artifacts associated with the so-called Châtelperronian industry, which archaeologists always presumed was the work of early modern humans. Now Hublin's analysis identified the bone as belonging to a Neanderthal. But rather than re-ascribe the Châtelperronian industry to Neanderthals, Hublin chalked up his findings to "acculturation": Surely the Neanderthals must have learned how to make this stuff by watching us.

"To me," says Zilhão, the University of Barcelona archaeologist, "there was a logical shock: If the paradigm forces you to say something like this, there must be something wrong with the paradigm." Zilhão published a stinging critique challenging the field to shake off its "anti-Neanderthal prejudice." Papers were fired back and forth, igniting what Zilhão calls "a twenty-year war" and counting. Then, in the middle of that war, geneticists shook up the paradigm completely.

A group at the Max Planck Institute for Evolutionary Anthropology in Leipzig, Germany, led by Svante Pääbo, had been assembling a draft sequence of a Neanderthal genome, using DNA recovered from bones. Their findings were published in 2010. It had already become clear by then that *Homo sapiens* and Neanderthals appeared in Eurasia separately—"Out of Africa was essentially right"—but Pääbo's work revealed that before the Neanderthals disappeared, the two groups mated. Even today, 40,000 years after our gene pools stopped mixing, most living humans still carry Neanderthal DNA, making up roughly 1 to 2 percent of our total genomes. The data shows that we also apparently bred with other hominids, like the Denisovans, about which very little is known.

It was staggering; even Pääbo couldn't bring himself to believe it at first. But the results were the results, and they carried a sort of empirical magnetism that archaeological evidence lacks. "Geneticists are much more powerful, numerous, and incomparably better funded than anyone else dealing with this stuff," Zilhão said. He joked: "Their aura is kind of miraculous. It's a bit like receiving the Ten Commandments from God." Pääbo's work, and a continuing wave of genomic research, has provided clarity but also complexity, recasting our oppositional, zero-sum relationship into something more communal and collaborative—and perhaps not just on the genetic level. The extent of the interbreeding supported previous speculation, by a minority of paleoanthropologists, that there might have been cases of Neanderthals and modern humans living alongside each other, intermeshed, for centuries, and that generations of their offspring had found places in those communities, too. Then again, it's also possible that some of the interbreeding was rape.

Pääbo now recommends against imagining separate species of human evolution altogether: not an Us and a Them, but one enormous "metapopulation"—shifting clusters of essentially human-ish things that periodically coincided in time and space. When they happened to bump into one another, they occasionally had sex.

Lunch happened at the mouth of Gorham's Cave, out in the sun. I ate a sandwich on a log, facing the sea, alongside Jennings and a few of his Liverpool students, while the young men and women from Spain mingled behind us, laughing and stretching and helping one another crack their backs. The language barrier seemed to discourage the two cohorts from talking much. And yet the students shared living quarters during the excavation and had somehow achieved a muffled camaraderie.

Jennings and his counterpart, José María Gutiérrez López, a veteran archaeologist from a museum in Cádiz, had a similar dynamic, despite working closely together for many summers at Gorham's. Neither was terribly fluent in the other's language, but their silence, by this point, seemed warm and knowing. Waiting for our ride at the end of one workday, I noticed them staring at a plastic bag snagged in the concertina wire above an old military gate. The bag had been there for a long, long time, Jennings told me. Then he turned and uttered, *"Cinco años?"* Gutiérrez López smiled. *"Sí,"* he said, nodding.

I, meanwhile, felt compelled to test out all of this as a model for human-Neanderthal relations. That contact obsessed me: What would it have been like to look out over a grassy plain and watch parallel humanity pass by? Scientists often turn to historical first contacts as frames of reference, like the arrival of Europeans among Native Americans, or Captain Cook landing in Australia—largely histories of violence and subjugation. But as Zilhão points out, typically one of those two cultures set out to conquer the other. "Those people were conscious that they'd come from somewhere else," he told me. "They were a product of a civilization that had books, that had studied their past."

Homo sapiens encountering Neanderthals would have been different: They met uncoupled from politics and history; neither identified as part of a network of millions of supposedly more advanced people. And so, as Finlayson put it to me: "Each valley could have told a different story. In one, they may have hit each other over the head. In another, they may have made love. In another, they ignored each other."

It's a kind of coexistence that our modern imaginations may no longer be sensitive enough to envision. So much of our identity as a species is tied up in our anomalousness, in our dominion over others. But that narcissistic self-image is a recent privilege. ("Outside the world of Tolkienesque fantasy literature, we tend to think that it is normal for there to be just one human species on Earth at a time," the writers Dimitra Papagianni and Michael A. Morse explain. "The past 20 or 30 millennia, however, have been the exception.") Now, eating lunch alongside the two parallel, incommunicative clusters of archaeology students, I considered that the co-occurrence of humans and Neanderthals hadn't been so trippy or profound after all. Maybe it looked as mundane as this: Two groups, lingering on a beach, only sort of acknowledging each other. Maybe the many millennia during which we shared Eurasia was like a super-long elevator ride with strangers.

Some paleoanthropologists are starting to reimagine the extinction of Neanderthals as equally prosaic: not the culmination of some epic clash of civilizations but an aggregate result of a long, ecological muddle. Strictly speaking, extinction is what happens after a species fails to maintain a higher proportion of births to deaths—it's a numbers game. And so the real competition between Neanderthals and early modern humans wasn't localized quarrels for food or territory but a quiet, millennia-long demographic marathon: each species repopulating itself, until one fell so far behind that it vanished. And we had a big head start. "When modern humans came," notes Chris Stringer, a paleoanthropologist at Britain's Natural History Museum, "there just weren't that many Neanderthals around."

For millennia, before modern humans poured in from Africa, the climate in Europe seems to have been exceptionally unstable. The landscape kept flipping between temperate forest and cold, treeless steppe. The fauna that Neanderthals subsisted on kept migrating away, faster than they could. Though Neanderthals survived this turbulence, they were never able to build up their numbers. (Across all of Eurasia, at any point in history, says John Hawks, an anthropologist at the University of Wisconsin–Madison, "there probably weren't enough of them to fill an NFL stadium.") With the demographics so skewed, Stringer went on, even the slightest modern human advantage would be amplified tremendously: A single innovation, something like sewing needles, might protect just enough babies from the elements to lower the infant mortality rate and allow modern humans to conclusively overtake the Neanderthals. And yet Stringer is careful not to conflate innovation with superior intelligence. Innovation, too, can be a function of population size. "We live in an age where information, where good ideas, spread like wildfire, and we build on them," Stringer told me. "But it wasn't like that fifty thousand years ago." The more members your species has, the more likely one member will stumble on a useful new technology—and that, once stumbled upon, the innovation will spread; you need sufficient human tinder for those random sparks of culture to catch.

"There was nothing inevitable about modern human success," Stringer says. "It was luck." We didn't defeat the Neanderthals; we just swamped them. Trinkaus compares it to how European wildcats are currently disappearing, absorbed into much larger populations of house cats gone feral. It wasn't a flattering analogy—we are the house cats—but that was Trinkaus's point: "I think a lot of this is basically banal," he said.

Showing me around the Gibraltar Museum one morning, Finlayson described the petering out of Neanderthals on the Rock with unnerving pathos. Gibraltar, with its comparatively stable climate, would have been one of their last refuges, he explained, and he likened the population there to critically endangered species today, like snow leopards or imperiled butterflies: living relics carrying on in small, fragmented populations long after they've passed a genetic point of no return. "They became a ghost species," Finlayson said.

We happened to be standing in front of two Neanderthals, exquisitely lifelike sculptures the museum unveiled last spring, on a sweep of sand in their own austere gallery. They were scientific reconstructions, extrapolated by artists from casts of actual fossils. (These two were based on the only Neanderthal skulls ever recovered in Gibraltar: that first woman's skull, sent to George Busk in 1864, and another, of a child, unearthed in 1926.) They were called Nana and Flint. Finlayson's wife, Geraldine, and son, Stewart—both scientists who work closely with him at the museum—had helped him come up with the names.

The boy had his arms thrown around Nana's waist, his cheek on her thigh. He was half-hiding himself behind her leg, as kids do, but also stared out, straight at us, slightly alarmed, or helpless. "I don't get tired of looking at them," Finlayson said.

He had commissioned the Neanderthals from Dutch artists known as Kennis & Kennis, and he was initially taken aback by the woman's posture in their sketches. She stood oddly, with her arms crossed in front of her chest, resting on opposite shoulders, as if she were mid-Macarena. But Kennis & Kennis barraged Finlayson with ethnographic photos: real hunter-gatherer people standing just like this, or even more strangely, their hands behind their necks or slung over their heads. As it happens, the artists had an intense personal interest in where human beings leave their hands when they don't have pockets.

I'd never thought about this before—I've always had pockets—and I wondered if artists might expose these perceptual bubbles more pointedly than archaeologists. Kennis & Kennis appeared to be major players in the tiny field of Paleolithic reconstruction. Scientists who had worked with them encouraged me to seek them out. "They're great people," one archaeologist told me. "Hyperactive. Like rubber balls."

The Kennis brothers, Adrie and Alfons, are each fifty years old: identical twins. They are sturdy, attractive men, with dark, wildly swirling hair, and live in the small Dutch city of Arnhem, southeast of Amsterdam. When I arrived at Adrie's house last summer, I found Alfons at the end of the driveway, glasses sliding down his nose, carefully filling a crack in the robin's-egg-blue butt cheek of a silicon Neanderthal mold.

Kennis & Kennis had gradually co-opted Adrie's house as a second studio. Most of their work and materials were here: full-scale headless bodies of various human species and a wall of shelves filled with skulls and heads. The heads were frighteningly realistic, with glass eyes and fleshy faces that begged to be touched. When the brothers fly around Europe to pitch their work to museums, they take these heads with them, like salesmen's samples. "On the airplane! We have heads!" Adrie shouted. "They scan things!" Alfons shouted. And slowly I understood: The brothers thought it was hilarious that airport security never questioned them about their duffel bags full of heads. "I never have to open my bags!" Adrie said, then he scampered to the wall, where a particular head had caught his eye: very dark-skinned, with a rough, bushy beard and rawness in its upper lip—a reconstruction of a primitive *Homo sapiens* skull found in Morocco. Adrie held the head in his palm and hollered, "Bowling!" while pretending to bowl with it. Then he laughed and laughed and laughed.

That was how it went for the rest of the day. The twins spoke in a bifurcated riot, seldom finishing sentences, just skipping ahead once they had spit out the key words. And if a thought escaped them or their English faltered, they didn't go silent; instead, they repeated the last word, or made a strange guttural drone, as if thrusting some heavy weight over their heads, to fill the space until they could go on.

Their first big commission came in 2006, for the Neanderthal Museum, on the site of Neander Valley. That sculpture emerged as a jovial, half-smirking old man, with woefulness, or maybe just exhaustion, behind his eyes. That jolt of Neanderthal individuality has been a trademark of their work ever since. It elevates Neanderthals out of a single homogeneous abstraction and endows them with personhood. (At one point, Adrie described watching a neighbor spend an entire day pressure-washing each brick of his driveway. He had an epiphany: "All the types of people around us, there must have been Neanderthals just like them." Alfons added: "Neanderthal neat freaks! Neanderthal Bill Gates!") What the brothers want, they told me, is for the viewer to catch herself relating to the Neanderthal—to recognize, in a visceral way, that Neanderthals sit at the fragile edge of our own identities. To feel *that*, Adrie explained, "they need to look you in the eye."

They were obsessed—the only word for it—and have been since age seven, when Alfons found a picture of a Neanderthal skeleton in a book, and it had instantly possessed them both. They spent a lot of time at their parents' restaurant, after school and on weekends: With nothing to do, they started drawing Neanderthals. They drew feverishly, combatively, each brother keenly aware of whose illustration of a rib cage looked brawnier, who had rendered more beautiful shadows on his Neanderthal's upper lip. "We were both the dumbest guys in the whole school!" Alfons said. "We couldn't count!" Drawing was all they knew how to do. As young men, they tried to teach art but couldn't find steady employment. Their family told them to give up their crazy preoccupation. They wouldn't. They made art at night and took custodial jobs at a psychiatric hospital. They organized the Christmas talent show and played Ping-Pong with the residents.

Initially they were painters, not sculptors. They made three-dimensional reconstructions only to have lifelike models to paint: They were *that* meticulous, *that* fixated on knowing how the musculature of a Neanderthal hung off its skeleton. Because they had to produce a three-dimensional individual, the brothers were forced to make decisions about what paleoanthropologists had the luxury of glossing over as spectrums of variation. Geneticists can suggest a probable scope of skin and hair colors for the species. But the brothers must imagine the wear on a particular Neanderthal's skin after a hard life outside, or the abuse his toenails would take. And would Neanderthals wear ponytails? Would they shear their bangs away, to get their hair out of their faces? "Every culture does something with their hair!" Alfons insisted. "There's no culture that does nothing with their hair."

This uncorked a frantic seminar on known global hairstyles of the last several thousand years. They began pulling up photos on Adrie's laptop, dozens of them, from anthropological archives or stills from old ethnographic films. These were some of the same photos they had shown Finlayson. The brothers had pored over them for years but still gasped or bellowed now as each new, improbable human form appeared on the screen. The pictures showed a panorama of divergent body types and grooming: spiky eyebrows; astonishingly asymmetrical breasts; a towering aboriginal man with the chiseled torso of an American underwear model, but two twigs for legs; a Khoisan woman with an extremely convex rear end. "People would never let us make buttocks like this!" Alfons said regretfully—to a typical, white European, it would probably look exaggerated and unreal. "But all this variation! It's beautiful!" shouted Adrie, refusing to look away from the screen. He *had* to look: These were reaches of reality that people's minds didn't travel to on their own. "If you live in the West, you'd never imagine," he went on. The brothers' delight seemed to come from feeling all these superficial differences quiver against a profound, self-evident sameness. Finally, Adrie turned to me and said very seriously, "These are all *Homo sapiens.*"

They showed me more photos. "It's real, it's real, it's real!" Alfons kept shouting. Adrie said, "Unimaginable, unimaginable, unimaginable!" It only registered later: I had spent the day with identical twins who, since childhood, have been stupefied by how different human beings can be.

At the rear of Gorham's Cave, past the hearth the team was excavating, there was a tall metal staircase. It led up to a long catwalk, which led to a locked steel gate. I waited there one morning while Finlayson fumbled around in his pocket. Then he turned his key.

The excavation had worked through this narrowed rear chamber of the cave years earlier and discovered, at the end of the 2012 season, an engraving on the floor: a crosshatched pattern of thirteen grooves in the bedrock. A tide of specialists flowed into Gorham's. They determined that the engraving was made at least 39,000 years ago and ruled out its having been created inadvertently—left over after skinning an animal, say. In controlled experiments, it took between 188 and 317 strokes with a flint tool to create the entire figure. "What we've always said," Finlayson explained, "is it's intentional and it's not functional. You can call that art, if you like."

The finding was published in *The Proceedings of the National Academy of Sciences* in 2014. The news media called the engraving "the hashtag." One scientist described the elaborate crosshatch as watershed evidence of Neanderthals' capacity for "complex symbolic thought" and "abstract expression." But several archaeologists told me they believe that there are many clearer signs of Neanderthals' capacity for complex cognition and symbolism, including a discovery in Southern France last year that seemed to dwarf the hashtag's significance. (More than a thousand feet into the Bruniquel Cave, Neanderthals assembled two rings of 400 deliberately broken stalagmites, with other material piled and propped around it—like a labyrinth, or a shrine.) But Finlayson was undaunted. He turned the hashtag into a logo for the Neanderthal-centric rebranding of his museum. There was a hashtag decal on the van he picked me up in every morning.

We stood and talked for a while until, finally, with great aplomb, Finlayson lifted a tarp and showed it to me. It didn't make a tremendous impact on me at first—it was lines in rock. But Finlayson went on, pointing to a spot near the entrance to this isolated anteroom, a few feet across from the engraving, where the team had excavated another hearth. Neanderthals built fires in that exact spot, on and off, for eight thousand years, he said—until their disappearance from Gibraltar. But few animal bones were recovered here; it wasn't a place they cooked. And the location of the fire was also puzzling: Neanderthals usually situated fires at the fronts of caves, to control smoke. And yet, Finlayson explained, "if you look up, this has a natural chimney." We flung our heads back: A chute coursed through the high, craggy ceiling above us.

It seemed the Neanderthals did their butchering and cooking at the front of Gorham's, Finlayson explained, then retired here at night. Lighting a fire at this hearth would block the narrowest point in the cave, sealing off this chamber from predators. You could hang out here, he told me, "have a late-night snack or something," then head to bed. "See there?" he said, motioning to a smaller opening to our right. It led to a second room, similar to this one. "This," Finlayson said, "is the bedroom."

I looked again at the hashtag. It wasn't on the cave floor, exactly, as it was usually described, but on a broad ledge, a foot or two off the ground. It made for a perfect bench, and it was suddenly easy to imagine a Neanderthal sitting on it, in ideal proximity to the fire. For all I knew, a Neanderthal had carved the hashtag to mark his or her favorite seat.

But Finlayson wasn't done. After the Neanderthal artifacts disappear from Gorham's sediment layers, there's a gap of many

thousand years—a thick stack of empty sand. Then other artifacts appear: Modern humans occupied the cave and built a fire
here, too, just a couple of feet from the Neanderthals' hearth.
They used the bedroom annex as well. They left a cave painting
on the wall in there: a gorgeous red stag, indisputably recogniz-
able to us—their descendants—as art.

Another 18,000 years passed, give or take. The Phoenicians
came. And they left offerings back here; there were shards of
their ceramics under the catwalk we had just crossed. Then
2,000 years after that, in 1907, a certain Captain A. Gorham of
Britain's 2nd Battalion Royal Munster Fusiliers arrived. Gorham
didn't discover Gorham's Cave, Finlayson told me; it had always
been impossible to miss. "*That's* what he found," Finlayson said.
"*That's* really Gorham's Cave." He pointed to the bedroom, and
we both turned, bathing it with our headlamps. Beside the entrance was written, in big block letters, GORHAM'S CAVE 1907,
with a chunky black arrow pointing to the doorway. Gorham had
written his name directly over the spot where, some 39,000 years
earlier, a Neanderthal had carved his or her own mark.

The full sweep and synchronicity of this history hadn't seemed
to occur to Finlayson before. Hesitantly, he said, "Maybe there
are special places in the world that have universal human appeal." I felt a similar, uncanny rush when I noticed that, at some
point while he talked, we had each instinctually taken a seat on
the rock ledge, next to the hashtag, and were now sitting side by
side, staring into space where the two ancient campfires once
burned.

It's not an especially spiritual experience when one human
being walks into another human being's kitchen for the first
time and correctly intuits where the silverware drawer is. At the
back of Gorham's, though, that same intuition was spread across
two distinct kinds of humans and tens of thousands of years.

Ultimately, why we are here and the Neanderthals are not can no longer be explained in a way that implies that our existence is particularly meaningful or secure. But at least moments like this placed our existence inside some longer, less-conditional-seeming continuity.

It was the day of the Brexit vote. After re-emerging from the cave with Finlayson, I would spend the rest of the afternoon re-jiggering my travel plans in a mild panic, trying to catch a ride out of Gibraltar and into Spain that night, so that if the Spanish exacted a retaliatory border-clogging after the results were announced, I could still make my flight home from Málaga the next day. I won't describe the scenes I saw that morning at the airport—the blankness on people's faces, phone calls I overheard—except to say that when I woke up four months later, on November 9, 2016, after our own election, I felt equipped with at least a faint frame of reference. Reality seemed heightened and a little dangerous, because for so many people, including me, it had broken away from our expectations. We had misunderstood the present in the same way archaeologists can misunderstand the past. Our assumptions about what was possible were suddenly exposed as grossly insufficient, because, to borrow Finlayson's metaphor, we'd never imagined that the few jigsaw puzzle pieces we were basing them on constituted such a tiny part of the whole.

Even some on the winning side seemed similarly stunned and adrift. Many, though, just felt vindicated. Later, I came across an essay for a British weekly by the actress Elizabeth Hurley, a fervent Leave supporter, who was now doubling down. "Knock yourselves out calling us ill-educated Neanderthals," she wrote, "and spit a bit more venom and vitriol our way. You are showing yourselves in all your meanspirited, round-headed elitist glory."

When I read that, I took genuine umbrage—on the Neanderthals' behalf. And while I hate to admit it, I also felt a cheap but delicious tingle of smugness, because I now knew that "Neanderthal" wasn't the insult that Hurley thought it was—although, I simultaneously realized, looking down on her in this way also closed a certain self-reinforcing loop and promoted, in me, the very round-headed elitist glory that Hurley was incensed by, thus deepening the divide. It was dizzying and sad and maybe inevitably human, but still no help to us at all.

Take Me Out

By the time I pulled into Spokane, I was furious at myself for coming to Spokane.

I'd had a bad pandemic, though not nearly bad enough that I feel entitled to complain about it, and definitely not to complain about it publicly. In the most important ways, my family was fine: healthy, housed, employed, and buffered from the crisis by circumstance, privilege, and luck. Relatively speaking, we were exquisitely comfortable and safe—literally on an island, the semirural suburb of Seattle where we live. We had space. We had trees. Until recently, the case counts were low.

Even so, at the onset of the pandemic, my wife and I were both working, and our daughters were eleven and six. While there were many moments of laughter and togetherness, life in our household also felt precarious and strained. Beneath the warm, opioid glow of family movie night, there seemed to be the potential for some darker disorderliness and pain. And so, I gradually put my career into an induced coma to prioritize our kids.

It was a luxury that felt like a necessity. But it carried its own complications, too. As our family's collective hard time eased, I began having my own personal hard time. The details aren't important. Let's just say, I felt as if I were moldering in place. Time passed. Summer came. I was slow to experience any of the combustive euphoria of the reopening while it lasted: I didn't fly anywhere, didn't eat inside a restaurant, didn't see a movie, scarcely set foot in a city, seldom managed to leave my small town. Then Delta swept in, and gazing out, I felt people were being reckless, and I was primed to take their recklessness very personally, on behalf of my one still-unvaccinated child. But I couldn't judge what, on the sliding scale of prolonged disaster, counted as reckless anymore.

Here's what I think was happening: It hadn't been too painful, initially, to settle into a small, circumscribed life—going grocery shopping, volunteering at our local vaccine clinic, getting together with friends outside. But it meant I'd never been forced, or forced myself, to acclimate to the virus as much as other people seemed to have done. I wasn't learning to live within the odds. This made me uneasy—personally uneasy, because I interpreted it as a lack of toughness, but also ethically uneasy, because I knew that in a broken society like ours, my comfort came at the expense of other people's demoralization and discomfort. Still, that's what happened. And while I'm sure this left me with an exaggerated sense of the risks of leaving my particular bubble, the real problem was, I'd started chronically undervaluing the rewards. I'd been forgoing so much that forgoing felt easy. Too many things I imagined doing began to feel skippable, arbitrary, not a tragedy to decline. Either I was approaching some new state of equanimity and contentedness, or I was depressed.

Then, as if I'd won a sweepstakes, this magazine offered me the seemingly wide-open opportunity to fly somewhere for its travel issue. By then, I'd spent almost seventeen months parenting two demanding children on an insular island. I needed to get back to work. And so, I considered the befuddling risks, stresses, uncertainties, childcare complications, psychic agitations, and relative irresponsibility of traveling anywhere at all and asked, "What if I drove to Spokane?"

Spokane, Wash.: birthplace of Father's Day; hometown of Bing Crosby; a city with a sequence of wide, rocky waterfalls pouring through its center like a Cubist boulevard, cracking it in two.

I'd been genuinely curious about Spokane for years. Though I heard a lot of liberals around Seattle disparage the city, young people kept rediscovering the place, opening businesses there, moving in. I also knew that Spokane was a city with a history of minor-league baseball that stretched back more than a hundred years, and I unreservedly love going to baseball games. A minor-league game felt like a manageable, belated step into the mid-pandemic lifestyle that people were calling post-pandemic life. I would be in a crowd, but a smaller-scale crowd, buffeted by currents of fresh evening air.

The problem was, in the two weeks leading up to my trip in mid-August, the Delta variant swamped the city. Spokane County had 535 daily cases per 100,000 people, a full vaccination rate that had stalled out at 50 percent, and its highest rates of hospitalization since the pandemic began. Still, there were a handful of counties in Washington State doing far worse. At some point during my six-hour drive to the city, the governor reinstituted a statewide mask mandate for most indoor public spaces, though it wouldn't take effect until the following week. In Spokane, there were plans for a protest downtown.

I arrived around dinnertime and found the classy, cavernous

lobby of my hotel packed with maskless strangers drinking and eating, but also not even drinking or eating—just lingering, loping through, working on their laptops, working in the restaurant kitchen, bellowing plosive consonants at one another, cavalierly clearing their throats. I went to my room and ordered a hamburger. And when the knock came, I fumbled to mask up, opened the door, and discovered a young woman smiling at me at close range, her bare mouth saying, with complete casualness: "How's your evening going? Getting up to anything fun tonight?"

This was foreign to me. I was agog. And at that point, my consciousness started thrumming, haplessly recalibrating to an unfamiliar magnitude of risk—this place called Spokane. I worried about carrying the virus home to my unvaccinated daughter or my in-laws, understood those odds were still quite low and manageable, but also understood that even a mild case in my orbit would create anxiety and disruptions to my family's already tenuous daily routines and require uncomfortable conversations with friends, foisting the same stress and nuisances on them. School was about to start—fully in-person this year. I didn't want my kid stranded at home or a ballooning network of other eight-year-olds needing to be swabbed, just because somebody's idiot father let his guard down in Spokane. "Heard the dad's a writer," I imagined some understandably infuriated parent writing on our community Facebook page. "He got paid to write about his feelings at a baseball game lol."

The Hillsboro Hops were in town from Oregon for a six-game series against the Spokane Indians. The name "Indians" was first used for a baseball team in Spokane in 1903. But in 2006, the current team began seriously grappling with how to bear that name respectfully and whether it should continue to use it at all. The baseball Indians reached out to the Spokane Tribe of Indians, whose people have inhabited the area for at least nine thousand years. A unique partnership was forged. When, for example, tribal leaders shared the urgency they felt to preserve their dialect of Salish—at the time, there were roughly a dozen remaining fluent speakers—the baseball team put Salish translations on the signage around its stadium. Since 2014, it has also worn the Salish word *Sp'q'n'i* (Spokane) across the chests of its jerseys. (The jerseys are auctioned off at the end of the season, and the team donates the proceeds to the tribe's youth initiative.) When I talked to the chairwoman of the Spokane Tribal Business Council, Carol Evans, she expressed great pride in the partnership and emphasized the fundamental difference between the Spokane Indians baseball club and other teams. "We are not their mascot," she said. "They're named after our tribe."

In fact, the Spokane Indians have four mascots: two dinosaurs, a superhero named Recycle Man, and a local species of fish. When I met the team's senior vice president, Otto Klein, on the field during batting practice, he told me about each of these characters, gushing with the blind fervor of a man bragging about his zany college-aged kids. Klein has worked for the Spokane Indians for twenty-nine seasons. His skill set was sports marketing, but his essential nature, it seemed, was "host." He saw his job as hosting the entire greater Spokane community in his welcoming, unpretentious little baseball stadium at the edge of town—impeccably engineering a cozy and communal feeling for everyone, every night. The mascots were part of that experience, of course. But everything was. "That's why, you look around, and it's immaculate," Klein told me. "I dare you to find a piece of trash." That's why there was a Kids Zone beyond the right-field fence, with hopscotch and chalk, and a Wiffle Ball field beyond the fence in left. That's why everything looked freshly painted, why the bathrooms were well lit and staffed by attendants. (Klein was confident I would have a "positive bathroom experience" that night.) That's why parking at Avista Stadium is free. "See that?" Klein said at one point. "You could eat off that." I thought he was gesturing at the seats behind home plate, but he meant the concrete floor.

What the Indians really offer their fans is their hospitality. At this level of minor-league baseball, Klein explained, the show has to be bigger than the nine guys on the field. The Indians are the High-A affiliate of the Colorado Rockies—three tiers down from the major leagues, one tier up from the floor. Players pass through the roster rapidly; virtually every week, someone is called up or sent down. (This year, three of the Indians' five starting pitchers vanished within weeks of Opening Day— just . . . poof, like a rapture.) That churn scrambles the usual sports-marketing logic, Klein explained. As soon as a ballplayer garners a little star power in Spokane—becomes a fan favorite, a potential bobblehead, a draw—he's spirited away.

Last year, the pandemic scrapped the entire minor-league season. Now, Klein said, people were returning, with relief and abandon, chasing that normal summer feeling of sitting at a game, even if the world still hadn't entirely returned to normal. "One of the things that I think sports allows us to do is escape our problems," he told me. "Right now, you're here at the ballpark, and you're not thinking about your cranky boss or the way your wife spoke to you this morning when you left home. It gives you an outlet to be kind of free emotionally and be a part of it." That's why I'm here, I said.

It was Dollars in Your Dog Night. With two hours to go before the first pitch, staff members in the stadium kitchen were wrapping hot dogs in foil and randomly inserting play money into some. These bills, in denominations of 1 to 100 dollars, were redeemable for real bills—a total of $2,000 would be given away during the game. Dollars in Your Dog Night was one of the most beloved promotions at Avista Stadium, and the Indians seemed to run a different one every night of the season. (Halloween Night, Pajama Party Night, Bark in the Park, when fans bring their dogs.) Hot-dog sales spike on Dollars in Your Dog Night. The $2,000 is sprinkled among hundreds of dogs—the potential for a payoff, for any individual hot-dog eater, feels attainable and real. "There's a really good likelihood that you're going to win money in your hot dog tonight!" Klein told me encouragingly.

After so many months of tracking Covid statistics and deciphering health-department dashboards, of being forced to visualize formerly mundane situations and make bungling calculations about distances, densities, air flow—the trajectories and life spans of billions of invisible aerosols eddying omnidirectionally through the air, and the odds of too many of them lodging up my nose—it was fun to imagine something random happening to me that was good. I might come home from Spokane with Covid, but I might come home with a twenty-dollar bill.

I haven't mentioned the smoke.

I saw the fire in the mountains north of Spokane as I drove into town, discharging its spectral, ashy cloud. The Ford-Corkscrew Fire had more than doubled in size overnight, chewing up 13,000 acres and forcing evacuations. Still, it had to be regarded as a relatively puny disaster compared with the megafires in California and even the other fires ravaging Washington State, some of which were also lofting smoke toward Spokane.

For days leading up to my trip, I watched the city's air-quality numbers rise on my phone, alongside its Covid numbers, tracking this data as compulsively as I tracked baseball statistics as a kid. It was another stressor that I couldn't control—another catastrophe we had largely inflicted on ourselves that seemed to be getting inescapably worse everywhere, just at different rates and on different scales, and which, therefore, seemed also to require a modulation of our discouragement and alarm. Then, the evening before I left home, the air quality in Spokane deteriorated starkly, edging above 200 on the color-coded meter: Purple. VERY UNHEALTHY. The Indians had a game that night and tried to wait out the smoke for an hour, while the crowd sat in the stands, swaddled in the abrasive, weighted blanket of Planet Earth's air. When the team finally took the extraordinary step of postponing the game, everyone booed. "It was kind of yucky, but we fans didn't care," Karen Kaiser told me.

Kaiser has been watching the Indians play in Spokane for fourteen years. She works as a curator at the Jundt Art Museum, on the campus of Gonzaga University, across the river from downtown. When we met in her office one afternoon, she set out a small, faded baseball card of a former Spokane Indians player for me to see. The back of the card described Jack Lohrke as "one of the luckiest boys in baseball." He was also Kaiser's dad.

Seventy-five summers ago, in 1946, Lohrke was the Indians' twenty-two-year-old third baseman and a standout slugger, hitting .345. On June 24, the Indians' owner received the inevitable phone call: Lohrke was being promoted to the Pacific Coast League. He should report to San Diego right away.

Lohrke was unreachable, however. The team had left Spokane several hours earlier, traveling west across the state for an away game the following day. Shortly after nightfall, the Indians' bus was climbing through the Cascades in the rain when the driver swerved to avoid an oncoming car. The bus skidded along the guardrail, scraping up a shower of sparks, then broke through the barrier, plunged off the road, and bounced 350 feet down the side of a mountain until it hit the riverbank below. Then the gas tanks exploded. Everything burned.

Six of the thirteen players aboard were killed instantly. Everyone else was severely injured; three more died in the hospital within days. But Jack Lohrke was totally fine. After receiving the call about his promotion, the Indians' owner had enlisted the help of the State Patrol, and a patrolman managed to spot the team's bus parked for hamburgers at a truck stop in the middle of the state. He relayed a message to Lohrke, who dispensed quick goodbyes to his teammates and began hitchhiking the 175 miles back to Spokane to pack his things. That is, Lohrke went east while the Indians continued west. Their bus crashed about forty-five minutes later.

It was an astonishing story, and the media ran with it. "Lucky Lohrke," they called him. But the nickname turned out to be even more apt than it seemed. Two summers earlier, Lohrke landed in Normandy with the 35th Infantry Division just after D-Day, then slogged through France and Germany, fighting in some of the grisliest campaigns of World War II. On four separate occasions, he watched the soldier standing next to him get killed but was never harmed himself. Then, trying to get home to Los Angeles after being discharged, Lohrke was bumped off an army transport flight at the last minute to clear a seat for a military VIP. He was miffed. Not only was he burning to return home, he'd never flown on an airplane before and was looking forward to the experience. The flight took off without him, then crashed, killing everyone on board.

Growing up in Southern California in the 1950s and '60s, Karen Kaiser did not hear any of these stories from her dad. He retired from baseball in 1953, after seven mediocre seasons in the big leagues, and took a job as a security guard. As a father, Kaiser told me, he was somewhat forbidding and withdrawn. ("Everyone would say: 'Jack, you've got six kids. You must really love children,'" she remembered, and Lohrke's line—always delivered flat—was: "Not especially.") Kaiser relished any time she could hold her dad's attention. She loved playing catch with him, even though he threw so hard he would turn her glove hand red. She described herself as a solitary, artistic child in a family of fanatical athletes, and it meant the world to her, she said, when Lohrke snapped at her brothers and sisters to leave her alone and let her draw.

Lohrke never talked about the bus crash, Kaiser said, and the only war stories she could remember the man telling were pat little anecdotes, like the time he had to sleep in a hay bale and woke up so stiff his legs wouldn't work. "Not a word about watching his friends die," Kaiser told me. "Not a word." It wasn't until she moved to Spokane after winning a scholarship to study art that Kaiser learned more of her father's history. She was still Karen Lohrke then, and people in Spokane kept surprising her by recognizing her last name. "I was amazed how many people knew about my dad," she said.

It was around this point in her story that Kaiser paused and asked me to follow her to the museum's loading dock, where Ken Spiering, a burly, genial older man in work pants and suspenders, was backing up his truck to unload some art.

Spiering, it turns out, is one of Spokane's best-known artists. He moved to the city in 1968 and has spent his entire adult life in town. In 1989, he created a twelve-foot-tall sculpture of a red Radio Flyer wagon that still sits in Riverfront Park at the very heart of Spokane, probably the most iconic piece of public art in a city that seemed to brim with it. (The wagon is a tourist attraction.) Now, at seventy-one, Spiering was transferring his personal collection to the museum, a transaction that Kaiser helped engineer. She and Spiering had been friends for decades. That's one thing she loved about Spokane, and its artistic community specifically, Kaiser told me: the intimate scale, the unpretentiousness of the scene. "It's folksy here," she said, stripping the word of any feeling of belittlement.

I helped carry in a couple of Spiering's printmaking matrices—detailed woodcuts of a boy sitting by a river, fishing. As we worked, Kaiser noticed her friend's fingers were bandaged and asked, "What'd you do to your hand?"

"Burned it!" Spiering said. "Right across these four fingers."

"A torch?" Kaiser asked. "You were making something?"

"No, on the grill," Spiering said, and began to good-humoredly outline a mundane barbecuing accident.

"Smells a little different than hamburger, doesn't it?" Kaiser said.

It was a nice moment, that's all. It made Spokane feel like a welcoming place.

Back in her office, Kaiser stressed that nobody, other than reporters, ever called her father Lucky Lohrke. He was deeply uncomfortable with the nickname. This was important to understand, Kaiser said. All these stories about Jack Lohrke narrowly escaping death didn't feel breezy and wondrous to Jack Lohrke. To him, they were traumas. They were stories about a succession of his closest friends not escaping death, all while Lohrke kept on existing, knowing they were dead or even watching them die. As a result, he seemed incapable of delivering the kind of light-hearted sound bite that reporters wanted. "I'm a fatalist," he told *The Los Angeles Times*.

"It was awful for him," Kaiser said. After the Indians' bus crash, Lohrke took it upon himself to drive one of his teammates' widows back to her parents' home in San Francisco. Then, continuing on to San Diego, he consoled another teammate's widow there. When he finally reported to his new team, the owner chewed him out for taking so long to arrive from Spokane. "Where have you been?" the man barked. Lohrke replied, "I've been delivering widows."

Suddenly, I heard myself thinking aloud in Kaiser's office, struggling to process my own, more banal good fortune as much as her dad's. How could Jack Lohrke—how could anyone with moral integrity—look back on his survival and feel unequivocally good and deserving of it and also not wind up racked with compassion and hypersensitive to risk? "I think," Kaiser said, "you'd have to be pretty egocentric to think there's some overriding meaning about the importance of your life as opposed to somebody else's."

"He was always worried about us," Kaiser went on. Lohrke usually seemed quite even-keeled, but he would fly into a panic whenever one of his children failed to get home before dark. Kaiser remembered one day, when she was seven or eight, her dad was up on the roof fixing something, and she begged pitifully to be allowed up to help. Finally, her father caved. "Dad said, 'Aw, bring her up here.'" And she was hoisted up.

Lohrke sat his little daughter down, pulled the extra denim of her pant legs away from her body, and proceeded to hammer nails through the fabric, all around, securing his child to the shingles so she wouldn't slide off.

"I was happy as a clam," Kaiser told me, "just sitting up there, just being where he was."

I bought two hot dogs in the top of the fourth but didn't win any money. In truth, I suspected I didn't even have a chance of winning money, because I happened to order my hot dogs at a moment when the smaller of Avista Stadium's two concession stands momentarily ran out of hot dogs—a fleeting and completely forgivable collapse of hospitality that, nevertheless, I'm sure will pain Otto Klein to read about here. Within minutes, workers scuttled in from the stadium kitchen, first with a tray of hot dogs, then with two bags of buns, to clear the backlog of customers. I watched the people behind the counter assemble and wrap them together as fast as they could. In their haste, they seemed to have abandoned the project of stuffing any dollars in the dogs. Later, though, I learned that this wasn't an oversight. All the money was disbursed in the early innings. I'd misunderstood and missed the whole thing.

Honestly, I didn't care. It was a trivial blip of disappointment at worst. I realized I hadn't been to a baseball game since I chaperoned my daughter's field trip to see the Mariners in the spring of 2019, and I felt grateful just to soak up all the usual, wonderful baseball stuff happening around me, the nuanced inflections of an experience that I'd known all my life. I was reconnecting with all the nostalgic clichés—the crack of the bat, and so on— but also subtler particulars: the helpless sensation of scampering to the bathroom and hearing, from the other side of the stands, a tense collective roar, then a terrible collective groan, and knowing I'd missed an opposing player's home run; watching a little redheaded girl, the age of my younger daughter, creep down the right-field seats toward the Indians bullpen clutching a green Crayola marker, flip through her program, and match the number on the closest player's back to his name, and then screw up the courage to ask Mr. Whoever-he-was for his autograph; the anesthetizing, stadium-wide wash of white noise and murmuring that can miraculously set in during the doldrums of a very long at-bat.

Otto Klein's people, meanwhile, were putting on their show, spackling every crack in the action with giveaways, games, and promotions. Down on the field, between innings, little kids tried to throw pizza boxes into fishing nets to win prize packs, or jumped up and down with pedometers strapped to their foreheads. These contests were relentless ("OK, guys! It's really simple! We're going to take those toilet seats and throw them like horseshoes!") and the mascots kept coming, too: the blue dinosaur, the other dinosaur, and, most beloved of all, making his traditional appearance in the middle of the sixth, Ribby the Redband Trout.

Ribby is an homage to an ecologically precarious subspecies of rainbow trout that spawns in the Spokane River. The fish tottered in from left field, anthropomorphically upright, then planted his feet to perform his signature dance: a quick, perfectly perpendicular vibration of the torso, executed with uncanny evenness and precision, as though there were not a human inside the Ribby suit but a pneumatic paint-can shaker from the local hardware store. My jaw dropped. People howled. The woman in front of me buckled over with glee. It was the most unusual thing I've ever seen a mascot do. "Hope you enjoyed Ribby!" the Indians' PR officer texted me proudly once the euphoria had passed. I replied, "That shake is really something."

I was enjoying myself! I was energized! The moon was low and radiant behind the stadium lights, and the air quality had eased to MODERATE. "Baseball is good!" I texted my wife. Still, concurrent with all that, I never stopped clocking my proximity risk. All this expert entertainment and distraction and I still couldn't mentally escape the pandemic as fully as those people just sitting around my hotel lobby seemed to have done. All evening, I would hop from one mostly vacant tract of seats to another, so I could take off my mask and feel marginally less self-conscious. Virtually no one else was masked, and there were small, unmasked children everywhere—a conspicuous violation of the stadium's policy that unvaccinated people must wear masks. I preferred not to breathe on them, just in case. I had never managed to embrace that one pandemic mantra: "It's probably fine."

The game went into the bottom of the eighth tied up, 3–3. The Indians' first baseman hit a grounder to the right side and reached first when the pitcher failed to step on the bag. Then he stole second. Then he bolted for home on a double to deep center field. The throw to the plate appeared to keep rising and rising. The Hillsboro catcher leapt but landed empty-handed. The Indians took the lead, 4–3.

The Spokane closer, Dugan Darnell, came in to stitch up the ninth. Darnell is a twenty-four-year-old Michigander who, after graduating from college in 2019, didn't have any opportunities to play professional baseball. So he made a résumé and eventually got a job as a "financial adviser recruitment consultant" at an analyst firm in Chicago, after interviewing for the position five times. He was midway through his second day of work when he got a call on his cell phone from the SouthShore RailCats in Gary, Indiana, offering him a spot in a small independent league. He quit his white-collar job on the spot and hopped two trains and a bus to meet his new team. He was lucky, he'd explained to me before the game. "I told my bosses I didn't want any what-ifs."

Now, Darnell was striking out the first batter he faced. Then another one, too. After the final batter lined out, the crowd exploded. The Indians' outfielders converged for a leaping, three-way high-five, then trotted in to hug and shake hands. The joy, for me, was Pavlovian. The home team won.

Soon the field was empty, except for Ribby the Redband Trout, whom I watched toddle in wide, pointless circles near third base—not fully performing anymore, but not exactly taking a break. Then "Don't Stop Believin'" started cranking on the PA, and the children appeared—a long parade of them, tightly clustered and impeccably straight, filing in from beyond right field where they'd been organized for one last, warmhearted Avista Stadium tradition—the chance to run the bases after the game. Presiding over this exercise was Otto Klein. Standing in front of home plate, he pointed the antenna of his walkie-talkie at the first child's feet and started flicking it sharply again and again, signaling to the kids, one at a time, when it was time to take off.

I watched them run and run: the young, clunky ones who slingshotted uncontrollably around first base, and the serious-faced tweens who crouched and sprinted, with something to prove. One or two scuttled by holding an older sibling's hand.

Suddenly, something surprising happened to me. I missed my own children, the same two girls from whom I'd wanted to peel myself away for a year and a half, who had infuriated me, depleted me, screamed at me, taken me for granted, picked insultingly at the dinners I cooked. I missed my younger daughter: a sweet, complicated, anxious, and stupefyingly talkative child, who had been marooned with a Chromebook at our kitchen table with an agonizing backlog of things to worry about and say. And I missed my older daughter—a contemplative and perceptive girl who, a few days earlier, when we had our first bout of summer smoke at home, looked up from our driveway and wondered aloud if her own children would think the yellow suns she drew as a kid were strange, because, by then, the sun would always look red.

In that moment, I understood that I was failing them. I don't mean as a father, not one-on-one. I mean as part of a society that seemed, with increasing bluntness, to be sending its children signals that it would not prioritize their well-being or their future—that it would not keep them safe. Why, from the very start of the pandemic, had I felt an inescapable responsibility to stay focused on my daughters even when I couldn't do it gracefully, which was a lot of the time; even when I felt resentful; even when it became obvious, I suspect to them as well, that this compulsion was neurotic and had left me feeling rudderless and stuck? It wasn't overprotectiveness. It was shame. It was grief. The one meaningful thing I had to give them was my attention.

I wish this epiphany had passed before the time came to write it down. I'm not sure I have a right to be so gloomy. But why bother re-entering the world and not being honest about how it went: that I traveled somewhere, tried to get a feel for the place, but struggled to feel much beyond the heaviness of my own head. That I was the melancholy doof in the mask behind the dugout in Spokane, feeling lucky—heartbreakingly lucky—just to be there and to feel as good as I did, while all the other parents crowded in around me, screaming for their kids to round third and run home.

Acknowledgments

I am grateful to all the people in these pages, for showing me the world.

Thank you, Wandee, Isla, and Rose. Thank you, Dé and Sterling Mackinnon, Tony and Young-Oak Pryor, and Susan Mooallem for stepping in to help when I've been away. Thank you to Jin Auh, who first had the idea for this book, and to Andy Ward, Kaeli Subberwal, Craig Adams, and everyone at Random House for the skill and positivity they brought to making it. Thank you to the editors, fact-checkers, and friends who've helped sharpen my reporting and writing (and, by extension, helped me become a more attentive, empathetic person), especially Sheila Glaser, Paul Tough, James Ryerson, Alex Star, Jake Silverstein, Bill Wasik, Jessica Lustig, Caitlin Roper, Aaron Retica, Joel Lovell, Hugo Lindgren, Gerry Marzorati, Rob Liguori, Jamie Lowe, Lia Miller, Doug McGray, Derek Fagerstrom, Haley Howle, Anita Badejo, Pat Walters, Megan Greenwell, Edward J. McGregor, Chad Millman, Mike Benoist, John Gravois, John Swansburg, Ben Austen, Dave Gilson, Roman Mars, Ira Glass, Jad Abumrad,

Robert Krulwich, Evan Ratliff, Chris Colin, Wendy MacNaughton, Laurel Braitman, Michael Pollan, and Jack Hitt.

The main thing I'd like to acknowledge in these acknowledgments is how lucky I feel to get to do this work and that you—a reader—want to read it.

ABOUT THE AUTHOR

JON MOOALLEM is a longtime writer at large for *The New York Times Magazine* and a contributor to numerous other radio shows and magazines, including *This American Life, The Daily, 99% Invisible,* and *Wired.* He is the author of *Wild Ones* and *This Is Chance!,* which was named a best book of 2020 by *BuzzFeed,* Brain Pickings, and Amazon. He lives on Bainbridge Island, outside Seattle, with his family.

jonmooallem.com
Twitter: @jmooallem